JOURNEY TO THE END
OF THE WORLD

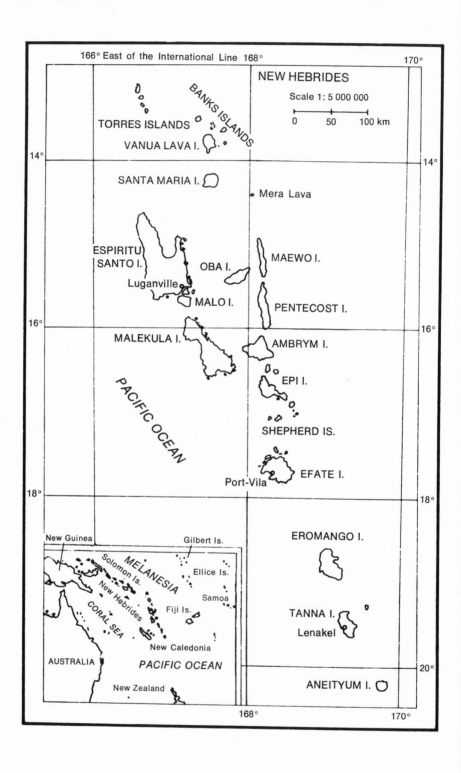

166° East of the International Line 168°   170°

NEW HEBRIDES

Scale 1: 5 000 000

0   50   100 km

TORRES ISLANDS

BANKS ISLANDS

VANUA LAVA I.

14°   14°

SANTA MARIA I.

Mera Lava

ESPIRITU
SANTO I.

OBA I.   MAEWO I.

Luganville

MALO I.   PENTECOST I.

16°   16°

MALEKULA I.   AMBRYM I.

PACIFIC OCEAN   EPI I.

SHEPHERD IS.

EFATE I.

Port-Vila

18°   18°

New Guinea   Gilbert Is.   EROMANGO I.

MELANESIA

Solomon Is.   Ellice Is.

New Hebrides   Samoa

CORAL SEA   Fiji Is.   TANNA I.

New Caledonia   Lenakel

AUSTRALIA   PACIFIC OCEAN   20°

New Zealand   ANEITYUM I.

168°   170°

Charlene Gourguechon's

JOURNEY TO
THE END
OF THE WORLD

*A three-year adventure in
the New Hebrides*

CHARLES SCRIBNER'S SONS   NEW YORK

Library of Congress Cataloging in Publication Data

Gourguechon, Charlene.
  Charlene Gourguechon's journey to the end of the world.

  Translation of L'archipel des tabous.
  Bibliography: p. 329
  1. Ethnology—New Hebrides. 2. New Hebrides—Description and travel. 3. Gourguechon, Charlene. I. Title.
GN671.N6G6813   919.3'4'04   76-46360
ISBN 0-684-14847-1

This book is dedicated to:

VIRAMBAT, the *Meleun*, Chief of Chiefs of the Amok Big Nambas, Malekula Island;

ALBERT GODDYN of Santo, the Frenchest Flemish man in the South Seas, my adoptive New Hebridean father, navigator, planter, three-star chef, and inventor of the Santo Sling;

CAPTAIN ERNST-WILHELM LAMBERTY, Pacific seawolf, Dutch author, French Foreign Legionnaire, solitary navigator, master of the *Konanda;*

DOCTOR ROGER MORILLERE, professor at the Sorbonne in Paris, authority on anthropological film making, whom I had the pleasure of meeting only after the end of this story but without whom it would not exist.

CONTENTS

INTRODUCTION

AUGUST 23, 1970. The luminous sky bleeds its red liquid sun into the blackening jungle. A few steps from Santo's pier, I ventured into the rising tide. I splashed through the warm white foam, trying not to lose my zories, trying to avoid the debris scattered in the white sand—bits of coral, battered Australian beer cans, rusty scrap metal left over from World War II American warships.

My friend John Miu, a Chinese shopkeeper, was sitting in his Land Rover, waiting to take me back to the hotel. A kind man, he waited patiently, as I insisted on watching the departure of the *Tasman Sea*, a New Zealand sailboat, until the last possible moment. My husband was aboard. We had been married only two days before.

Jacques pulled in the anchor and Kal hoisted the mainsail. A few minutes later, I couldn't identify either of them. I assume the silhouette that waved to me with large gestures was Jacques, but I'm not sure. It might have been the captain.

Sometimes when people are sad they tend to focus their attention on anything at all to avoid facing up to the cause of their sadness. I fixed on the old saying "Red sky at night, sailor's delight, red sky at morning, sailor take warning," murmuring it softly like an incantation. A dumb thing to be reciting, I realized even at the time, as a red evening sky in that part of the world is not particularly a sign of good weather.

They were leaving. My husband, Jacques Gourguechon (Jacques Marie Leon Jean Gourguechon), and our companion, Kal Muller. They were headed for the south of Malekula, planning to penetrate the island's interior as far as the villages of the Mbotogote tribe, where we had been the first outsiders to set foot. They had to get there as quickly as possible, with all the movie cameras and photo equipment, for an important ceremony was being prepared. They had been lucky enough to find a sailboat going in the right direction. One of our usual problems was that we often wanted to go precisely to those remote shores that were beyond the normal service of the island trading boats.

The next day I too would be on Malekula, but in the north, making my way toward the Big Nambas plateau. They were also preparing a ceremony. Jacques and Kal had suggested that I go alone to gather the particulars from the chief. Afterwards, I was to charter a small boat to the south of the island and find a guide to lead me to the others in the mountains. I had already made this journey all alone with no more than ordinary difficulties—a boat that went under and the coast people in the south who had not wanted to supply me with a guide.

Despite my desire to stay with Jacques, to maintain at least for a little while the illusion of a romantic tropical honeymoon, I wasn't unhappy about having to manage on my own in the jungle and with the New Hebrideans. But my melancholy was undeniable. You've got to know what you want, I reminded myself, annoyed with my own ambivalence.

The *Tasman Sea* was no more than a tiny shadow when the night swallowed her completely. It was over. John turned on his headlights to show me the way. I got into the car.

Santo. Darkness. But it was no later than six-thirty. The tropical night. The purity of the air. The humidity. The scent of frangipani. Only ten lights, and two of them on boats. A gentle wind. Not a single star.

I got out in front of Chez Albert. The harsh light of the bistro and the unchained laughter of ex-bushmen warring against a pinball machine overcame me in the street.

"Thanks, John. Tell Moumouille I'll stop by before leaving tomorrow morning, and ask her to wrap up about fifty tobacco sticks."

Albert's loud gruff voice came forth to meet me. "Well, my dear, so your husband's already walked out on you, huh? Don't worry. If he sleeps with a Small Nambas tomorrow night, it surely won't be the first time!"

My laughter was forced.

"Aw, don't lose your sense of humor. You know me, I'm just kidding. Come on, cheer up! You're invited to have dinner with us tonight, in the kitchen."

"Thanks, Albert, but I'm really not hungry. Could I have my key, please?"

"Oh, no! You've gotta eat something. And first, you and I are going to have a drink. You can use one. Let's live it up! The drinks are on the house!"

I laughed despite myself. Good old Albert. If my father in Chicago knew this adopted New Hebridean father of mine, he wouldn't like the looks of him at all.

Stretched out on my bed, I watched distractedly the movements of the cockroaches up and down the wall, and the stillness of a velvety gray moth, large as a bird, that had alighted on the curtains.

I thought no more of Jacques, but of Virambat, the Big Nambas "chief of chiefs" whom I was to see in about two days' time, assuming all went well. I imagined the traditional ceremony he was organizing, during which his eldest son would take a superior grade in the Nimangki, the hierarchical men's society. The idea of seeing another pig slaughter, the bloody sacrifice that accompanies every ceremony, really didn't please me. But I consoled myself with the thought that at least there would be no ritual man slaughter. I vowed to make Virambat tell me one day about the sacrifice of men on stone beds and about cannibalism, subjects the Big Nambas as a rule avoid with strangers to the tribe. A guide, of Big Nambas origin but under missionary influence, once explained this reticence to me.

"It's not that they're ashamed," he said. "To the contrary, they think that you're not capable of understanding."

There *were* things we did not understand yet, things we hadn't seen or even suspected yet, despite all the bamboo doors which the Big Nambas and other tribes had already opened to us.

But their confidence in us was constantly growing. More and more we were subject only to the ordinary taboos against women and uninitiated men, just like members of their society. With greater frequency we were being spared the special taboos, those against nonmembers of the society. And I knew without a doubt that before the end of our stay we were to see and learn far more, to discover unimaginable secrets. In the New Hebrides, above all else you must not be impatient. And we weren't.

Two years! Already! Two years since an idea tossed out in my Lincoln Center office in the course of a simple conversation had so drastically changed my life. I had gone on to spend months and months in the jungle with "primitive peoples," weeks in trading skiffs (which really were primitive); I had been subjected to cyclones, earthquakes, shipwrecks, and malaria; I had shared a hut with rats and swine.

An Ambrym native once asked me, *"Village b'long you, what name b'long him?"* New York, my village.

Midtown Manhattan. A beautiful spring afternoon. At the Vivian Beaumont Theater, where I did public relations and press work, we were putting on a new production of *Cyrano de Bergerac*. I was preparing an article on the eventful history of the play. I had unearthed a gentleman on East Fifty-second Street who had, in his family album, pictures of Constant Coquelin and Sarah Bernhardt playing the principal roles in London in 1900. It took me a good two hours and five cups of tea to persuade him to let me borrow the historic photographs, then more than half an hour of polite listening to his reasons for disliking modern theater.

At three o'clock, I rush out of my taxi in front of Lincoln Center Plaza. I run past the Henry Moore sculpture, without checking the progress of its verdigris coat, without, for once, so much as a glance. I bolt into the theater through the actors' entrance.

"You're late," announces the Puerto Rican doorman.

"Yes. For the rehearsal!" I reply, already well down the hallway.

"Don't run so fast, sweetheart," he calls after me. "The days are long, y'know! And they're all the same!"

Stopping in my office to leave my precious photos, I find a note slipped into my typewriter: "I'm at the printer's. What a mess! The posters are terrible. An Ethiopian director sent by the State Department is arriving at three with his interpreter. Can you skip the rehearsal and take care of them? S." S. is Susan Bloch, head of the public relations and press department, my boss.

I call Reception. They're there. They were even a few minutes early. I show them in. I no longer remember the director's name, though he was a charming man. But the interpreter was Kal Muller.

When a question asked out of simple politeness provokes an unexpected response, you don't forget it. "Are you in theater, too?" I asked.

"No, not at all. Hold on . . . look," said Kal, pulling from his briefcase several color photographs of painted blacks, naked except for a small mat of straw, their somber moon eyes glowing mysteriously. "Does this interest you?"

At night I think again of those pictures, which had a portentous attraction for me. They will not release me. I cannot put my finger on what holds me. I am gripped by anxiety. I think of my work, Lincoln Center, New York, all that I have enjoyed so much . . . of my life, as if it were something outside myself, a separate entity I could measure. I instinctively understand the relationship between my troubled feelings and those confounded photos. I have presentiments which I don't dare admit to myself.

Two days later, at the West End Inn, Kal spreads out on the table before me index cards, notes, photocopies of anthropological texts, and the photographs I had finally asked to see again. He tells me everything he knows, adding that he knows very little, and that is why he plans to return to the archipelago in the near future.

"You know," he suggests, "it's someone like you we need. We're not allowed to spend much time with the women because of the taboos. They live completely apart. In fact, I don't even know what they do all day long."

"You really make me want to go."

"Good, but I'd better warn you it wouldn't exactly be a pleasure trip for you. There's a difficulty. There are many, in fact, but one in particular for you. Women count for absolutely nothing in that society. They are truly sub-men."

I laugh.

"Don't laugh," continues Kal in a professorial tone. "Women are inferior, not only to men but also to pigs. Women don't even have names; the pigs do. And I'm sure a foreign woman wouldn't be more privileged than a Big Nambas woman."

A week passed. Kal phoned me at the theater. "I've just seen Margaret Mead at the American Museum of Natural History. She gives us her blessing but could only pledge five hundred dollars. It's rather symbolic. But if we hang around trying to get rich, we'll never leave. I'm going to order the tickets. Have you made up your mind?"

"I haven't stopped thinking about it."

"People who think too much never do anything."

I handed in my resignation at the theater the next day. With all my power, I resisted the arguments of my friends at Lincoln Center. My parents raised every possible objection. They thought I'd gone mad. I didn't hear any of them.

Departure in one month.

"What's your French film maker's name?"

"Jacques Gourguechon."

"Excuse me?"

"Jacques Gourguechon."

"That's a funny name."

Kal reminded me of this little dialogue yesterday, to make fun of me, just before the marriage ceremony at the French Delegation in Santo.

I envision the moment Jacques and Kal met as if I had been there myself, they've told me about it so often. Paris, 1968, the May Revolution. Everything fluid, everything possible. People not hesitating to take what chance offers.

At the Guimet Museum, Kal, having just arrived from New York, is conversing with Roger Morillere, professor of cinema. They talk of the Pacific. Jacques arrives, in transit, to retrieve some of his films on Japan which had been screened at the museum. He pricks up his ears. The Pacific! He knows the Pacific.

He's interested. Kal and Roger are on the subject of the Big Nambas. Jacques, his films under his arm, one foot on the stairway, makes a half-turn to join them.

Roger Morillere makes the necessary introduction and states the evidence. "What do you know, Kal! You're looking for a film maker—here's your man! Jacques, unless you've got something important going, here's an interesting project for you."

Jacques is in fact planning a trip to central Asia, where he had already spent many months. But the stories of the Big Nambas intrigue him. Moreover, he and Kal feel that immediate and rare rapport between two people who have much in common.

An hour later the two of them were seated in a Chinese restaurant deep in the heart of the Latin Quarter. Between the bird's-nest soup and the egg rolls, the matter was already settled. They would leave together for the New Hebrides. Central Asia could wait for another time. Who knows, perhaps they'll go together?

This quick agreement wasn't surprising. Both of them had already traveled widely. Jacques had just finished a series of programs for French television called "Camera Stop," for which he had gone around the world. Kal had spent two years in Africa with the United Nations. They were able to compare their experiences in the Middle East and South America. For them, the expedition to Malekula was but another stop in the life of a traveler.

They were full of confidence and enthusiasm. I was full of doubts, but enthusiasm, too.

1

The Far West of
the Pacific

Santo. Way down there, on the right. A loose fringe of corrugated metal roofs blinking at the sun through a tangle of aggressive greens held back along sharp, irregular curves by the royal
blue sea. Beaches. Blond vibrations. The tender turquoise of shallow water over bright coral sand. Vivid white scratches here and
there: the reefs.

The long wake of the only boat in sight splits the ocean. Before
us, the vast expanse of Espiritu Santo Island, the gigantic, incredi-
bly dense rain forest, reaches back toward distant misty peaks. A
far cry from the image of the island as a dot on the map.

We skim the treetops, the leaves engulf us, and the plane jolts
to a stop just at the edge of the jungle. The air is so heavy with
humidity that it's almost visible. We pry ourselves out of our
seats. We are three, but the third is not yet Jacques, it's Tom.
Lanky, bearded Tom Milkwood, a friend of Kal's from the University of Arizona, a geologist who had had enough of mineral
hunting in the Far West of the States and wanted to try his luck at
a new kind of hunting—in the Far West of the Pacific Ocean.

I recalled the sumptuous Faaa Airport in Tahiti, the tranquil-
izing countryside around the Tontouta landing strip in New Cale-

The village of Santo: surrounded by rich vegetation, with a mixture of wooden tropical houses and Quonset huts built by the Americans during World War II. *Jacques Gourguechon*

donia. No comparison. Here we were really at the end of the world of civilized nature.

I remembered having read something about the problem of termites in the tropics. Looking at the "air terminal," a shack made of corrugated iron and corroded wood, I immediately understood the amplitude of the ruin these insects can wreak. The façade of the terminal sported a hand-painted sign: SANTO, in two-foot-high red letters.

We're separated by a chicken-wire fence from the people waiting for the plane. There are three or four Europeans and a handful of natives. (In the New Hebrides there are only two categories of people, native and European. You're native if you're Melanesian; you're European if you're French, British, American, Chinese, or Martian.) The Europeans are dressed in baggy planter's shorts and Tahitian shirts with huge dark perspiration patches under the arms and over the shoulder blades. The New Hebrideans are dressed the same way, only their Hong Kong–made, imitation

Tahitian shirts are dry, if dirty and ragged. There's a minimum of movement, barely enough to brush away the flies.

One European woman, a hefty redhead, suddenly recognizes Kal and begins to shriek his name. With one hand she waves; with the other she wipes away the sweat dripping from her forehead and flowing down her bosom to the low-cut neckline of her dress. Flies buzz all around her, but she has no third hand with which to shoo them away. So that's Elsa Ravon. She and her husband run a bistro on the ocean front and had offered to rent us low-price rooms. Kal had talked to me about her, but his description hadn't been very detailed.

Inside the shack, decorated by a few washed-out airline posters and a map of the Pacific, we are greeted by a French gendarme and a British constable, fresh enough for a parade. Each is surrounded by a contingent of French- or English-speaking New Hebridean subgendarmes or subconstables. The formalities established by the Anglo-French Condominium of the New Hebrides, undoubtedly the strangest government in the world, are brief but memorable. I had obtained a British visa in New York, but the gendarme tried to explain to me that I was welcome to opt for French "protection." Not to be outdone, the constable retorted that since my native language was English, I would certainly prefer British protection.

Apparently I was obliged to become an honorary Frenchwoman or Englishwoman for the duration of my stay so that I would be subject to French or British law. (Without which, if I killed someone on New Hebridean soil, the Condominium would have to deliver me to the nearest American consul, in Fiji, when he's present.) I promised them both that I would carefully evaluate the situation. I had no idea of what their "options" might really entail. There had to be a catch; otherwise, why would they be competing?

We left by the other door, beyond the fence. Elsa was waiting for us in front of her jeep, which dated from World War II. She gave Tom a warm smile, me a cooler one. An energetic handshake for him, a limp one for me. The New Hebrideans watched us load the pile of baggage into the jeep. Their puzzlement as to why so much freight accompanied three people was visible. Except for two small suitcases, everything unloaded from the plane was ours.

Condominium boats, the only ones in the world that sail under two flags. *Jacques Gourguechon*

"Ready?" asked Elsa.

"You don't mind," Kal said to me, getting into the front seat next to Elsa.

Tom and I climbed onto the baggage in the back. We were off in a hotrod roar.

"Watch your door, Kal," mentioned Elsa. "It doesn't close very well." She also warned us that the car had had no brakes to speak of since the previous summer.

The gravel road snaked down toward the coast. Beyond the coconut palms glistened Santo. Three or four piers stitched the greenery to the blue, to the wide Segond Channel.

Santo. I'm wide-eyed, excited. A long road bordered by wooden shanties and renovated or run-down World War II Quonset huts, spread out pell-mell. An anarchistic vegetation climbs toward an all-powerful sun. The road hugs the coastline. About a mile out is another island, Aori, all green and blue. We pass several cars and a few helmeted natives on motorbikes. The black shadows walking along the roadside turn their heads at the sound of each approaching vehicle. But it's like a film in slow motion. No one moves quickly. People hardly seem to be stirring at all.

I lean forward to tap Kal on the shoulder. "Where's the center of town?"

"Right here!"

The second city of the archipelago—its commercial center—and "downtown" you'd swear you were still in the country.

Lo Po, Fung Kwan Chee, and Wong, the Chinese stores, dark and dilapidated, line the overgrown grassy footpath which might euphemistically be called a sidewalk. All the buildings are one-story, white cement-block structures that seem proud of their own ugliness. We passed the French and British delegations, lost behind coconut palms, banana trees, and bougainvillea. A boat docked at the main pier did fill the void somewhat.

The jeep struggled through the sand along the beach. Beyond a curtain of tropical flowers and bushes we arrived at a large Polynesian-style hut. A sign stuck into the ground beyond a ditch announced our destination: Tearoom "A la Marine."

A man emerged from the hut to welcome us with open arms and a big smile. I guessed it was Elsa's husband, Jean Ravon, whom Kal had mentioned in passing.

Ten A.M. The bar was in full swing. The local planters had already begun their regular sequence of rounds and we were invited to join in. Messieurs Coulon, Simonsen, Procureur, Leconte, and Thibault, their faces tanned and lined by years in the South Seas. And René Romero, of whom Kal had also spoken, a one-time sailor, now Santo's resident jack-of-all-trades. He works at the bank, exports New Hebridean art, paints, and is an accomplished clarinet player, interior decorator, and travel agent. He is bad-mouthed by some as a double-dealing rug merchant. He has an engaging smile and looks very young. It was hard for me to believe that he has ten children.

The owner of the bar, who clearly enjoys his work, served us our beers with enthusiasm. His wife discreetly poured herself a stiff whiskey. I don't know whether it was in our honor or not.

I was thirsty. I drank a little of my beer and suddenly felt queasy. I tried to ignore the feeling. I didn't want to spoil our arrival. The planters, each in his turn or all at once, jumped at the chance to tell us the anecdotes that all the locals must have heard time and again. I was overcome by a wave of nausea and dizziness. Was I going to faint for the first time in my life? I tried to convince myself that it was nothing, that it would pass unnoticed. I tried literally to keep my chin up. But Tom noticed. "What's the matter? Don't you feel well?"

Everyone was watching me. I couldn't hide it any longer. Elsa led me into her room. I collapsed on the bed. She brought me a couple of pills and a glass of water. Panic-stricken, on the defensive, I had to know what the pills were. "Quinine," she said briskly. "Take them."

"But I already took antimalaria pills. And anyway I can't have malaria yet!"

"Here we take them every day. You don't know what you're talking about. Come on. Drink up."

I took my medicine, but the water didn't rinse away the bitter taste. In less than an hour it had passed. I rejoined the others, refreshed as if I had just awaked from a good night's sleep.

"What she needs," cried one of the planters, "is a gin and tonic. In these parts, young lady, it's the best medicine for fevers. You only need twenty-five of them to get your daily dose of quinine. Come on, Jean, serve the little lady and then bring the same for everybody."

I protested that I wasn't thirsty, but the drink arrived all the same.

Mr. Thibault and I began talking, or, more precisely, I listened to his monologue. He is very much the gentleman-planter of the group: a handsome man, graying at the temples, with a slightly arrogant manner and dressed completely in white as if to play the role in a movie. He let me know he was the only educated person in this motley crew and recommended that I read without delay *Erromango* by Pierre Benoit. It's a novel, he explained, that traces the decline of a sensitive, cultivated planter, too sensitive to resist the nefarious influence of the islands. I found it hard to understand his French and made an effort to listen closely. René whispered to me later that Thibault had a very thick Marseilles accent. But apparently that wasn't the reason for the linguistic problem, as Mr. Thibault was Parisian and had never been to Marseilles in his life.

In our honor, the planters stayed for lunch. The food was

heavy and the wine plentiful, the kind of meal that knocks out
even the heartiest of eaters when the thermometer hits 100 degrees
in the shade. The Marine's bamboo walls and pandanus-leaf roof,
which let in whatever air there is, don't help much on such a day.
But in this country, the noontime meal goes hand in hand with
the siesta, the daily period of convalescence.

I didn't want to take a nap. I wanted to see something more of
the island than the inside of a bistro on my first day. I went out to
take a walk. "Mad dogs and Englishmen go out in the midday
sun." But there were, in fact, only a few lazy lawnmowing cows
beneath the coconut palms.

When you see a coconut grove for the first time you're tempted
to roam into it, drawn by the graceful palms. I didn't know what
even the youngest of the island children know—the ripe coconuts
fall from these trees with enough force to kill a person instantly.

I wandered along the beach, stopping in front of the British
Delegation to smell the delicate perfume of the frangipani and to
cut a hibiscus flower for my hair, already fancying myself a

Charlene Gourguechon. *Kal Muller*

daughter of the islands. I went as far as the pier, anticipating some activity, but no one works in the early afternoon. The only boat was a cargo ship from Osaka, the *Chiba Maru*. A lone Japanese sailor, half-asleep, stood guard on the bridge. Fenwicks, small wagons loaded with bags of copra, and a few trucks were scattered around the pier, undoubtedly abandoned helter-skelter when the lunch-and-siesta whistle blew. The hum of the boat machinery in the overheated air was the only sign of life in what was otherwise a vacuum. In the main street of Santo, not a soul, not a single car, all the stores sealed up tightly. My head was on fire, my bare arms beginning to tingle—it doesn't take very long to get a suntan here. I returned slowly, ever so slowly, to the Marine.

Jean and Elsa were already settled in with their after-siesta drinks. Jean was morose. He was washing and polishing glasses and banging them down on the bar. Elsa told me not to pay any attention to him; he has his moods. He yelled "shut up" and raised his fists. He was perfectly correct with me, but I didn't have the least desire to witness a scene between them. I asked Elsa where our rooms were.

I learned then that we had more than simple rooms. We had our own private little cabana on the beach, made of wood and sheet metal, about a hundred yards from the Marine. The entrance was full of wasps.

In the evening we went back to the Marine for a light supper. Outside the generator purred. It existed only to provide energy for the three naked lightbulbs that illuminated the hut with a feeble though annoyingly stark glow. Candles or oil lamps would have been cheaper and nicer. We ate quickly. No one spoke much. Elsa gave us oil lamps for our rooms.

A mosquito net ballooned over my bed. I had no intention of lowering it, not on such a hot night. The flickering shadows on the wall evoked all kinds of associations. I fell asleep happy, yet vaguely troubled.

When you wake up here, it's like being outside, as the "window" is no more than a hole in the wall. No need to get out of bed to see what the weather's doing. But it's so beautiful you want to get outdoors right away. Grimacing, I remembered the inevitable grind of waking up in New York.

Seven A.M. and we were in the café, where generous slices of papaya were set before us. Jean Ravon already had a beer in his hand (only the second of the day, he insisted with a wry smile) when René came in, followed by a sleepy New Hebridean named Anatole. Anatole was René's factotum, his "boy." René suggested that we go into the "bush" (the local word for jungle) to visit the head of an indigenous movement called Na-Griamel. It would be a good introduction to island life, he explained.

For about five miles, the crushed coral road wound through plantations and lush forests. Then we turned off onto a bumpy trail interrupted occasionally by closed gates and cattle crossings. The car choked on in the dust and the heat for another five or six miles. Anatole's duty was to show the way and open and close each gate. I had time to admire the rich and rampant vegetation—climbing to the sky over gigantic trunks entangled in the webs and waterfalls of lianas. We came upon an area where the jungle had been pushed aside for human beings. Bamboo fences painted white led us to an enormous banyan tree. The land directly around the banyan had been meticulously cleared, forming a kind of village square. Beyond, footpaths led to leaf huts, geometrically arranged amid banana trees. The atmosphere was more like that of a military camp than a village. A native stopped the car in front of what might be called a guardhouse. A sign read:

VANAFO

NA-GRIAMEL HEADQUARTERS

J.T.P. MOSES STEPHENS, CHIEF PRESIDENT

He put his head into the car and asked, "You got knife? You got musket?"

"No got! No got nothing," replied René in as carefree a tone as he could manage.

Accompanied by three or four sentries carrying enormous clubs and wearing Na-Griamel insignias on their grimy t-shirts, we were directed toward a hut. A few near-naked tribesmen came out from behind the banana trees to smile at us as we entered the hut. A chair and table made out of crates, the only furnishings, loomed like a throne in the exact center of the room. Our guides signaled us to wait. They sat down on the crushed coral floor. They looked tired. The hand-drawn posters, leaning up against the bamboo wall, attracted my eye. Two poorly executed, childlike pictures were lessons in protocol for the instruction of visiting natives. The first represented the table and chair, which were drawn in heavy pencil, with stick figures sitting on the gravel. In the second, a radiant, almost visionary personage had taken the seat behind the table and the stick figures were standing at attention before him. I was wondering whether women were also supposed to rise when a Chief President arrived. Moot point. I hadn't even had the chance to sit down when he appeared.

With his abundant gray beard and his prophet eyes he looked nothing like a New Hebridean. European? Polynesian? Maybe he had some Melanesian blood, but it certainly didn't seem to predominate. An unctuous smile. I studied his face. Was it the look of a sage or a trickster? René introduced us, but the Chief President had to make his own introductions in his own way. "I am Jimmy Tubo Patuntun Moses Stephens," he said haughtily. "You can call me Jimmy," he added with a wink.

He surveyed our film and photography equipment and looked impressed. He knew we were Americans, and that seemed to please him. "I'm going to the UN with our case. I'm sure you can help us."

We put him straight on that right away. We were neutral and didn't intend to help anybody for the moment. Jimmy reassured us. "Of course, you're honest people. Take your time. But you'll agree with my point of view in the end and you'll get me good publicity."

Thus he set to the task of explaining his position. It was fairly confusing. He preaches the return to Melanesian customs but, belonging to a mission, wants to Christianize the tribal pagans and make them wear clothes. He told us there are members of his movement throughout the islands. All you have to do is pay the dues to join. And what does the Na-Griamel do with this money? "We improve the condition of the New Hebrideans."

The only subject which was clear was the reclamation of European property. Jimmy explained to us that this land had been bought at a time when a square mile could be had for a couple of cigarettes, that all the original sales should be reviewed, and that he wasn't talking about the cultivated lands but the vast uncul-

Kalman Muller was seven when his parents left Hungary. He spent some time in France and Switzerland, where he learned French and English, before rejoining his family in Tucson. After studying at the University of Arizona, he left for Africa where he traveled for a year and a half. His next trips were in Europe and the Middle East, followed by South America. He became an accomplished photographer and, during his stays in the United States, obtained a doctorate in French literature. In 1966, leaving Los Angeles in a sailboat, he crossed the Pacific for the first time, stopping at the Marquesas Islands, Tahiti, Bora Bora, and the New Hebrides. Fascinated by this archipelago and its inhabitants, he promised himself he would one day return for a longer stay. *Jacques Gourguechon*

tivated areas whose titles are still in the hands of European individuals or companies.

We took some photographs and a few feet of film.

We didn't know the country yet and were in no position to evaluate its problems. We told Jimmy as much. We would certainly return later with more exact questions. Jimmy understood.

In the car on the way back to Santo we talked about what we had seen and heard. Kal was a priori in favor of the Na-Griamel; Tom had no opinion; and I was wary of the Chief President but felt there was something to the movement. René, certainly much more knowledgeable than any of us, had no ideas on the subject, and Anatole didn't dare express a point of view. In any case, we agreed that we would have to get some information on Jimmy, the Na-Griamel, and the condition of the New Hebrideans in general before going back to Vanafo. Above all, we mustn't return too soon. We were sure that Jimmy would take advantage of our presence if he could. We didn't wish to be anybody's puppets—Jimmy's, the Condominium's, or the New Hebrideans'.

Back at the Marine the regulars were sprouting like weeds around the bar, but a lovely crocus blossomed amid them. The young man with fine features, curly chestnut brown hair, magpie eyes, and wearing a beach ensemble in brilliant turquoise and white was Charles Matignon, head of the antimalaria team.

Charles was very interested in our project and was willing to do anything he possibly could to help us. It took very little time for him to corner Kal. Their tête-à-tête at the back of the bistro, punctuated by Charles's crystalline giggles and Kal's artificial guffaws, was very animated.

After a while, Kal went up to Elsa to tell her he wouldn't be there for lunch, that he was leaving with Charles. "Where are you going?" asked Tom, who had overheard. The tone of his question made it clear he thought he had the right to know.

"We're going back to Vanafo," said Kal, rather embarrassed. "Charles knows Jimmy well and he's going to help me get something from him."

"Don't you think that's a bit premature?" I asked. "We just decided we shouldn't go too fast with Jimmy. You agreed we have to find out more about him. And don't you think we ought to find out about the Big Nambas first? That's why we're here."

Kal shrugged his shoulders. "It can't hurt," he mumbled without looking at me.

Charles kissed Elsa's hand. Jean offered his hand as well. Everyone laughed aloud. Charles turned red and tried to laugh along with the rest of them. He and Kal left very quickly.

"I don't care," said Tom.

"I care a great deal," I answered. This was to be my first disagreement with Kal.

That evening Charles's hired car dropped Kal off in front of the Marine. Kal came in, carrying a sculpted object.

"What's that?" I asked.

"A ceremonial mask from Malekula. Charles gave it to me."

"That's good," I grumbled. "I see you haven't wasted your time." And I wasn't about to drop the subject. I wanted everything up front. Kal couldn't see the contradiction between our joint decision made that morning and what he had done alone in the afternoon.

"Why are you so upset? It's not important anyway," he concluded nonchalantly.

"If this is the way we'll be working together with the Big Nambas, you'll see the importance!"

I was in a hurry to leave for Malekula, but nothing moves quickly in the Pacific. The *Tahitien* was behind schedule, and Jacques had sent us a telegram from Tahiti saying he would be a week later than expected. While we were waiting, we prepared for the journey as fully as possible. In the Chinese stores we bought a minimum of supplies: blankets, since the nights are cold on the Big Nambas plateau; a case of canned meat, which we could trade or eat ourselves from time to time; flashlights and batteries. Despite our strict budget we bought a Polaroid camera so we could give the Big Nambas photographs on the spot. And we disregarded the suggestions of people in Santo to get a tent. We thought it would isolate us too much from village life; someone was bound to offer us some room in his hut.

Since Malekula isn't far from Santo, we expected to be able to get some valuable information about the Big Nambas in town. It wasn't easy, though. Everyone does have an opinion, but there are as many opinions as people. Some say their culture has already died, that they're Christianized, that there's nothing interesting to see. Some warn us that it's still very dangerous—why, just the other day they shot at one of the native police; they're as savage as ever. The New Hebrideans living in Santo respond to our questions with a typical cry: "Ouuu-iii!" We finally realized that no one in Santo knows these famous Big Nambas personally.

Theoretically, before going off into the other islands, you must pay your respects to the French and British delegations, but for the time being there was no one in either office. Nothing moves quickly in the New Hebrides.

We took advantage of our stay to really get down to studying pidgin, the universal solvent of the islands. An Australian linguist, specialized in the Pacific area, told us later that there are approximately two hundred languages and dialects in this small archipelago that counts only some eighty thousand inhabitants. It is not simply from island to island but from valley to valley that people cannot communicate in their native tongue. Hence the need of a vehicular language. Even the British and French often use pidgin when speaking together, as neither group is inclined to take the trouble to learn the language spoken by their Condominium co-administrators.

For us, pidgin was quite misleading at first. You hear English words and think you've understood something, but you never get the gist. Although the vocabulary of this variety of pidgin is based on English, with French and Melanesian words thrown in, the structure and use of the words is entirely Melanesian, as is its rapid musical rhythm. There is no direct expression even for the most basic ideas. Everything is paraphrase, and you have to understand Melanesian reasoning more than the vocabulary. I'm hungry: *Belly b'ong me he sing out, he wannem something go down long him. Me wannem kaï-kaï* would be technically correct pidgin, but a well-brought-up Melanesian wouldn't say it. *Kaï-kaï* is a key word nonetheless, which we learned at once. It means "to eat" or "food."

The Santo Europeans had some fun giving us a few examples of "classic pidgin" for objects of Western civilization. A saw: *Something b'long white man you pushem he go you pullem he come he savvy kaï-kaï wood*. A piano: *Something where he got black teeth b'long him he got white teeth b'long him you killem he cry out*. *Killem* means "to strike something or someone"; *killem dead finish* means "to kill."

We were forewarned that most Big Nambas don't speak pidgin anyway. Our guides and porters certainly would, but we would have to learn what we could of the Big Nambas language during our stay.

It started raining before sunrise and continued all day long. The rain was fine, regular, incessant. Everything was damp; the humidity penetrated our very bones. We took apart and cleaned the equipment. In this climate camera lenses get moldy quicker than fruit on the kitchen table. Elsa and Jean were tense, drinking more than usual. They were bored. With weather like that, they don't get any customers. "Thank goodness you're here," Elsa said. She needed to confide in someone and began talking about her husband as if he weren't there. While mixing a generous anisette for Jean, she told us how he becomes violent when he drinks too much, how he breaks this or that. Jean played along, laughing, yes, I'll never forget the time I smashed the record player. . . .

"He thinks it's funny," continued Elsa, "but it's not. He really goes wild. He goes out of his mind!"

"Okay, Elsa, that's enough," said Jean, still smiling. "Don't push it too far. No one's interested in your sob story."

"Let me finish, Jean," she said, without looking at him. "You really can't imagine what it's like, he's ruined most of my things, and I had such pretty things, presents and souvenirs. He becomes a real brute. He——"

"I said that's *enough!*" No more smiles. Jean didn't want to play any more. And it *was* enough, but not for Elsa.

"All right, Jean, all right . . . oh, but I just wanted to tell you about this one night. He beat me and kicked me out of the house. I had to sleep at my son's house. My arms were already black and blue and my son wanted to call the police, but I said no."

Jean jumped off his stool behind the bar. That was it. A violent wave of anger swelled up inside him. Was this what Elsa had tried to provoke? Jean wanted to hit something, to break something, to let loose. He screamed and threatened his wife bodily. But, his hands trembling, his face purple, he controlled himself. His anger subsided.

Kal, Tom, and I looked at one another. It would be best to leave, but where could we go in that rain?

After a few minutes of heavy silence, Elsa became nostalgic. She had been a singer. Taken by a sudden desire to share the joys of her past, she ran into her room to find her album of old photographs and yellowed press clippings.

The comparison was poignant. She had been a pretty girl, a lovely young woman. The Elsa Ravon before us was a grotesque caricature of the charming, Gloria Swanson–style singer of the thirties. Her husband also saw the decline, but unlike us he wasn't embarrassed. On the contrary, he jumped at the occasion, laughing raucously, mocking her cruelly.

Under the pretext of being hungry, we asked if we couldn't eat an early lunch so that we could work all afternoon. Elsa dragged her flaccid legs toward the kitchen. Jean was pleased; he had had the last word.

The rain finally stopped toward evening, but we learned that the rain had been a bad sign. The rainy season would probably start early that year. We too had become irritable, having been cooped up all day. We were pacing like caged animals when Charles came in. There was going to be a dance that night in Santo. Kal wasn't interested. Needing a little distraction, I said that maybe I'd stop by. Charles was horrified. All alone? You mustn't! A girl like you! It's not so much the natives as the mestizos. You have to be careful. What would people say? I began to suspect that around here "people" always had something to say. All the same, I was amused that Charles should be so concerned with my welfare. And in any case, Tom also wanted to go. So, finally, the two of us left, trailing footprints in the ebb-tide sand.

We could hear the Tahitian-spiced American rock and American-rolled Tahitian music far down the otherwise silent road. It was coming from a large cabin overlooking the sea. An event for everyone in Santo. People swarmed inside and out Chez Mao. Pauline, an imposing Tahitian, drowning in shell and flower leis, a crown of frangipani on her head, greeted each new arrival exuberantly while keeping her eye on the behavior of the noisy revelers at the bar. She was the boss. Mao, her husband, Tahitian as well, a handsome man in his fifties, was perfect for his role as bandleader. He crooned his South Pacific melodies to every woman who passed in front of him. A carnival of pareu colors, Chinese silks, perfumes, laughter, and drums in counterpoint. Fireworks bombarding all the senses.

Across from me, gulping his beer through bushy red whiskers, sat Tom. We danced together two or three times, and then I danced with a local mestizo—very correct, may I have the pleasure of this dance and so on. From the bar Charles followed my every movement. Over my shoulder I spotted Tom asking a very pretty girl to dance. Refused flatly, he slinked back to his beer. When I got to the table, he was sulking; he didn't want to dance any more.

My own spirits were soaring. I wanted to dance. No one was refused. A Frenchman. An Australian. A Tahitian waltz with a tipsy Fijian sailor who insisted ten times that he *would* marry me, but didn't make a scene. While whirling with a New Caledonian, I watched a Wallis Islander dressed in a pareu and white shirt. He was pretty high, dancing all alone, his hips swaying back and forth suggestively, Polynesian style. He wasn't bothering a soul, but Pauline didn't seem to care for this sort of thing in her establishment. She showed him to the door without too much difficulty, being the stronger of the two. Faster and hotter the music burned.

Tom had had enough. As we were leaving, I blew Charles a kiss. He had never stopped watching me. He smiled feebly and nodded good night. Tom and I silently found our way up the coast to the Marine.

Santo on Sunday is deader than usual. Everyone seems to disappear, even to go into hiding. All the store windows are boarded up, all the cafés closed. The only activity in Santo on Sunday is the siesta. So when Charles and René came to the Marine in the morning to invite us to a picnic on the beach with some friends, we didn't hesitate to accept.

We stopped by René's house to pick up his wife, Yvette, and his youngest children. Yvette shook our hands with a shopkeeper's smile and offered us a tour of her boutique at our earliest possible convenience. She is a featherweight European with a piercing oriental voice.

On the way, we stopped in front of a cage on plantation grounds to look at two flying foxes. We had already heard a lot about these enormous bats, and René warned us that we would be seeing a good deal of them in the islands, especially at dusk when they glide high above the forest. Strange animals. They do look a lot like foxes—the same head and body, but with powerful bat wings and fine pitch black claws that seem made of plastic. I bent over them to look at their faces. Hanging upside down, their heads nestled in their necks, they scrutinized me with intelligent, dreamy eyes. You'd think their magnificent wings would be a burden. I couldn't imagine myself eating them, though I already knew that flying fox meat was an island delicacy.

At the beach, the other picnickers were already there—and they were gendarmes. Right away, one of them started talking to me.

Was I enjoying my visit to the New Hebrides? Would I be in Santo two weeks from now? No. Oh, that's too bad. He was planning a field tour and would have been delighted to take us along. What are we doing here exactly? What are our projects, our interests?

Little by little I realized the questions were getting more and more precise. I was actually being subjected to a police interrogation! Our contacts with the Na-Griamel worried him more than anything else. My answers weren't very reassuring. To the contrary, I was laying bait. "Oh yes, we're very interested in the Na-Griamel. We're going to do a more serious study."

"You must be cautious, mademoiselle. Very, very cautious."

"And what do you personally think of the Na-Griamel?"

"You can't judge such things too quickly now, can you?"

René had told everyone that I had written a children's book. The gendarme asked me the name of my editor in New York.

"Walker," I replied.

"Wo-kerr? Wo-kerr?" That name meant something to him. "The *Dai-li Wo-kerr?*"

The other officer was tossing his knife into the sand so that it stood upright. His eight-year-old daughter wanted to learn how to do it, and he gladly repeated his performance. Then, when he was tired of that stunt, he started stabbing trees.

By the time lunch was over, everybody was in high spirits. René and the gendarmes got a game of volleyball going with the women and the children. Kal and Charles settled down for a nap. Tom and I went off to take walks, but not together.

The champagne-colored beach curved to the horizon. There was something poignant about the eternal void of the ocean. I focused on one small point in the water and then another. Nothing. Only waves washing over more waves. It was deliciously hot. The gentle song of the Pacific completed my universe. I wanted to collapse into the warm sand larded with tiny shimmering shells.

A few feet from me, the jungle stops, contained by the water. The sun disappears into the green but is refracted in every direction from the chasm of foliage. Green, silent hostility in all its thickness. Not recommended for the casual stroller. I had just heard the story of a Santo Frenchman who had gone off hunting in the jungle two weeks before. He brought his dogs, but the na-

"Black-palm" tree fern. *Jacques Gourguechon*

tives who usually go with him hadn't gone this time. The planter had gotten off to an early start and told his wife to expect him for lunch. He still hadn't returned at sunset. His wife called the police, who immediately sent out a search party.

It wasn't until midnight the next day that he found his way to one of the plantations. His dogs had run away and it was impossible for him to catch them in the labyrinth of lianas. Meanwhile, the search party hadn't found a single trace of him. Our man was turned completely around, desperately lost, and headed away from the edge of the forest. He had completely lost his sense of direction. Finally, at nightfall of his second day out, he found a fence. He was saved and he knew it. A fence can wind along for miles, but it always leads somewhere. This incident wasn't unusual. European residents of Santo, who think they know the country well, get lost in the jungle with extraordinary regularity. During the war, numerous Americans died in this very manner, only a few miles from their base.

I ventured into the jungle following something of a trail that went along the fringe of this virgin forest. I didn't go very far. I knew I was within shouting distance of the picnickers, but I suddenly wanted to flee the shadows and find the reassuring warmth of the sun. In the depths of this obscure crypt, this wild proliferation of leaves, the few rays of light that reached me seemed sinister. My imaginings left an aftertaste of fear. Hearing the far-off laughter of our friends, I felt I was saved.

Back by the sea something was floating in the water, bobbing in the advancing and receding foam. From a distance, it had a strange form. A solid mass with a long flapping tail. I walked toward it. It was just at my feet now, and I still didn't know what it was. Animal matter in any case. Covered with a thick violet membrane, compact, round, and fatter at one end. What I had taken for a tail was no more than a continuation of the same, an empty tube, torn, turned a sickly yellow. Like a fetus, or an organ ripped from I don't know what animal. I didn't want to ask the others what it was. I didn't want them to see it. Why did the existence of this thing bother me so much . . . almost like a guilty secret?

I joined the others. They had given up volleyball for French bowls.

Ernst-Wilhelm Lamberty, captain of the *Konanda*, the largest trading boat of the islands, came to lunch at the Marine. He came especially to see us. He had heard we were looking for boat passages. It would be possible, he told us, but not this time. He was not going to Malekula just yet.

Ernst, or Ernie, as he is called, is Dutch. He speaks French, English, and German fluently. He's over fifty years old, and his waistline isn't too far from the fifty-inch goal. He's gruff and jolly and looks the part of the South Seas captain. We hadn't heard his story yet, but we knew we were dealing with a personage.

We had drinks at the bar. The rule of each man paying for his round no longer applied. It was Ernst who proposed "one for the road" over and over again. The road was the distance from the bar to the table.

"So. You intend to go back to the rat race after seeing all this?"

We admitted that life in the tropics had its charms.

"You don't know it yet," he continued, "but you're done for. Once you set foot in these parts, you never get away. This life grabs you in your gut and won't let go. Look at me. I came to the New Hebrides for two weeks and I've been here fifteen years now!"

The conversation turned to one of his favorite subjects, women.

"European women, and American women too, they're all the
same, a pack of hens. All they want is to find themselves some
poor sucker who'll earn lots of dough. They waste hours polishing
their nails. I know all about it. And they spend their lives chasing
after the newest-style clothes. Every year, they throw out last
year's dresses like rags. You think that's normal? And the poor
bastards who bring home the bacon and pay the bills! Oh, I've
had enough of you 'civilized' people." He sighed with a smile and
not a little pride that he'd avoided their fate.

Tom was in complete agreement with Lamberty. Kal dropped
an "uh-huh" or a "could be" from time to time but wasn't at all interested in the topic. For me, it was good entertainment.

Feeling that both Ernst (for his own amusement) and Tom
(perhaps with a grain of hostility) were putting me on the spot, I
thought I'd give them a hand. "So, Captain, according to your
theories, what am I doing here?" He took my hand. No trace of
nail polish.

"No lipstick either, and none of that clown paint around the
eyes."

Elsa, who wore heavy makeup, did not seem pleased.

"Obviously you didn't come here to wear the latest fashions,"
he said, with an approving glance at my blue jean cut-offs and
t-shirt, "and you didn't come to catch a rich husband either.
Women! I'm always happy to find the exception. But you're in-
dependent-minded! Native girls know a woman's place—in the
kitchen or in the bed. You don't know that!"

"No, you're right there."

Elsa asked Tom if he was really interested in native girls. "Oh
yeah, I sure would like to meet some!" Elsa interpreted this in her
own way and set the thing up with the seventeen-year-old daughter of her house cleaner. At first Tom was very happy. He talked
with her in pidgin, how-are-you-fine-how-are-you. He offered her
a soda.

But Elsa was growing impatient. "What are you waiting for?
Take her to your room!"

The girl smiled. Tom understood. He was mortified. All at
once, he felt terribly ill and went off alone.

Kal returned from the Chinese stores with an abundant supply of presents for the chief of the Big Nambas: knives of all sizes, axes, tobacco sticks, cartons of cigarettes, rifle cartridges, flashlights, batteries, all kinds of canned food, two bottles of rum, and more.

"You're not going to give him all that, are you?" I exclaimed.

"Not right away, anyway."

"Why not?"

"He'll think you want to buy him."

Kal thought this could only make matters easier. I felt it would be best to arrive with a few small presents, explain our position, and openly ask his permission to stay with them. We could always offer other gifts later on. Again, Kal and I weren't seeing eye to eye, but Kal was the head of the expedition, so the decisions were his. All I bought were candy for the children and a few bottles of cologne for the women.

Finally, over the radio, we learned that the *Tahitien* had reached Port-Vila, the tiny capital of the archipelago. Jacques would join us; the team would be complete, and we could leave for the interior.

I was in a bad mood. Both Kal and Tom were getting on my nerves, each for different reasons. When Kal asked me if I wanted to go with them to get Jacques at the airport, I said no. I set my typewriter up in a corner of the bistro and began typing my notes. A friend of Kal's, I reasoned sulkily, would never be a friend of mine.

But I was wrong and knew it right away. Jacques Gourguechon shook my hand vigorously when he arrived. He has an open smile and playful, intelligent eyes. Everyone intuitively had a favorable first impression of him. Elsa and Jean wanted to keep him all to themselves.

And, of course, with the arrival of a new person in any group, the configuration changes. Kal and Jacques got on as well as when they had first met in Paris. Jacques and I quickly developed a good rapport which, I'm not quite sure why, immediately eased the tension between Kal and myself. Tom was always fine with everyone or no one. But in a team of four, if three are relating well, that's already quite a lot.

Jacques Gourguechon was born in Poissy, France, and at an early age began filling his schoolboy notebooks with drawings of sailboats and exotic scenes. The French government launched his career (involuntarily) by sending him for his military service to Algeria, where his deep interest in other cultures was affirmed. On his return he met the explorer André Migot, a specialist on Tibet and vice-president of the Society of Explorers. With Dr. Migot, Jacques Gourguechon learned his craft. In 1964 he undertook a voyage across central Asia, which led him to spend several months at Uzbekistan and in the northeast of Afghanistan around Pamir. He returned with a film, *On the Silk Route*, shown on French television, which then sent him around the world in 1965–66 to shoot several dozen shows in the series *Camera Stop*. He visited the Amazon, Kyoto, the Philippines, and the black ghettos of Los Angeles, where his work interested the Carpenter Center at Harvard which invited him to collaborate on some commercial films. In 1968 he met Kal Muller in Paris and together they undertook an expedition to the New Hebrides. *Kal Muller*

I learned the importance of getting along when you're not only working together but living together as well. Funny, but liking or disliking, loving or hating someone seems to have little to do with it. Maybe it's communication that counts. Jacques knew how to draw Kal out and make him talk. At that time I didn't realize it, but I missed talking. I like to talk. With Kal, I had been able to express myself if I had a considered opinion to offer, but easy-going conversation is not his usual style. Kal and I eventually got to that point, perhaps thanks to Jacques. Friendships can fall into place when a team such as ours functions well. As for Tom, he and

I never had much to say to each other, and nothing comes of nothing.

For the moment there were no boats going to Malekula, so we would have to take the Air Melanesia Navaho as far as the Norsup plantation in the northeast part of the island. The agent told us that there were no bookings at all for Wednesday, two days later, and therefore there would be room not only for us but for our equipment as well.

We were going to have lunch with René at Chez Albert. His wife didn't want to join us. René explained nervously, "I can't stay too long. If Yvette doesn't want to come, that means she would rather I didn't either."

Cocktail time once again. And we found ourselves with the same group of planters planted behind their whiskeys. I concluded that when they're not at the Ravons', they're at Albert's.

From the door behind the bar emerged a shouting phenomenon, as big as a football player, his shirt opened wide to show off his sturdy tanned chest. This septuagenarian had a pirate face and strangely, at the same time, resembled a General De Gaulle who had spent half a century in the tropics. The likeness was confirmed by the portrait of De Gaulle which reigned over the line of bottles against the wall behind the bar. Rough and ready, a bottle of Amstel beer in his hand, he yelled over his shoulder, "Anna! Goddamn and blast it, are you coming or what? We got customers!" A bang of his fist on the bar. A guttural voice. It was hard to tell whether he was yelling in French or English or pidgin.

Apparently, I wasn't the only one who had difficulty understanding him. Albert is Belgian and his native language is Flemish. His French is often more picturesque than correct. But you get used to his language quickly and understand that his character is more French than that of the French themselves.

René introduced us. The old hooligan gave me the once-over and a devilish smile. "So, my little bird, are you poken?"

"Excuse me?"

"Poken, poken! Is she poken, or what?" he barked at the room in general.

René laughed and said I was American. He explained to me that "poken" comes from the shop sign "English spoken." It's local slang for an English man or woman. As Santo hadn't yet invented a colorful label for U.S. citizens, throughout my stay I was simply called "the American."

Albert didn't yield the floor to René for very long. "The Americans!" he howled. "I knew them during the war. I took General Rose to Guadalcanal on my boat. And this General Rose says to me later, he says, 'Albert, I don't know what we would have done without you.' "

Louis Ancess, an old mestizo planter, had a word on the subject too. "I don't say this is your case—but I was invited to a dinner by a captain and found myself seated next to a lieutenant who refused to give me a light because I didn't have white skin! I won't have anything to do with Americans, they're all racists. Present company excepted, mademoiselle," he added gallantly.

"You," continued Albert, pushing a steel finger into my shoulder, "you can't know, you're too young. But it's a good thing he was around. Him." The finger now pointed toward De Gaulle's shoulder in the portrait. "That great man was there to keep an eye on you. If not, the Yankees would have fucked up the whole works!"

René gave me a discreet nudge with his elbow and a wink. "Albert, talking about De Gaulle, I heard the other day in Vila that he never shook your hand and never called you 'Albert,' that it's all a lot of hot air."

"You son of a bitch! Bring me the bastard who told you that, and I'll smash this stool over his head. It was '66 when he came, in '66, and I've got witnesses. Not the likes of you either."

A loud, pointed laugh preceded the arrival behind the bar of a majestic black woman, dressed all in red and purple silk, gold earrings accenting a half moon of sparkling teeth. It's Anna, Madame Albert Goddyn, the queen of the establishment, with cocoa-skinned little girls, about three and fours years old, clinging to her skirt.

"G'd afternooooon," she drawled regally, all smiles, her voice resounding from her three-hundred-pound frame.

Screeching brakes announced the assistant director of public works, the fire chief, the president of the Boxing Club, the vice-president of the Veterans' Association, and the gourmet-in-residence of the New Hebrides. Five people rolled up into one—

André Augonnet. "Tell them, André, you know the story. Tell them how De Gaulle shook my hand. Anna! Take care of the customers!" With that, Albert disappeared into the kitchen.

"I don't want to tell them that, Albert," called André. "I'd rather tell them about the Queen of England."

"Bloody po*kens!*" bawled Albert from the other side of the wall, amid the terrible din of pots and pans.

Everyone chuckled, including Anna.

Jacques asked, "What's this about the Queen?"

"One day, Albert was returning from Port-Vila . . . ," began André. He seemed to be thoroughly enjoying the story in advance.

"It was a Saturday morning," chimed in one of the planters, "that's why there were so many natives and even some pokens."

"Yes, a Saturday," continued André. "Albert arrived in a taxi and over the front door of the café he found an enormous banner which read TODAY IS ENGLISH WEEK. He tore it down and stamped on it. He screamed and yelled. And inside the bar what do you think he saw? He couldn't believe his eyes. The portrait of De Gaulle had been replaced by a photo of the Queen of England!"

Albert dropped a pan on the cement floor, surely to punctuate the tale.

"So, our poor Albert was beside himself with rage. He took the photo and threw it on the ground. I will not repeat the vulgarities which flew from his mouth. He picked up the picture with its broken glass and went into the bathroom and hung it up over the toilet. But that wasn't enough for old Albert. He went into his bedroom, got his revolver, and emptied it into the picture. Then he waved the gun over his head with a nasty look in his eyes and announced to us, 'The next time anyone makes fun of the General in my place, he'll have to deal with me! And the bastard'll never be the same again!' "

"Weren't the English who were there furious?" I asked.

"Oh, everyone knows Albert. But someone must have complained because the next day Albert was brought before the French Delegation. The Condominium always needs to keep up appearances. But since Albert is no diplomat, he repeated everything he had said in front of the Delegate and in the end he almost set off an international incident!"

I noticed René was getting impatient. He looked at his watch, thinking of Yvette, probably. "Hey, Albert, what are we eating?" he cried toward the kitchen.

Albert dragged his feet to the door, without hurrying. In one hand he held a huge steak dripping blood, in the other a giant butcher's knife. With his eyes he held René. "Shit," he replied calmly.

We were as far as our dessert, after a more than plentiful meal, when a tiny woman on a bicycle rode up in front of the open café door. Yvette! Straddling the bike, she glanced into the den of iniquity where her husband was hiding.

"René!"

Lifting his arm to glance at his watch one more time, he knocked over his wine. "Yes, dear, I'm here. We're almost done. Won't you have coffee with us?"

"Thanks a lot, I've been waiting for over an hour. I'm your wife, not your maid. You've got work to do. Are you coming home or not?"

"Yes, angel, right away. I'll be there in five minutes."

"If you dawdle, let me warn you, it'll be bad!" She was off in a huff. René fell back in his chair. He was visibly shaken.

"This lunch is gonna cost me a helluva lot," he sighed.

The next morning at eight we boarded the Air Melanesia plane for Malekula.

2

"One Photo, One Pound"

A L L I'm telling you isn't history from a book. It's the truth. I remember it like it was yesterday. Now, listen. The old chief, Velvel, accepted my father almost like a member of the tribe. And the day Velvel sent him a gift wrapped up in banana leaves . . ."

"But Monsieur Theuil," interrupted Robert Figa, "what about the Corlette boy? The one they ate? Wasn't he a relative of yours?"

Pierre Theuil visibly enjoyed being asked questions that anticipated his thoughts. He straightened up in his chair. He pushed back his straw hat with a thumb and scratched the receding hairline. "Of course. He was one of my first wife's brothers. Let's see, how old would he be now? . . ."

We were on the eastern coast of Malekula. Robert Figa, the bookkeeper at the Norsup plantation, where we had landed, had invited us to stay at his house until we would leave for the Big Nambas plateau. He had brought Jacques and me (Kal and Tom not caring to come along) in his Land Rover, along the coastal trail, to meet one of the planters in the region, a real old-timer. Hardened by half a century of labor under the hot Malekula sun, Pierre Theuil still lived in the same dilapidated cabin where he'd been born.

Robert Figa insisted, "Tell Jacques and Charlene what happened to the Corlette boy."

"Well, it happened right over there at Tautu," said Mr. Theuil, pointing toward a promontory just north of us, "on the Bridges plantation. Bridges was an Englishman. When I think of it . . . I could have been there, too, that day. My father often took me up there to play with his kids. I was five or six at the time. That, my friends, is Fate, and you're looking at a lucky man. Anyway, Bridges was eating lunch with his four children and the Corlette boy who was visiting. His wife, a local native, had gone off to see her parents. She was lucky, too. Then they stormed the house."

Jacques asked whether "they" were the Big Nambas or the Small Nambas.

"Big, Small, they're all the same when it comes to a massacre. For the record, these people were Dirak, a group of Small. The Big are more apt to strike the west coast. They entered the Bridges' cabin and fell on him and the children with their hatchets. Maybe the same hatchets Bridges had sold them. Only one of the kids was able to escape, the Corlette boy. He fought his way through a mangrove thicket down to the water and tried to wade out to the Bridges' canoe. But they caught him. They took the body back to their village. They cut it up and sent the cooked chunks of meat to the northern villages. For days, even here on the coast, we heard the rumble of tom-toms from the jungle, the tom-toms that announced their victory."

Theuil laughed softly at this old memory from which he was now detached, but which must have indelibly marked his childhood.

"And the worst thing is," he continued, "that a chief who receives such a gift has a moral obligation to return one in kind. It's like a debt. We understood that, even the kids like me were aware of this custom. I remember I used to pretend they were chasing me. Kids like to be scared, it's a lot of fun. But I still had terrible nightmares that made me wake up screaming."

"But why?" I asked. "Why was the whole family killed? Was it vengeance, or what?"

"I guess we'll never know. They couldn't possibly have had anything against Bridges himself. He had a reputation for being honest and on the level with everybody. And it wasn't Corlette ei-

ther. He knew the natives like no other planter did. He even
spoke Dirak. But maybe it was a vengeance against whites in general. What I mean is, when they're wronged by a white, say
someone on a boat who kills or kidnaps a native, if they can't get
their hands on the guilty man, the blood of any other white will
do. That's their justice. And they're not sentimental about their
choice either. They take the first one they can get hold of, a missionary, a planter, anyone. On the other hand, there's no mystery
at all in the case of Mazoyer. We know very well what they were
avenging."

Pierre Theuil kicked a dry coconut shell and watched it roll
along the ground. Then he just looked at us and didn't say another word. He didn't impose himself. If we wanted him to go on
with his story, we had to show him our interest by asking questions. We were willing. "Who was Mazoyer? What happened to
him?" queried Jacques.

"Paul Mazoyer had a large plantation on Aori, the island across
from Santo, but he used to go to north Malekula to recruit his laborers. He didn't get along with anybody, not his workers, not
his neighbors, not even the administration. No one went to his
house. He had thirty mastiffs to protect him and always had a
shotgun handy. Basically he wasn't a bad guy, you just had to get
to know him. He started out with nothing. He was born in New
Caledonia and built up his plantation from scratch. But he had a
savage streak more savage than even the savages. In a word, he
was a brute. During the First World War he volunteered for the
dirtiest detail. He was one of the guys who finished off the
wounded enemy soldiers in the trenches. You see what I mean?
He was a giant, strong as a bull. Not a man to tangle with! But
when he drank, which was pretty often, it was hard to avoid a
quarrel with him. He beat his laborers so badly that the government had to intervene. And I'm talking about this government,
which usually leaves the planters alone. And most of them aren't
angels either. The administration took away his Tonkinese workers. Mazoyer never came clean in his dealings with the Malekula
natives. And that was a grave error. He never understood that
you have to watch your every step with those people. If you don't
keep your word, you're sure to regret it. One day he beat one of
his Malekula plantation workers to death. The others found out

about it. For that and all his cheating, Mazoyer's stone bed had been ready on Malekula for quite a while."

"His stone bed?" I repeated.

"Yeah, his rocks. Oh, of course, you don't know about all that," smiled Pierre Theuil. "You've just gotten here. Well, you'll see how the Big Nambas cook—on a layer of white-hot stones. And when they condemn a planter to death, they send him an ambassador to warn him that his stone bed is ready. You get the picture! Now, Mazoyer wasn't afraid of anything. He even laughed about 'his stones.' He talked about them with the writer Pierre Benoit, whom he met in Santo. 'The thing is, those animals keep their word whenever they can.' All the same he was haunted by the thought of his motorboat breaking down one day off the coast of Malekula. But fate is fate, after all, as I said before. Though now that I think about it, that man always seemed to do his damnedest to provoke incidents.

"Anyway, the end of the story, the definitive end of his story, came one day when he was recruiting. He took aboard three Big Nambas women from the village of Mrawe. They went voluntarily, but the chief wanted them back. He offered Mazoyer a fine tusked pig in exchange for them, and Mazoyer accepted. So the chief sends the pig over to the boat. And Mazoyer double-crosses him. He tells the chief, 'I'll keep the pig and the women, too. That'll show you who's boss around here.' That was the last straw. That night five Big Nambas boarded the boat, shot Mazoyer to death, and ransacked the boat. We don't know whether the crew was in cahoots with the natives or not, but there were no witnesses. Mazoyer's body was found riddled with bullets. The fingers of one hand had been cleanly chopped off with a machete. He must have tried to hold on to the hood of the deckhouse and get out of his cabin while they were still on the bridge."

Silence. No one had anything to say after this story.

The day was fading away. The leaves of a huge mango tree in front of us began rustling. There was no wind. I saw pieces of the tree break away toward the sky and take on the form of flying foxes. Flapping away into the dusk, with their sharp cries, these beasts lost the gentleness I had sensed in them that bright day in Santo when I saw two of them in a cage. They were truly macabre animals.

Robert Figa started the ball rolling again. "A little while ago you started to tell us about Chief Velvel."

"Ah, Velvel, my father knew him well."

"You were saying he sent a present wrapped in banana leaves. . . ."

"Oh yeah, you're talking about the special laplap! You know what a laplap is?" he motioned to Jacques and me. "It's the daily bread of all these natives. It's like an enormous pancake made from grated yams. For special occasions they put a piece of pork, flying fox, or some kind of meat inside. That wasn't the first time they'd given him such a laplap. They did that from time to time. Well, on this particular day, I remember how papa bit into the sandwich—because we didn't have the right, only the head of the family—and said, 'Must be a ceremony or something going on, there's meat in it.' He nibbled a little more. Suddenly he turned white and his eyes bulged out of his head. He tore off the leaves and ripped the laplap open. And what did he find? Son of a bitch, a human hand!"

"Whose hand?" asked Robert Figa. "Did they ever tell you?"

"That, my friend," sighed Pierre Theuil, "God only knows."

Between them Claudie and Robert Figa personify the war in the Pacific and the resulting peace. Robert's mother was a New Hebridean, his father Japanese. Claudie's mother, who still lives in Santo, is from the New Hebridean island of Aoba, where the Polynesians passed through and where, more recently, the French left a few buds on the branches of her family tree. Claudie's father is American. She never knew him, but she does know that his name is Lambert and assumes he's still living somewhere in the States. Claudie explained, without a trace of bitterness, that he stayed around just long enough to see his son and daughter born before leaving for the U.S. of A.

Claudie and Robert are in charge of the plantation store, are the representatives for the small Air Melanesia planes, and run the plantation movie theater. Yes, there's a movie theater, said Robert, smiling. Most of the films are westerns dating back to the fifties, all scratched, torn up, and stuck back together, but the workers like them.

We spent an enjoyable evening at the Figas', in their large, colonial-style, painted wood house, built to let in the breeze when there is one and to keep out the omnipresent heat. The electricity is turned off on the plantation at nine o'clock, but the Figas have several oil lamps and a battery-operated record player. All night long we listened to Tennessee mountain music of which Claudie seemed especially fond, although she couldn't understand a word of it.

The Figas invited us to stay on for a closer look at the plantation. Of course, we were interested, but we refused politely. Above all else we were in a hurry to reach the Big Nambas plateau. The plantation could wait for another time.

Early the following morning Robert drove us to the village of Mae, a couple of miles away, to find porters and a guide. "Listen," he warned us, "let me negotiate. They're sure to ask for the moon to go up there, but I'll get a fair price in the end."

It's a sad little village. Tiny Melanesian shanties with a few corrugated metal roofs, the inhabitants dressed in mission-approved but ragged and filthy clothes. The Europeans have imposed cloth on the natives without teaching them that cloth needs washing and mending. Children, naked, noses running, surrounded us freely. All this amid the most luxuriant natural environment imaginable.

Our guide's name was Alphonse. He was one of the village elders. He came toward us immediately. The people of Mae seemed to have been waiting for us.

Robert Figa quickly told us a little about Alphonse. "By his name alone you can see he's dependent on the Catholic mission. He would be called Ezekiel or Jacob if he were with the Protestants."

They bargained about the price for a few minutes, but Alphonse didn't dare go too far with Robert, who knew the going prices. "Okay," Robert said finally, "it's fixed at a pound a person plus kaï-kaï." (An Australian pound is about $2.50.) Alphonse was to decide how many men we needed.

We brought him back by car to the Figas' house. We had thought a half-dozen porters would do. But after weighing each parcel, satchel, and suitcase in his hand, Alphonse said we would need fifteen. Now, our crew really wasn't rich. Kal, Jacques, and Tom immediately selected the things they would carry themselves. Alphonse looked over what was left and announced magnanimously that nine porters would be an acceptable minimum. Departure was the next day at dawn.

The Figas offered us a tractor with a trailer to take us up to the edge of the jungle. Otherwise it would have taken us over an hour just to walk across the plantation.

As the tractor slowly covered the miles, we made out in the faint light of dawn the forms of coconut palms. At sunrise we arrived at the boundary, the definitive line of demarcation. A menacing wall of dark green rose directly in front of us. *Savage* . . . the word came to mind as it never would again in regard to the inhabitants of this environment, despite their sometimes cruel customs.

Suddenly, I was afraid. A primordial fear, irrational and overpowering.

The porters set to cutting bamboo and lianas with their machetes to carry the packages and suitcases. The lighter parcels were tied one at each end of a bamboo stick and slung over the shoulder. The heaviest packages were tied to one end of a length of bamboo and carried behind the shoulder, the stick giving the porter some leverage. Jacques, Kal, and Tom each carried a camera case or a bundle of photographic equipment. From my neck hung a camera and in my pocket I had a light meter, no more.

The dawn sky changed to daylight. We looked up at the vivid blue tropical day before plunging into the black-shadowed vegetation.

Little by little my anxiety took form. I tried to reason calmly, but it wasn't reassuring. The porters were on familiar ground. They just went forward, avoiding the pitfalls without even having to think about them—as I used to do before (and "before" already felt like eons ago), crossing Broadway anywhere, sensing the cars from both directions, their distance, their speed, while the timid wisely waited at the lights. Kal, Jacques, and Tom were no nature children either, but they were far better trained than I for jungle walking. No problem, no inferiority complex, I was indeed the weakest.

But don't let anyone tell me so! Was it self-respect, pride, or stubbornness that drove me on? Probably all three, because I was certainly determined. My weakness would not show and no one need know about it. Above all, especially since the others would have been all too sympathetic, I did not want to fall back on the only ready-made excuse I had: *it's hard for a woman.*

I was obsessed by the idea of maintaining a good position in the line. I didn't want to walk in front of the porters for fear of setting too slow a pace. I didn't want to walk last for fear of falling behind and getting lost. I inspected my shoes regularly. If I ever had to stop and retie the laces, I would lose my place.

The lianas that crisscrossed the footpath, hidden by the underbrush and dead leaves, threatened to trip me at every step. But in that kind of situation you learn fast. I learned to watch the man in front of me and literally follow in his footsteps whenever possible.

I learned not to ford streams with my shoes on. I tried it once and failed. A black-and-blue mark on my thigh, large as a grapefruit; a crushed can of film in my hip pocket, looking like it had been run over by a steamroller; my clothes soaked, quick to mildew, slow to dry, in this climate—one spectacular fall with your feet pointing upward toward the sun is the best of teachers.

I learned that when you see sunlight through the trees ahead, you're coming to a descent. In that area the hills are always treacherously steep, slippery, and muddy. Realizing that I was less afraid for myself than for the fragile camera I was carrying, I was not too proud to ask Jacques, Kal, or a porter to carry it to the bottom of the slope for me.

The New Hebrideans, despite their heavy loads, had a certain dignity in negotiating these descents. Their backs straight, their heads held high, they were like living statues moving only from the knees down. I often ended up on my backside. However I got there, I was pretty glad just to have made it.

I also learned what *nangalat* is. One of the porters, who had noticed my inflamed scarlet arms, showed me the nettle which was to blame, or at least two or three of the endless varieties of this plant. So, on top of everything else, I had to start studying the leaves to avoid those nasty red-veined ones.

Hours. And more hours of walking.

We passed through clouds of minuscule insects that attacked our every exposed orifice—eyes, nose, ears. We closed our mouths, but the gnats glued themselves to our lips.

Even before hearing the roar of waves, we reckoned how close the sea was. The breeze, unexpected, so welcome, caressed us and evaporated the dirty perspiration from our skin.

Coming out of the dark jungle onto the coast we were, literally and figuratively, dazzled. I wanted to throw myself into the pure blue water. And I wasn't the only one. Everybody needed to bathe, refresh, purify. But we didn't, as the porters warned us it was a shark-infested coast.

We walked along the endless white powder beach that in a more hospitable country would have long ago been the site of a luxurious Hilton. Then we plunged back into the jungle. This time it was just an afternoon stroll, a flat terrain and a sandy trail. We stayed in the coastal region.

The path led us directly to Aori, a Presbyterian village, where we were to spend the night. The inhabitants came from their gardens to greet us, some timidly, some boldly.

Aori is prettier than Mae. Corrugated metal hasn't gotten this far yet, and before the village lies a magnificent beach. But I sensed the same sadness in both villages. I didn't draw any conclusions because I wasn't yet familiar enough with these "man-salt-water" as the coast people are called in pidgin, as opposed to "man-bush," the people of the jungle. "Man-salt-water" also happens to be synonymous with "Christianized natives," which all the coast people are. The Europeans call them "pasteurized natives."

A man of fifty-five or sixty, with enormous buckteeth, introduced himself. *"Name b'long me Stanley. You fella you savvy talk-talk inglis?"* I realized a little later that he thought he was expressing himself in perfect English. He confided in me: *"Me happy too mass talk-talk inglis, but olgeta long place here he talk-talk pidgin no more."* What could I say? I simply said, *"Me happy too mass too."*

Stanley wasn't the village chief, since there are no longer any chiefs in Aori. But he's the "teacher," a sort of subclergyman who represents the island Protestant missions, which comes down to the same thing. Whether his origin was Big Nambas or Small Nambas was impossible to say. He certainly preferred to bury his pagan heritage. He didn't waste much time before speaking to us of God: *"God: him he big fella on top papa b'long you-me."*

He asked us casually, as if asking us where we came from, what our religion was. But he made the mistake in the asking of catching Kal's eye. Kal said, smiling and firm, "None." Poor Stanley was profoundly shocked. Then he found his equilibrium, laughed, and tapped Kal's shoulder, saying, "*Ah! you-you-story-on too mass!*"

Stanley informed us that we would need a second guide to climb to the Big Nambas. Alphonse agreed. There was no pride involved. Alphonse was happy to let a brother earn a pound if it didn't cut into his own earnings. We shook Willy's hand. He was no more than three inches over four feet, with a weasel head and a very broad smile. He was excessively friendly. We mistrusted him at once. But we were to get to know and appreciate Willy. His philosophy was simple: you can be friends and help each other, but it's understood that you cheat each other whenever you can. Willy is a former Big Nambas so he was familiar with the labyrinth of trails on their plateau, and, of course, he spoke the language fluently. We were glad to know that.

We ate with the porters, Stanley and Willy, in the village dining room, a shack furnished with a long table and benches. Stanley begged our pardon. We're poor, he said. We assured him that everything was fine. Yes, but . . . you understand. In the end, we did understand. The people of Aori know how to eat at the table like Europeans, but from force of habit they still use fingerware. The village owns only three forks and one bent spoon. We protested: we don't need any of that, we have fingers like everyone else. But Stanley insisted gravely that it would not be *correct.* I was given the honor of the bent spoon. In the intervals between prayers in pidgin, we ate yams and taros. (Imagine a platter of giant potatoes—they grow up to six feet in length—overcooked, tasteless, and gluey, no butter, no seasonings.) We took a few cans of mackerel from one of the bags to offer to our hosts. For us, exhausted and starving, it was a three-star dinner. And for our friends, too, who opened our cans like Christmas presents.

"Don't you ever go fishing?" I asked Stanley.

"Ah, no, missis," he said, "*salt-water he no good, me fright long him, he savvy kaï-kaï man.*"

He didn't need to add that the salt water scared him off from taking baths, too.

After dinner he brought us to his hut and graciously offered it to us for the night. There were two small rooms. Kal, Jacques, and Tom were to camp in the first. Stanley kindly offered me the second one, his own bedroom. He is probably the only native in northern Malekula who has a bed. He's very proud of it. It's a plank of wood, supported by four posts about a yard high, with a mat about as thick as a sheet of paper in the guise of a mattress. I thanked Stanley with all my heart.

It was eight-thirty, two and a half hours after sunset and well after the usual village bedtime. The man-salt-water have gotten into the habit of using oil lamps to light up the night. However, since the oil is delivered by boats that arrive irregularly and is fairly expensive, and since "civilized" people don't sit around a simple campfire, one goes to sleep early. Kal and Tom adopted this principle and lay down on the earth floor, each wrapped in a blanket, sighing, evidently content to stretch out. Jacques and I weren't sleepy. I was tired after walking all day, but the excitement of being there woke me up. We sat down in front of the hut on a tree trunk laid out like a bench.

The beach glowed in the moonlight, disturbed only by the shadows of the rock. Breaking waves lapped at the edges of the jungle. The sea was silver, stretching to infinity in the gigantic chasm that was night.

We talked softly, without seeing one another, mostly watching the sky. I was fascinated by the stars. They seemed to be an optical illusion. Were they protruding or were they holes in the midnight blue? I laughed. Maybe, reason *numbah one* for their existing, they had been destined to be above all else the compass face for Stanley's ancestors. Did he sometimes think, despite his aversion for the sea, that his forefathers had been some of the very best navigators ever?

Jacques told me what a hard time he was having with pidgin. I responded that it was nothing to worry about. He hadn't been in the islands as long as we had. And since English wasn't his native tongue, he couldn't hope to learn pidgin as easily as we could. However, he could hope to learn it better. An English speaker faces the hard task of willfully deforming his own language, whereas a French speaker can absorb pidgin as a totally new, and not too complicated, language.

We had a little impromptu lesson in our magnificent open-air classroom. *You* is "you alone." *You-fella* is "you guys." But there are traps. To say "everybody," it's not *all fella*, which means "old person" ("old fellow"), it's *olgeta*, "altogether." "Here" is really pronounced *ia*. "By and by" becomes *bambaï*. And so on.

Then it was Jacques's turn to be teacher. My French was very bookish then. I had studied Racine but hadn't met the best-loved cartoon characters. I enjoyed learning the French equivalents for expressions like "far out," "groovy," "gross," "no shit." I still didn't understand the precise meaning of the vulgarities I had heard in Santo, but I had gotten the gist and didn't care to ask Jacques for the details.

I have no idea when we went to bed. I had lost all sense of time. The sensation was not displeasing.

We tiptoed into the hut and whispered good night. I reached Stanley's bed mumbling to myself in newly learned slang about how well I was going to sleep. Beddy-bye, *dodo;* forty winks, *roupiller;* shut-eye, *to snore with your toes spread out like a fan.*

But I spent the night trying to accommodate my stiff muscles and my bruised thigh. Half-asleep, I believed I was on the operating table. I was pleading with the surgeon, it's nothing. I'll be fine tomorrow, please don't touch me. Through the wall, a simple trellis of leaves, I heard snoring. I envied the others. The earth has to be a softer mattress than a wooden board.

There's a river not far from Aori. But going there to wash up in the morning was out of the question. Everyone was anxious to reach the Big Nambas. I was planning to disappear discreetly into the bush for a few minutes when Stanley took my arm and declared triumphantly, *"He got small house long place here."*

"Yes, yes, he good," I said, understanding nothing and wanting to get away from him as soon as possible. But he dragged me behind him to point out two tightly sealed outhouses. Before even opening the door the offensive odors almost knocked me out. Stanley was watching me from a distance, proud of the modern conveniences he had to offer. It was a disgustingly filthy oven whose contents were slowly simmering under the morning sun. I counted one-and-two-and up to ten. Twice. Holding my breath. I'd still have to slip off somewhere if only I could get out from under Stanley's friendly surveillance.

We were offered an orange-leaf tea and cold leftover yams for breakfast.

I had already understood that it takes a moment to find a good walking rhythm. In fact, it takes about half an hour. Still, it wasn't very hard that morning. We were constantly going up, but without steep climbs. There was no trail to speak of, at least no visible trail. I settled behind Willy's heels. The pushed-aside undergrowth would close in on its space as the sea refills the wake of an insignificant boat.

After about two hours of forging ahead, I saw the sky through the trees in front of us. I knew what that meant. Down we go. But this time it was different. Everything seemed to be illuminated from far off, light streaming from everywhere, every facet of the leaves glistening. The air suddenly thinned. The regular cooing of jungle birds ceased. I had the surprising sensation of hearing wind but not feeling it. That can't be another hill slope, I thought; that has to be a real abyss. It was.

Because of the trees, you can't see the cliff until you're practically standing at its edge. Two vertical walls of vegetation, with I don't know how many yards between them, two hundred maybe. Green walls with black stripes. Where there's a gorge, there are bound to be naked slopes of slippery mud. Bending over as far as you dare, you see the stream.

I made it to the bottom like everyone else. Less dexterously, perhaps, but that was all right with me. The stream wasn't even two feet deep. Such a deep fissure in the earth for so little water! But so crystalline, cold, and delicious. On our hands and knees, we let the current fill our mouths. Strange how thirsty you get in such humid country. We took the time to bathe, as we didn't know when we'd have such luxury again. I modestly moved downstream behind a big rock. The porters were even more modest than I was. They washed only their heads, arms, and their legs up to their shorts. They found the spontaneity of Jacques, Tom, and Kal hilarious. Naked as can be, the three of them were joyfully splashing water everywhere.

Climbing the other cliff, we found a totally different kind of vegetation, dominated by trees towering a hundred feet over us. Here and there we saw a banyan with its air roots forming numerous trunks. There was little undergrowth, but the ground was covered with layers and layers of dead leaves.

Following a narrow trail. Rounding a bend. And all of a sudden it's really happening. We're face to face with two Big Nambas. At

The nambas, a bushy mass of red-violet pandanus fibers twisted and used as a penis sheath. *Kal Muller*

last! A man of thirty-five or so and a boy of about twelve. They talked with Willy in their language.

I had seen the costume in Kal's photos, but that didn't make it any less striking in the flesh. Even though the word *nambas* is translated as "penis sheath," it's not exactly a sheath. At first glance it is a bushy mass of red-violet pandanus fibers, twisted around the penis, the end of which is brought up and tucked under a wide bark belt. Oddly, they seem to be more naked in this costume than they would be if they were completely nude.

We were only able to get the words "Mrawe," the village where we were headed, and "Amok," the village where the important chief we had heard so much about lived. I gathered that this man and boy must be from Amok.

We waited for the translation. When it finally came, it was much more terse than the original. Willy finally turned toward us and announced, *"Mrawe finish. Olgeta man Mrawe he go long salt-water. One man—no more—he stop."*

Kal was visibly disappointed. So the village of Mrawe doesn't even exist anymore. He had been counting on seeing the same people he had known a year and a half before. "Too bad," he said. "We'll go see what there is at Amok."

The path followed a woven cane fence. Beyond was a garden where several Big Nambas women were working. But we were able to see them only an instant. As soon as they noticed us, they ran to the end of the garden, giggling and shrieking, and hid behind a grove of bushes. We called to them in friendly tones, but they wouldn't budge. It was like trying to attract wild does. I recognized their costumes, too. Very graceful. A pandanus-fiber skirt slung low on the hips and a long wig of the same material, which flows like a waterfall over the shoulders and down the back to the waist or even below the hips, like a long shock of purple hair.

The next incline—steep, muddy, rugged with exposed roots, and interminable—was one of the hardest, but it turned out to be the most rewarding. For once we had struggled our way to the top, we saw there was no return descent. We were on the Big Nambas plateau.

Tall grasses and wild cane alternated with a lower, dense vegetation. The trees never grew taller than fifty feet. We were following a veritable labyrinth of paths going in every direction. Willy laughed maliciously. *"Suppose me-fella no stop, you-fella, you go you go you go you no savvy go long Amok!"*

The confusion was intentional. Only the inhabitants of a village know all the paths that surround it. And an enemy has less chance of arriving at his goal or of leaving alive. Moreover, there are the taboo paths: those reserved for women, those reserved for the chief and his family. Another wild cane fence and behind this one a cluster of huts. Then more bush. I asked Willy if we were really in Amok. *"Longway little bit"*—a typical pidgin answer that can mean anything from five minutes' to a whole day's walk.

Emerging from the bush, we came to an isolated hut with a small clearing in front. A knee-high fence surrounded the "front yard."

Willy informed us: *"Okay now, house b'long govmin. Me think bam-*

baï you-fella you stop olgeta long place here." It wasn't simply the "government hut," it was more precisely Mr. Wilkins's hut. The British Delegate had had it built for his excursions into the bush. It seemed the French Delegate never ventured as far as the Amok plateau.

Kal was irritated by Willy's news. "That," he exploded, "is precisely what I do not want! We've got to live right in the village, with the people."

Willy shrugged his shoulders. *"Me no savvy,"* he said, squinting slyly at Kal. *"Me think-think no more. Bambaï Meleun he tellem long you."* He explained to us that *Meleun* is Virambat's title and means "chief of chiefs."

In front of the hut we crossed a large open space overgrown with wild grass in the middle of which were four or five vertical drums. Kal told us this was the ceremonial ground and that it is cleared just before each ritual. There must have been a ritual very recently since the grass grows back fast in this climate.

I looked at the drums with a morbid curiosity. I already knew a good bit about them. Tom Harrisson, a daring Englishman, had lived with the Big Nambas (never at Amok but in numerous other villages) during the thirties and explained the use of the drums beyond their musical function. If they're slightly taller than man-size and in the stylized form of a man, that's no coincidence. During the cannibal ceremonies, the human victim was bound to a drum, and the drummer set to work in a fury. Not a single sound emanated from the instrument, only the screams of the man-shield as his bones were shattered, which, according to the local cuisine, tenderized the meat. Harrisson himself was present at these ceremonies.

We plunged back into the bush. We passed by gardens where no one was working and came out in front of a long fence about three yards high. I suppose there were huts on the other side. Willy told us to wait for him there. He was going to look for the Meleun. We lay down on the ground.

Kal yelled, "Shit!" and propped himself up on his elbow.

"What's wrong?" I asked lazily.

"A leech—it tried to get into my eye."

I bolted upright.

Willy didn't hurry about coming back, and when he finally did get back, he told us we would have to return to the isolated hut and wait there for Virambat. The law is the law, and we had to respect it. Kal frowned but didn't say anything.

We sat down with the porters on the ground and on a couple of tree trunks in front of the hut. About an hour later the welcoming committee arrived: five men, one young man about fifteen years old, and two boys. Kal sensed right away which man was the Meleun and went forward to greet him. Cheers, Kal, I would have thought it was one of the older ones. Virambat was forty at the most. A little later, I noticed he was the only one wearing the tips of two pigs' tails in his pierced ears.

Kal spoke for us and Willy interpreted. We had been told that Virambat understood pidgin, but if so, he didn't want to let on. Maybe he thought he could maneuver more freely by dealing with us indirectly. Kal explained our position. We wanted to stay with them, participate as fully as possible in their lives. And later we would want to take photographs and shoot film.

During this entire speech, Virambat was obviously amused. He tossed comments to the others, who laughed outright.

"What are they saying?" we asked Willy, but suddenly he didn't understand pidgin either. He didn't want to answer us. His only friendly gesture was to make an effort to stiffen his face so that he wouldn't break into laughter like the rest of them.

Kal took a carton of cigarettes, a package of tobacco sticks, an ax, and a knife from one of the satchels. He offered them to Virambat. The Meleun examined them all very closely, lifted an eyebrow, nodded, and handed the booty to one of the other men, mumbling, *"Y pass."* In this context *y pass* means "okay" or "good" as we would say "thank you." We understood very quickly that *y pass* also means hello, good morning, good evening, good night, and good-bye.

Virambat and his crew continued to talk and laugh among themselves.

Not knowing how much French or English Willy understood, we tried as much as possible to use slang or popular words among ourselves. "Should I lay the booze on them, or what?" asked Kal.

Tom and I thought not. After all, it is illegal. Jacques suggested, "Better to share a hit, like the Indians pass their peace pipe."

I got out a bottle of rum and an enameled tin cup which we had
bought from the Chinese in Santo. Virambat nodded again and
murmured, *"Y pass."* I filled the big twelve-ounce cup over halfway, intending to offer it first to Virambat and then pass it
around the group. Virambat grabbed it, closed his eyes, threw his
head back, and emptied it in a single gulp. I saw what he was
doing, but I couldn't react. My surprise froze me stiff.

The Meleun let out a royal cough, and a red-violet hue, the
color of his nambas, tinted his brown cheeks. He wiped away the
tears that were streaming from his eyes. With dignity he cleared
his throat and began to talk. We understood that he was about to
pass his chiefly judgment. Would we or would we not be invited
to stay in Amok?

Willy translated. *"Chief he say you wannem stop long Amok, you stop
long house here. He say more, you wannem takem photo, one photo, one
pound one man."*

"A pound each man for all the photos we want to take?" questioned Kal.

Virambat with his number one wife. The pigs *"b'long Meleun." Kal Muller*

"No," replied Willy with a smile and a superiority about him as if he himself were the chief of chiefs. *"One photo, one pound."*

It took us a good long time to assimilate that one, and to realize we were being put on. An Australian pound—almost $2.50—for each photograph! But where did that outrageous idea come from? They certainly hadn't done any business with rich tourists. Do they take whites in general for people with unlimited funds? Maybe they just don't know the value of money. That would be expected, after all. But something told us they knew it all too well.

Kal regained his self-control and calmly answered, "One photo, one pound? Fine, we won't take any pictures."

We entered into a none-too-promising series of negotiations.

"Can we go into the other huts? The chief's hut?"

"Taboo."

"Can we at least see the gardens? Just to watch the people working?"

"Taboo!"

From a basket one of the men brought out a pig's jawbone with two curved teeth protruding like tusks. This is an object of value among all the New Hebridean tribes. He handed it to Kal. At Mrawe, two years before, Kal had been offered many identical jawbones as a gesture of friendship. I smiled, believing it to be a gift in exchange for ours, and thus finally a display of goodwill. Kal was smarter. Suspicious. "How much?" he asked the Big Nambas.

"Ten pounds."

We presumed, and rightly so, that the government had suggested this simple method of discouraging the few hardy tourists who might come and disrupt their lives. An effective method, I'm sure. Therefore, we thought we'd better explain the difference between such "tourists" and ourselves right away. Kal went to it.

"We have come here because your customs interest us. In our countries, we don't have the same customs. We don't know about them. We want to stay here a long time to learn your customs. If we take pictures, we will give you some of them. Your children and your grandchildren will be able to see how it was before. If in our countries we are paid for these photographs, we will give you some money. But we do not have much money now. We spent a lot of money just to come here. And we aren't here to do business with you. We're interested in 'custom b'long you-fella.' If we never pay you anything for the pictures we take, 'sorry too mass.' Your grandchildren, who may wear shorts like the Europeans, who may not work anymore in the gardens, who may no longer have the same ceremonies, these grandchildren will be happy to have photographs of their grandparents. And if you don't want us to stay with you, then we'll go to another tribe!"

While Willy was translating, Kal found the Polaroid and took a picture of Tom. He certainly wasn't going to pay a pound to take Virambat's picture. A minute later, Tom's photo was passed from hand to hand. The old men didn't know how to look at it, they didn't associate the photograph's black-and-white surface with reality. They turned the photo in every direction, knowing there was something there that they should see. Then they tried holding the picture still and turned their heads, covering as much of a 360-degree arc as possible. Virambat's active eye discerned the image right away and he confiscated the picture, slipping it between his bark belt and his skin.

Nonchalantly, Kal asked, "Who wants his picture taken?" Virambat stood up at once and posed stiff as a board, not with a "cheese" smile, but rather with a nervous, somewhat fierce expression. Kal pushed the button—and it jammed. Kal looked like a fool and obviously felt like one, too. He tinkered with the camera but couldn't locate the problem. It's nothing. Kal will fix it, we told Virambat. Kal ended up sacrificing the roll of film, tearing it out angrily and putting in another. He finally succeeded in getting a picture of the Meleun. Virambat for the first time showed some consideration for us and invited us to move into the hut.

"Okay," Kal said. "We all agree. Jacques, Tom, and Charlene will sleep here, in this hut, and I'm going with the Meleun!"

The response was predictable. "Taboo!"

Because the hut is "special" it contains a crude table and benches as well as two low platforms, made of split bamboo, which are intended to serve as beds. These platforms are laid out head to head or foot to foot, as you like, at the back of the hut opposite the door. Evidently, we would sleep two to a cot. For a couple of minutes we discussed whether it would be better to have our heads or our feet against the wall. (We were not about to sleep all in the same direction, with the feet of two tickling the ears of the others.) I suggested that we would be more peaceful with the heads against the wall; the others agreed. I joyfully pulled my damp, muddy boots off my damp, muddy feet and curled up. A quarter of an hour later I rolled over to see which of my three companions I had for a neighbor. Without completely admitting it to myself, I would have been disappointed to see Kal or Tom next to me.

The very first night we met the other inhabitants of the hut: rats and fleas.

During the following days, we lived together tranquilly. The Big Nambas came to see us whenever they wanted to, but we rarely were allowed to go anywhere with them.

Kal was getting impatient. He kept trying to push things. He never missed an opportunity to pound home to Virambat, in every tone and from every angle, his desire to visit the other huts and gardens. But the Meleun remained intransigent. Jacques and I, on the other hand, found this period of quarantine perfectly normal and told Kal as much. After all, they didn't know us. Let's just be thankful they're letting us stay where we are.

In the morning and the evening Virambat or members of his family (male members, of course; we hadn't yet seen a woman) brought us yams, taros, and bananas. We quickly established one basic rule about this: we would not pay, in kind or money, for food. We were very happy to share what provisions we had brought, canned goods, tea, sugar, and so forth, and we also wanted to offer tobacco, but never in direct recompense for their yams. If they wanted to share their kaï-kaï with us, we would be very pleased. Virambat, having reflected, found our attitude fair. Every evening he came with one or two brothers, sons, and cousins to eat with us. We were always about ten squeezed around the table. Other Big Nambas came, too, but just to watch. I got the impression they didn't have the right to join us in the presence of the chief's family.

During those evenings we had a chance to observe Virambat. A personage. Physically, he is a handsome man, well built and muscular. When he wasn't next to one of us, he gave the impression of being taller than he really was.

We heard the Meleun call, more than once during a day,

Virambat's number two wife, in her long purple pandanus wig, weaving a skirt out of the same fiber. *Kal Muller*

quietly but firmly, "Wi-liii!" And Willy would come running to hear his instructions. Willy wasn't the only one. Everybody obeyed the chief without discussion.

Several times I tried to talk to Virambat about his wives, as I was eager to meet them. But it seemed to be a taboo subject, even for another woman. The only thing Willy would tell me was that Virambat had seven wives. He used to have thirteen, but the others had died.

There was one guy I didn't want to get to know at all, whom I wouldn't have wanted to meet in some dark corner of the woods, and that was Rabi, Virambat's cousin. So as not to confuse him with the other Rabi, Virambat's second son, a twelve-year-old boy, we called Cousin Rabi the Terrible Hermaphrodite. Over six feet tall, he is the biggest Big Nambas. His arms and legs are extraordinarily long and thin. But he has a round belly, thin waist, and the breasts of a young woman. His hairless face was perpetually scowling. His character was that of an old shrew. He seemed to have a certain amount of power in the tribe. And he clearly didn't like us.

We had brought a short-wave radio that everyone wanted to listen to in the evening. Classical music didn't move the Big Nambas, but if we found some jazz or rock, they wouldn't let us turn the thing off. One evening, as thanks for an Elvis Presley concert transmitted from Australia, Virambat proposed a little concert of his own. As the Big Nambas sang, we taped, and then we played it back. They couldn't believe their ears! For once they didn't think of asking to be paid.

Tom and Kal arm-wrestled regularly. The Big Nambas were an enthusiastic audience. They had never seen this kind of contest before. Kal always won and each time he gallantly announced, *"Tom he strong too mass all same."* But for the Big Nambas *"strong too mass"* doesn't mean anything, it's the strongest that counts. Tom played the role of a good sport as well as he could, but it was a rather transparent mask.

The men left us around nine o'clock. They lit their way with reed torches. They were undoubtedly headed toward the *nakamal*, the men's hut, to drink *kava*, the Big Nambas ritual beverage. Kal had tried it at Mrawe, and he said so to Virambat, hoping to get invited. I knew that such an invitation would not come easily. It would be hard enough for Kal to obtain permission just to enter the Amok nakamal, let alone to participate in what went on there. Virambat couldn't care less that Kal had been able to come and go as he pleased at the Mrawe nakamal. At Amok it was strictly taboo!

Having succeeded in discouraging the attempts to sell us yams and bananas, we tried to eliminate all forms of commerce. Several Big Nambas brought us various objects, announcing their prices without delay. We didn't make any exceptions. We never said no. We simply said, "Not for the moment, we haven't come here to buy things." But the Big Nambas are a persevering people. One day, a young man, Ari, who talks a little pidgin, came to see us with a magnificent sculpted ironwood club. He announced proudly that it had been his father's, and that his father had killed eleven men with it. When we reminded him gently, as if he didn't already know, that we weren't buying anything, he interrupted, saying, "O, something here me no sellem! Something here, he something b'long papa b'long me! Me sorry too mass. Me likem you-fella too mass. Allsame me no savvy sell him here something."

We started to say, "Well that's good . . . ," but Ari didn't give us the time to finish the sentence. "Me no sellem," he repeated with a sly look, "all same me givem him here club long you fella . . . suppose you-fella givem long me twenty pounds!"

We were a little disheartened. But something told us that this was all just a show, that they tried to sell us objects whose only importance was their exchange value. I was sure that no matter how much money we offered them, we would still not be allowed to break a single taboo. We tried to question Willy about this, but he pretended to know nothing.

Our relations with Willy got a little better the day we insisted he stop calling us "mastah" and "missis" and start using our first names. He was flattered. We had already told him to do so a number of times, but apparently he didn't dare. The Amok Big Nambas weren't used to the "respectful titles" the planters imposed on the natives in general. Their contacts with the Europeans were still too sporadic. Up until that day, they had avoided calling us anything directly. I didn't know how they referred to us among themselves. Probably, "the bearded one," "the tall one," "the small one," "the chick," or some such epithets. But from that day on, everyone got a big kick out of pronouncing "Tom," "Kal," "Zak," and "Sarrlin" as often as possible.

Nonetheless, despite all of Willy's consideration for us, we remained wary of him. We learned why he was allowed such liberty with Virambat. His sister, who had died a few years before, had been one of the Meleun's wives. And one of Virambat's sisters had married one of Willy's brothers. We were convinced that Willy was taking advantage of his role as interpreter.

Because of this, we wanted to learn the Big Nambas language as soon as possible. Even though no one wanted to provide us with the ethnological information that interested us, and though we still hadn't been able even to see the things we hoped to film and photograph, everyone was very happy to teach us the rudiments of their language. For once, there was no taboo! It was fascinating work. The vocabulary isn't too difficult to learn, but the principles of the grammar were. We pounded our heads against the wall of verbs. "Bring me a coconut" translates literally as, "You go climb, coconut you take, you come toward me." If the object in question is water or sugar cane, the entire structure of the sentence is different and the verbs are not necessarily the same. We had the impression that a totally different thought process, as well as the means of expressing it, was opening up for us. Each tiny discovery was a pleasure. *Pai* means "yam," but it also means "year"; *nal* signifies "moon" and "month"; there is no word for "week." We learned how to count—logically, Amok means one or first—and we learned that the years are not counted. Thus, the Big Nambas have no idea how old they are.

Pai y nal nal means "plenty yams." We certainly had plenty of opportunities to repeat that expression, morning, noon, and night, with *y pass* tagged on after it.

During one language-learning session Kal decided he wanted to learn the names for the various parts of the body. When he got to the sex organs the Big Nambas reacted like children, smirking, poking each other in the ribs, and tapping each other on the back. Willy, embarrassed and smiling uneasily, tried to be the first to supply us with the words in question. But the others shouted him down. And he finally explained that for each part of the sexual organs there is a proper word and a vulgar word. They were teaching us the vulgar words. Willy, who took the missionary message very seriously, was offended. He was even more upset when, having explained the thing to us, we laughed as much as the Big Nambas.

Fawn-eyed Mano, a sweet eight-year-old son of Virambat, cuddled up against me, running his fingers up and down my arms and legs, whispering very softly, *"Ounet! ounet!"* I didn't understand. At first I thought he must mean "skin," but it wasn't that. He seemed to be fascinated and finally I understood. *Ounet* means "veins." Obviously, through the Big Nambas' darker skin, you can hardly see the veins and they don't look blue like ours. Mano beamed, pleased with his discovery and pleased that I had understood him.

Aside from these lessons, the hours we spent rambling on about this or that with the Big Nambas were a pleasure for everyone. For Jacques, Tom, and myself, it was not lost time; we thought of the human contact we were establishing. Kal, however, was always thinking of the photographs we were not taking, the film we were not shooting, and the documentation we were not getting.

I noticed that the Big Nambas now seemed to make a distinction between us and the few other Europeans who had visited them. The others never stayed, whereas we were becoming more and more a part of the landscape.

Kal, acting on a sudden impulse, asked Virambat how he could get a nambas and a belt. Virambat broke into laughter. But Kal insisted, said he was serious. The Meleun said a few words to his ten-year-old son Ulen. The boy shot off like an arrow and came back fifteen minutes later with three nambas, three belts, and one skirt, but no wig.

"How much?"

"A pound."

This time, since he had asked for the goods, Kal was inclined to buy. I told him right away not to take the skirt for me. I didn't want it, or not under those circumstances anyway. So that there would be no misunderstanding, I asked Willy to explain to the Meleun that I did want a skirt *and* a wig, but later, when I would know the women. Virambat gave me a penetrating look and smiled. He didn't say anything.

Cascades of laughter accompanied falsetto screams—"Ouoouh!" the Melanesian expression of unbridled hilarity. The men taught Kal, Jacques, and Tom how to put on a nambas. The result made me laugh, too, though I didn't really know why. I had never had any desire to laugh at the Big Nambas. Was it the light skin with the tanned appendages? Was it the body hair? Whatever it was, they looked like overgrown babies in red diapers. Virambat couldn't contain himself either. His asides raised a chorus of "ou-ooouh!" that shook the room. Gleefully, he reached out to pinch Kal's nipples.

It was a gesture I had noticed before, as well as other physical play between men. This never surprised me, as the Big Nambas are known not only for their wars and cannibalism, but for their homosexual practices as well. Homosexuality is not simply tolerated in their community, it is an accepted norm.

In this society, the grandparents do not nurture the memory of an amorous youth. They continue, it is their duty to continue, to lead a sexually active life until they are physically incapable of doing so. A boy is initiated sexually in most cases by his grandmother, but her role in his sex education is quickly over. She then plays the matchmaker and eventually even takes care of the future wife of her grandson. Her godmotherly attentions often earn her expensive presents.

The grandson, meanwhile, retreats to the bosom of his grandfather. He must go to bed with his *bumbu* ("granddad"), whom he calls from then on *ndvyek* ("my flesh"). It is believed these relations are essential to the growth of his genitals. The boy plays the role of the wife—indeed, the slave—of his grandfather, working in his gardens, looking after his pigs, and so on. And it isn't an empty ritual, acted out coldly. Scenes of jealousy are common, particularly if either of the two decides to sleep with another man or woman.

This vernal-hibernal marriage is over when the boy becomes an "adult." He is circumcised, and the grandfather publicly dresses him in his first bark belt. Before that he wore a nambas, but it was simply knotted around his waist. From this moment on, he must be content with women. But, having developed a taste for men, he impatiently awaits the birth of a grandson, so that it can all start over again.

A little girl of the Big Nambas tribe, wearing the traditional wig. *Kal Muller*

When everybody had had the time to admire Kal, Jacques, and Tom dressed in big nambas, Willy, certainly on a cue from Virambat, proposed a walk to the stream to "go swim." I presumed correctly that he meant "bathe." The closest source of water is an hour away if you trot like a hare, which the Big Nambas do naturally. The stream where we were headed was reserved for the chief and his family, whereas the communal one was a bit farther on. But Willy told us it was all right since the Meleun had invited us.

Where two paths crossed, Willy pointed out a forked stick stuck in the ground at the start of one of the trails. He told us that this means "taboo" and that no one except the chief has the right to use that path.

"Why—b'long wanim—he taboo?" we asked.

"Me no savvy," lied Willy, and he scampered up to the front of the line to avoid any more questions.

The stream was no more than a creek, but in front of a steep slope in the waterbed they have cleverly laid a length of bamboo to channel the flow of water. It made an ideal shower.

With us were one of Virambat's brothers, two of his cousins, and his oldest son, Nisaï. Virambat decreed that Kal, Jacques, and Tom would bathe first. Nisaï wasn't allowed to watch them. The others watched avidly between peals of laughter.

Virambat and his men went next. Nisaï did not have the right to look at them either. The men do not even take off their scant coverings. They simply fix a large taro leaf in their belts to protect their nambas. Willy didn't bathe at all. He had the right, but not the desire. He had evidently gotten into the habits of the man-salt-water and preferred to remain comfortably dirty.

No one had the right to watch while Nisaï bathed. ("Not even his own father?" I asked Willy. "Taboo!") In fact, we had to move away. We climbed back up the bank and sat down on the ground a few yards from the edge. When Nisaï came back to join us, I saw that I had not been forgotten. Virambat waved me down to the water and Willy assured me that they would wait for me. I pondered over Nisaï's special role. After all, he was about fifteen years old. Why was he set apart from all the men? It was only later that I realized he still wasn't wearing a bark belt at that time.

Back at the hut, Jacques abandoned his nambas for his own clothes. Kal and Tom kept the native dress on and continued to wear the costume during the following days. And two or three days later I overheard Tom ask Jacques rather aggressively, "Why aren't you wearing a nambas like us? What's the matter, are you too shy or something?"

His eyes laughing, Jacques asked, "Can you picture Virambat

dressed in a suit and tie? Me in a nambas is about the same thing."

This started a conversation among the four of us. I saw that we had fundamentally different points of view. Kal believed firmly that we should share in the life of the natives as much as possible, sleep with them, eat with them, wear the same clothes, become in a sense members of the tribe. Tom seconded his opinion. Jacques and I thought that we could never get under their skins, that we are not Melanesians, and that playing out such a farce could never lead to mutual respect. Jacques and Kal had both traveled a great deal and were familiar with the life of a wide range of peoples. Tom and I had no such experience behind us. But each of the four of us believed totally in our respective positions.

"I want to become a real part of the community as much as you do, Kal," Jacques continued. "I know that for the moment we're really on the fringe, but I'm convinced this will change. However, I disagree with you completely on another level. I want them to accept me without having to act a role. Do you understand what I'm trying to say? We can imitate everything they do, but you and I, no matter how long or how hard we try, we'll just never become Big Nambas! So . . . you do what you think best."

"But at Mrawe," Kal protested, "very quickly—right away—I was almost like an adopted son."

"I know you feel that way," said Jacques. "But I wonder how they really feel about it."

Kal wanted to visit Mrawe even though the village had been abandoned. And anyway, we had been told there was still one man there. Maybe he knew this man. Maybe there were a few others who had decided to stay. We headed for the village, led by Willy and Virambat. The cane fences along the approach to the village were in a state of disrepair, which gave us a gloomy idea of what was ahead.

Mrawe was a shambles. The jungle had invaded everywhere. The large drums on the ceremonial ground were drowning in the tall grass. Roots were growing through the walls of the huts, and the roofs were beginning to cave in.

"Good Lord, only two years ago," murmured Kal. "Two years." He reacted like a man who had found his hometown again after a bombardment. He plowed his way through the ruin, guided by his memories, telling us what everything used to be.

That's where we ate, and that hut over there, that was the naka-mal where I slept with the men. Good God, over there, between those huts, there was a garden, we weeded it together.

A little farther on, under a lean-to, we found the inhabitant who had stayed behind. I recognized his face from the photos, but he had aged considerably in two years. In the pictures, I would have said he was sixty-five, but now he looked at least eighty. He was toothless and half blind. When Kal spoke to him, a torrent of words spewed out, but he didn't remember anything. Willy told us, *"Head b'long him no good."*

"Did they leave him here all alone to die?" I asked.

Willy pointed out a recently used trail which led to the lean-to. He thought the old man's family must be bringing him food, but that he wasn't able or didn't want to walk as far as the coast.

Tracking down the good times of the past is a dangerous sport. On the way back, Kal joked, trying to camouflage his profound disappointment. He probably would have felt better if he had let out his feelings. But that isn't his style.

The memory of Mrawe continuing to haunt him, perhaps, Kal announced that he was not satisfied with the progress we had made in Amok so far. There were still too many taboos for his taste, and he doubted that we would ever get much further with Virambat. And in any event we ought to see what was going on elsewhere in the archipelago. We had heard stories of other tribes, the man-bush in the interior and the Sakau on the north of the island of Santo, the Small Nambas in many other parts of Male-kula. Kal decided to go prospecting and to go alone since everyone else, including Tom, wanted to stay.

We were to get back together a month later, in Santo, to com-pare notes. Perhaps we would then return to Amok, perhaps we would go somewhere else.

Kal's disillusion was multiplied when, arriving at the coast, he met some of the men from Mrawe including Tina, his "protector" and best friend. They were happy, very happy, to see Kal again. But they didn't welcome him like the returning prodigal son.

3

"Y Pass!"

T H E Big Nambas are the only tribe in the New Hebrides who have a hereditary chieftainship. This confers a considerable power on the chief. But he does not reign until his death. His power is transferred to his oldest son when the son is about twenty years old, and the father adopts the role of royal counselor. Thus the former chief reinforces the new one, and this prevents any lapse in authority. Traditionally, each village or group of villages is the seat of an independent chieftainship.

These villages were constantly warring with one another. At the beginning of the century, the Amok domain became the strongest in north Malekula quite simply because the people of Amok were the first to obtain rifles from the Europeans. They used them to decimate entire villages, to annihilate enemy populations. Around 1930, during the reign of Nisaï, Virambat's great-grandfather, Amok had some eight hundred rifles. Virambat's grandfather, Tusaï, continued in the warrior tradition. Virambat's father, another Nisaï, died when his son was still too young to take on the chief of chiefs role. His uncle, Kali, became regent. Kali's aim was to make himself as formidable as his ancestors. He even tried to intimidate Virambat since he didn't relish the idea of becoming simply "the chief's uncle." Finally, Virambat claimed his rights and took on the official title of Meleun.

But Virambat was to be the last warrior Meleun. The great tribal wars had come to an end, although the peace was not the result of the Condominium's policy of pacification, a European policy that the Big Nambas have mocked for generations. War had simply become too dangerous for them. The traditional technique of Big Nambas warfare was not direct assault but ambush, never mass murder but eye-for-eye slayings. You don't kill ten men of an enemy village when the death of a single man effects the desired revenge. For hundreds of years the Big Nambas had maintained an equilibrium by following this principle, but after the introduction of guns, the rule was too frequently violated. It became too easy, too tempting, even too agreeable for those traditional warriors to pull the trigger, and they finally realized that the whole region from the plateau down to the coast was becoming depopulated. A good number of surviving tribesmen took refuge with the missionaries and became in a single blow "ex–Big Nambas" like Willy.

Virambat had been a dauntless warrior in his youth, brought up on the idea that the menu of any feast required human flesh and that a chief's son had the right to a tender piece from the upper inside thigh or, according to his preferences, a choice morsel out of the head, the favorite being brains. But the last time Virambat had a vengeance to satisfy, about twenty years ago, he decided not to take a human victim. His armed men attacked the village that had wronged him (the inhabitants having fled before their arrival). They burned the huts, killed the pigs, and devastated the gardens. That night the Amok tom-toms thundered through the usual village silence. This was odd, as there was no prisoner, and no one knew quite what to make of it. Since then, the aggressive instincts of north Malekulans have been suppressed by a regime of peace.

As a child Virambat had been a Melanesian little prince, a youth pampered according to local custom. The deep wrinkles that now claw his brow must have been engraved when he was still an adolescent. Before he wore a bark belt—that is, before he was a man free to dispose of his body as he pleased—he had become a confirmed pandanus skirt chaser. Virambat already had seven wives, three of whom were able to fulfill the physical functions of a mate. But he hadn't chosen his wives, and it was the wife of another whom he preferred.

When a young chief of chiefs indicates that he wants a married woman, she drops her husband (whom she hasn't chosen either) and goes to the chief. She isn't risking anything since the moment a woman steps into the yard of the chief's hut her husband loses all his rights over her. From then on she belongs to the chief, and the husband isn't even compensated. This is exactly what happened to the woman who sent young Virambat's heart aflutter. And the husband couldn't protest. But it wasn't a simple romantic triangle of the sort so well known in our society—it was a romantic rectangle, Big Nambas style.

The only person concerned who raised his voice—indeed, raised a downright storm—was none other than Virambat's grandfather, the mighty Tusaï. This scandal erupted during the period of sanctioned homosexual relations. Virambat was sleeping with Tusaï, working in his gardens, and acting as his all-around faithful servant. Tusaï didn't object to Virambat's seven wives since this was normal and moreover it was a sign of wealth. What he did object to was that Virambat was attracted to one woman in particular, and that he preferred to make love with her instead of with his grandfather. That was intolerable.

Out of spite, Tusaï almost started a war against his own grandson. He was a traditional warrior, but in at least one respect he was already a modern man. He headed for the government Delegate to accuse his grandson of being a sexual pervert. And since it is a crime against humanity to offer to a woman what was due to the grandfather, shouldn't Virambat go to prison? The Delegate was decidedly nonplussed. For him it was a complete reversal of accepted morals and he didn't know what to do. So he didn't do anything. The village elders finally convinced Tusaï that Virambat was quite ready to wear the bark belt and thus end his sexual relations with his grandfather. In a solemn public ceremony, Tunaï placed the belt around Virambat's waist. No doubt he continued to feel jealous, but he saved face and avoided a civil war.

Kali's jealousy had to be dealt with, too. Kali did everything possible to keep if not the power at least the authority of his regency. He cooperated with the young Meleun in one single area:

opposition to the government. The Condominium would have liked to speed the Big Nambas' pacification and, in general, to control this aggressive tribe which recognized no administration but its own. The Big Nambas were pacifying themselves because they wished to do so, but they had no intention of being controlled in any way by the Europeans. Kali and Virambat, who were underestimated by their adversary, didn't even need to employ violence. They were too cagey. They played the French against the English, the English against the French, and threw everybody off balance by playing on the ambiguity of their relative importance. When Kali appeared before the Delegate, he was the chief and would promise the Condominium anything they wanted to hear. The instant he had disappeared back into the jungle, they learned that Virambat was the real chief and all Kali's promises were worthless. Before the same Delegate, Virambat protested modestly that he couldn't promise anything without his uncle's approval. They had worked it out so that they would never be together in the presence of Condominium representatives. Having no other recourse, the Condominium feigned indifference.

In the role of Meleun, Virambat has known troubles much more complicated than the problems of personal jealousy. Traditionally, the Big Nambas society revolves around wars and the chief of chiefs is also the commander-in-chief of the tribal army. Inevitably, peace brings changes to a militaristic society, and if certain violent customs are eliminated, others become difficult to maintain.

The Meleun has the power of life and death over his subjects. Virambat's father would have exercised this power without hesitation. Virambat might have exercised this right when he was in his early twenties, but even then he would have hesitated to do so. Now, at about forty, he hangs onto this theoretical power like a precious souvenir.

A woman must bow deeply to pass before the Meleun and must audibly whimper, *Boterkana! Boterkana!* ("Cut me! Cut me!") Much of the meaning of this form of Big Nambas politeness, a way of publicly recognizing that the chief could crush a woman like a fly, is now gone. Women still bow low, even to the ground, before the Meleun, but it is done out of respect and tradition rather than out of fear.

According to "custom-law," the death penalty is the unquestioned sentence for the violation of certain important taboos. For this kind of crime the Big Nambas generally execute by strangulation. But a stiff fine is now usually considered a harsh enough punishment. Not a money fine, not yet—though that may come to be. For the time being the guilty still pay in pigs. And if the death sentence is really justified, the Big Nambas count on the spirits to intervene.

One group still stands apart: the clans called *nembalian*, whose members carry out the important function of circumcising the boys. In the cannibalistic era, no further back than Virambat's youth, the nembalian had a second function that complemented this first: they furnished human victims in compensation for the blood they spilled during circumcision. To make peace a defeated chief sent his opponent one of these men with the ritual words "Here is your meat!" If the victorious chief kept (kept, killed, cut up, and distributed the pieces of) the victim, the peace was accepted. The nembalian still administer circumcisions, an operation held to be necessary for the proper growth of the child, but they no longer owe a blood debt.

Today, Virambat preserves his authority within the tribe. His every whim is still an order to be obeyed without dispute, but in peacetime, any general's stars tend to tarnish. If one of these days someone decides to defy Virambat, he'll be able to do so without being clubbed by the nearest loyal warrior. In any case, nowadays an insurgent has an alternative. He can go down to the coast, dress in shorts and a shirt and cry out indignantly against the savagery of the man-bush.

However, we were to see that the Big Nambas traditions live on, proving to us that deep-rooted ancient beliefs do not disappear from one day to the next. For fifty years the missionaries have tried to break this society, and they believed the end of the wars would be the end of their difficulties. They were wrong. The backbone of this tribe is strong.

Soon after Kal left (but I don't think it was a result of his leaving) the taboos against us began to be relaxed. Very early one morning Virambat came to our hut. Looking straight into our eyes, he gave Willy an order. *"Chief he tellem suppose you-fella wannem look-look long good-fella pig b'long Chief, you-me go now."*

The honor of this invitation did not escape us. Virambat was proposing to show us his personal treasure, the Melanesian equivalent of the crown jewels. Pigs are the currency of exchange among all the traditional tribes of the New Hebrides. You can buy anything with these animals—a woman, prestige in the society, even a privileged position in the beyond.

The natives pull out the pigs' upper canines to make the lower ones grow out in tusklike curves. The monetary value of the beasts depends on this curvature. The teeth can form up to a three-tier spiral, but this is a rarity. A perfect circle represents a small fortune. The owners of such pigs are considered wealthy men indeed.

Virambat keeps his treasure in front of a high cane fence behind which he keeps his wives. Two pigs were tied to two trees, a liana bound tightly around one front paw of each. Virambat introduced us. Their names were Kelia and Pouxel. The third pig, called Still, was sheltered by a small lean-to. It was he who had the most beautiful teeth, forming about a circle and a quarter. Although these pigs look like boars, they are in fact pigs, of a species found throughout Melanesia, originally from South China.

Pigs are the only money in the world that can be hypnotized. Molinma, Virambat's younger brother, gave us a demonstration. Approaching Still, he spoke soothingly, his hand tracing geometric designs in front of the pig's eyes. Still stared fixedly and began to hum like an idling engine. Then he staggered as if drunk and fell onto his side. His feet kicked feebly. He finally rolled over on his back, his legs pointing upward. Looking at his stiff body and his wide-open, immobile eyes, you'd have said he was dead. Molinma looked at us with pride. It had taken him only two or three minutes to accomplish the feat.

I was impressed but I didn't understand. "Why do they do this?" I asked Willy.

"Pig," Willy explained, *"him savvy makem bad. Savvy kaï-kaï man. Suppose pig he no good, man he no killem pig [killem, "to strike"]. Suppose man killem pig, man maybe spoilem pig, spoilem teeth b'long pig, losem plenty shilling. Orright. Man makem pig sleep no more."*

"They've thought of everything," said Jacques. "If they could do the same thing with snakes and lions . . ."

Willy seemed to have understood.

"Big Nambas," he said proudly, "*him savvy too mass something.*"

Back at our hut, I decided the time was ripe. I had asked Virambat more than once, politely, if I could see his wives, but the answer was always the same: taboo! Encouraged by the fact that we had been able to see the pigs, I braced myself, took a deep breath, and howled, "Wi-liii!" mimicking Virambat's tone. Willy had never heard me talk like that and he was all ears. Virambat perked up, too. He was intrigued to hear a woman speak so imperatively.

Confronting Virambat, face to face, eye to eye, I commanded Willy sharply, "Tell the Meleun I want to see the women. I'm a woman, too, and I've had my fill of always being with the men. I want to see the women immediately!"

My heart was pounding. Virambat could very well use my initiative as an excuse to send us packing. Jacques and Tom were dumbfounded. There was a strained pause, after which Virambat softly murmured, "*Mich.*" Willy didn't need to translate, I understood. Tomorrow. My heart slowed down to a more normal pace. Virambat and I looked at each other, suppressing grins, like sly accomplices.

"Y pass! That's great," I said to him as warmly as I could. I wanted to kiss his cheek, but I didn't know what he would think.

"Wi-liii!"

"*Chief him tellem Tom more Zak he drinkem kava long him-here night.*"

Y pass, y pass, y pass! We were thrilled. Tom and Jacques were finally going to be able to enter the nakamal, the men's hut, and partake in the kava ceremony, too. Kal should have been a little more patient.

Willy tried to squelch my joy. "*Taboo b'long you,*" he told me. "*You stop long place here. Suppose you go long nakamal, my word, you dead-finish quick-quick.*"

But I didn't have the least desire to break the traditional taboos. I just wanted to get rid of the arbitrary ones, the taboos against nonmembers of the tribe who are not accepted by the tribe.

That evening we ate with Virambat, his brother Molinma, his sons Nisaï and Rabi, a cousin, and an uncle. And Willy, of course. But the hut was overflowing with Big Nambas, men we had never seen before. They must have known there would be two guests for that evening's kava session. From our dwindling supply we drew two cans of sardines to pass around. Everybody was pleased.

The Terrible Hermaphrodite was there. As a member of the chief's family, he could have eaten at the table with us, but he didn't seem to want to join us. Without unwrinkling his brow, he appropriated, with bony index finger and thumb, two fat sardines. (The others had served themselves only one or half of one.) He examined each very closely, as if looking for traces of poison, then nibbled at them delicately and finally wiped his hands on his thighs.

A man whose portrait would be a perfect illustration for Jack London's cannibal stories stood at one end of the table during the entire meal. His hair and his beard fairly burst from his face. Tortoiseshell hung from his ears. A wide hole pierced his septum. He directed a sinister, undeviating stare at us, saying nothing, eating nothing, just sitting motionless, watching us. Once the meal was over, Jacques took a pack of cigarettes and gestured toward this man to offer him one. He accepted. But when Jacques pulled one cigarette slightly forward, to make it easier to take, and extended the pack, the man recoiled as if he had been offered a white-hot iron bar.

Willy, who had witnessed this little scene and Jacques's surprise, explained that the strange hairy man was the *taboo-man*, the sorcerer. "*Him he no savvy putem something long mouth b'long him,*" Willy said. "*Suppose one man he touchem allsame something before. Taboo! Poison-man he stop longway long house b'long him, he makem kaï-kaï b'long him. He no savvy kai-kai something b'long you-me. Him he strong too mass.*"

Jacques pulled out a new pack of cigarettes and offered it to the man, saying to Willy, "Tell him to take one. No one has touched them. The pack is still sealed."

The taboo-man, or poison-man, without a word or a smile, tore off the cellophane wrapper, grabbed about ten cigarettes, and tucked them into his bark belt. His eyes defied us to try and take them back.

"Him he glad too mass," announced Willy.

I asked Willy what the sorcerer did to earn his keep.

"Suppose algeta me-fella wannem rain, him he savvy makem rain. Suppose you sick-sick him he savvy makem orright body b'long you. Suppose you rubbish-man him he savvy spoilem body b'long you. Him he talk-talk long man-he-no-man, man he no got body allsame you-me [a pidgin definition of spirit]."

Then Virambat gave the signal. It was kava time.

The men lit their reed torches and disappeared into the jungle night. Virambat didn't budge. On the contrary, he seemed to settle more comfortably on the bench. After having gotten the others on the road, Willy said *ta-ta!* ("good-bye") to me and headed for the door. Confused, I called him back to ask if the chief wouldn't be going, too. At first Willy seemed surprised, but then he remembered that I didn't yet know how many things worked in Amok. "Meleun," he explained, *"he come bambaï. He no savvy come first time. Taboo!"*

I asked Willy a few more questions, during which his impatience mounted, but I finally understood that the Meleun did not have the right to be present for the preparation of the kava. When the kava is ready, the men wait for him and the ritual drinking begins as soon as he arrives.

Virambat stayed alone with me for almost an hour after the others had left. He didn't pay any attention to me and amused himself by examining our belongings closely. I watched him steadily and felt strange being alone with him. I decided I would intervene if he started fooling with the cameras, but he was more interested in the can openers and Jacques's watch. The sound of a watch was familiar to him and seemed to please him. When I turned my back for a moment I felt his fingers on my head. I realized he was studying the barrette that held up my hair. I took it out to show him. He appreciated the clasp, testing it several times. Then he tugged at my hair, to be sure I wasn't wearing a wig.

Then Virambat remembered the radio and went to touch it. After I showed him how it worked, he tried all the stations before stopping at one that seemed to be Chinese. In pidgin, I told him I didn't understand a word. He smiled, moved the dial, and found some Ray Charles, which pleased us both. It brought back my high school days in Chicago—how strange to hear the same music now in Amok—and I wondered what Virambat could be thinking of, listening to it.

At last he'd had enough. It was time for a drink. He said, "Y pass" and lit his torch. I reminded him that we had an appointment tomorrow to see his wives. He smiled enigmatically and left.

As soon as he was out the door, I couldn't even hear his footsteps. I heard only the crickets. As long as the oil lamp was lit, the rats would leave me alone.

I heard Jacques and Tom returning and lit the lamp. "Y pass," I yawned. "How'd it go?"

Then I saw their faces. I understood right away. The least you could say is that they looked tired.

Tom immediately crawled onto the bamboo bed. Jacques tried to talk to me, but the words didn't come. To call his eyes simply bloodshot would be an understatement. Moreover, he had lost all control of his eyelids.

"Are you okay? You're not sick, are you?" I asked, worried.

He was just in front of me and he took my hands. But I wondered if he saw me.

"I'm okay," he replied, trying to make his voice sound normal. "I don't feel a thing." He headed toward the bed and followed Tom's example without even taking off his shoes.

Twenty seconds later he had slipped into a profound sleep. The next morning, or rather a few hours later, Tom and Jacques were alert and fresh. They got up early as usual. No dragon breath. No hangover. Nothing.

I made tea and Jacques told me about their evening.

"When we left you last night we had no idea what we were getting into. It's not so much drinking the kava as waiting for Virambat to not want to drink any more. We didn't know we'd be spending half the night in the nakamal, sitting on a log, half asleep, our eyes popping out of our heads with the smoke. What time did we get back here?"

"Two-thirty."

"And we got to the nakamal at about nine. Only five and a half hours? It seemed more like ten. Anyway, Nirambat, Virambat's brother, was there to welcome us."

"So, what's it like inside the nakamal?" This sacred hut which I had glimpsed through the curtain of banana, croton, and *namouila* leaves intrigued me. It's as taboo as the Chinese emperors' forbidden city toward which a woman could not even look under penalty of death.

"At first, we didn't see much at all," continued Jacques, "except the fire burning in the middle of the hut and the sparks that flew off toward the smoke-blackened walls. The bamboo roof shone like black enamel. And then we realized we were almost hypnotized by a pile of skulls that grimaced back at us in the play of shadow and light. They were the ancestors' skulls, covered with soot, dust, and spiders' webs. They were enthroned at the back of the nakamal on a large, flat rock shaped like the apse of a church. And we felt like we were in some kind of savage sanctuary, even a church, where the men indulge in their homosexual practices too—although that doesn't change anything, it's only a part of the whole. And the spirits are there! They're really there. And the kava ceremony is the means of communicating with them."

"But is there really a ceremony?"

"Yes, in the sense that it's a ritual and because the men drink the kava in a special way and in a special order. Wait, let me tell you exactly how it went. As soon as we got into the nakamal, Virambat had us sit down close to the door of the hut—I mean the hole in the wall that's used as a door. You have to stoop down to pass through it and you have to step over a wide partition of logs laid out horizontally. Behind these there's a kind of screen you have to walk around, a screen about as tall as a man, made of young tree trunks. It's meant to prevent an enemy or an enemy's spear from getting inside easily. It's the same idea of defense as the labyrinth of paths around the village. The hut—say fifty feet long, fifteen across, and twelve feet up to the highest bamboo beam—was built to withstand arrows, spears, gunshot, and cyclones, too. The roof's thick layer of pandanus leaves is literally sewn with a kind of reed to the bamboo framework. That, in turn, is solidly attached to the supporting posts and to the thick whole-log walls. The amount of work that went into it is incredible. What craftsmanship! It's solid and supple at the same time.

"The area closest to the entrance is the place of honor. Because of the screen you can see what's going on outside without any risks. When Virambat is in the hut, that's where he sits. We were seated on tree stumps in front of two old men and one younger man squatting around a banana-leaf spathe which was used as a bowl. It was about two feet off the ground, propped up by six or seven sticks. The three men were chewing kava roots and spitting gluey pellets into the spathe. Because we showed so much interest in the unappetizing spectacle of these toothless old men spitting into the bowl, we were quickly given the honor of some roots of our very own to chew."

"I hope you didn't let on how you really felt," I said.

"Not at all! Believe me. We knew it was an honor and said 'y pass' at least ten times before stuffing the roots into our mouths. These pepper roots have an anesthetic effect. Almost immediately your mouth goes numb like after a shot of Novocain; you can't feel your tongue or gums and your lips are about as sensitive as a chunk of rubber. It's hard work chomping away at those damn roots. After a while I could feel my temples throbbing with the effort. About a half hour later, when the men decided we had done enough chewing and salivating, they gave us a welcome sign to spit the pellets out. There were already about ten of the sticky reddish balls in the spathe. Then a man took a bamboo pole and slowly poured a couple of gallons of water into the bowl, judging the exact amount needed. After that one of the old men worked the pellets around in the water. I had the impression he was washing his hands more than anything else. The liquid had turned a muddy color, like water squeezed out of a dirty dishrag. He put a handful of chewed root in a coconut. Then, carefully, with his fat fingers, he skimmed off the bits of wood that were floating on top of the liquid. The kava was ready.

"Just at that point, as if it were some well-staged play, the Meleun, Virambat, made his entrance with that great supple, pantherlike walk of his. I almost felt like applauding. We could tell he was glad to see us there. He spit on the ground, kneeled, and in twenty seconds drank so much kava that the level of the liquid in the spathe went down at least two inches. He got up and ceremoniously gestured us to go drink.

"Drinking kava for the first time has got to be the same thing as going into battle. Your only refuge is in the frantic activity of the front; you can't trail behind. I inhaled through clenched teeth, thinking that the more I drink this first time, the sooner the work would be over. Like Virambat, I made as much noise as I could. It must not have been ridiculous because the men watched me most approvingly. I returned to my tree trunk, three steps from the watering-hole, almost in the place of honor, right next to the Meleun.

"Kava is a strong, very sharp brew. It has a bitter but fresh taste and lies heavy in your stomach. It affects you very quickly, and before all the men had taken their turns at the spathe I was pretty high. I felt like I was floating. My imagination soared. I was very proud of myself: I was the Great Explorer who had penetrated the Big Nambas holy of holies, their sacred nakamal, deep in the Malekula jungle; who had dauntlessly befriended the fierce Cannibal Tribe.

"The flames threw shadows on the men seated or stretched out on split bamboo and branches. I glanced at the skulls at the other end of the nakamal from time to time. About an hour had passed. The kava tenders were back at work. Some of the chewed roots which had been put aside in the coconut now served as a sponge which was squeezed and resqueezed into what was left of the liquid in the spathe. Then the young man on water duty refilled the bowl. Virambat jumped to his feet to go drink again. Then, everybody had the right to go to it again. Our memorable experience was quickly becoming an endurance test. Neither Tom nor I could sit up straight any longer. Taking the first long hit of kava, we had thought the first round would be the only one. No one had warned us that as the evening goes along the drink is replenished again and again. The more you drink the more there is. From the four corners of the nakamal came the voices of the reclining men. We could barely distinguish them in the glimmer of the fire which was stoked only once in a while. At first the narcotic effect of the kava was pleasant, but that euphoria induced to communicate with the spirits didn't last for us novices. All we could feel at the end was lead in our stomachs and a powerful desire to sleep."

"Why didn't you ask permission to leave?" I questioned.

"Willy had warned us that you can't leave the nakamal till Virambat has. So we stayed, to drink and listen to the Big Nambas. They all talked softly and peacefully—everyone seemed to be agreeing. Finally at about two-thirty, we couldn't even keep our eyes focused on the fire. Our chins were heavy on our knees. Virambat told us that if we wanted to sleep, we could leave."

"And the rest of them stayed?"

"Oh yeah! They all seemed to be in good shape."

"Maybe they didn't want you to see what happened next. That's possible."

"Meleun only knows!"

Virambat is a man of his word, and around ten o'clock he picked me up for the promised visit to his wives. In a little bag I carried lollipops, chewing gum, a pack of cigarettes, and a little bottle of perfume. I knew the high cane fence behind which the women lived, the same fence to which the royal treasure is tied. It was really something to finally clear this barrier. Parallel to the exterior fence there is an identical interior fence. They form a narrow corridor down which we walked. The Meleun's wives are well protected.

At the end of the passage we came into a large clearing. In it were six huts, a lean-to, and a cane box about as big as a hut, resting on stilts. (This, I learned later, is a storehouse for yams.) The ground in the middle had been carefully swept. A few scattered banana trees provided shade and a decorative touch. The women who were in the yard dropped what they were doing, ran to their huts. And squatted in the middle of the entrance holes, watching us. The children who were playing in the yard did not run away, but they did drop their games to look at us. Ulen and Mano, two of the chief's sons, whom I knew, came to meet us. Ulen, bold as ever, grabbed my hand. Mano walked on my other side timidly. I offered him my other hand. He took it with a smile.

I followed Virambat and Willy to the lean-to. A large woman who didn't seem to be afraid like the others was cooking. She looked about forty years old, but I suspected that she was probably younger than that. I guessed correctly that she was the Meleun's first wife.

Witar-ambat, Chief's-Daughter-Number-One. *Kal Muller*

Two naked and wide-eyed toddlers clung to her skirt. There were also two pretty girls, one about fifteen and the other about thirteen. The older one, who was already more a lovely woman than a pretty girl, had a great deal of poise.

Virambat spoke quickly and I didn't get a single word, but I understood I was being introduced. He signaled me to shake hands with his wife and then with the girls.

I asked the wife's name. Virambat and Willy did not seem to understand. The name, the name. She doesn't have one. But what do you call her then? Chief's wife, the First. Rarely she might be called Aori since she comes from that village.

And the girls? What are their names?

Witar-ambat and Witar-ptarrn.

What does Witar mean?

Chief's daughter.

They are thus called Chief's-Daughter-Number-One and Chief's-Daughter-Number-Two.

I tried to get more details and discovered that in effect Big Nambas women do not have names. They are simply called daughter or wife of so-and-so.

I remembered that pigs do have names. Kal had warned me about the relative importance of women and pigs, and he hadn't been mistaken.

I wanted to shake hands with the other women. With a wave of his hand, Virambat gave me the go-ahead. I went from hut to hut, but the women never moved from their thresholds and giggled in embarrassment. In front of the last hut, I indicated that I would like to enter. Wife-Number-Six laughed wonderfully, but either she did not understand or didn't dare let me pass. Then, squatting so I could get through the low entrance, I waddled forward. She had to back into the hut so I wouldn't knock her over.

I think she had probably not understood my request because she seemed very happy to have me in her hut. It took me a moment to get accustomed to the darkness. Three or four children had followed me inside and couldn't take their eyes off me. I had the impression of being in a doghouse. The "door" was also the window and the chimney, and there were no other openings. There really wasn't much to see: the ashes from last night's fire in the middle; a pile of wood against a wall; a pile of yams against the opposite wall; a stack of neatly folded mats; and in the back of the hut, banana leaves spread out over the earth floor—the bed, no doubt.

You can stand only in the center, since the hut is a yawning A-frame. I examined the underside of the roof. It is very well built—cyclone-proof, earthquake-proof, arrow-proof.

I presumed that Big Nambas women spend most of their lives outdoors. When I went back outside (Virambat had grown impatient and sent Ulen to get me) Willy said that I was right and explained briefly. The hut is used mainly as a shelter for sleeping. A Big Nambas man can have several wives, though it is generally only the chiefs who can afford such a luxury. But he must furnish each wife with her own hut. Willy said no more, so I drew my own conclusions. Virambat visits one of his wives whenever he feels like it without the inconvenience of finding them all together in a communal hut. When he doesn't want female company or (given the social behavior of these people) prefers to be with men, he sleeps in the nakamal.

I sat under the lean-to with Aori, Witar-ambat, Witar-ptarrn, and the children. Two other women found the courage to come and join us. I emptied my bag. Since Virambat had told me that the women enjoyed smoking, I passed out the cigarettes, which they lighted immediately with an ember. Usually they roll wild tobacco in a dried leaf or fill a clay pipe like the men. I asked Aori (through Willy) if she liked the cigarette. She said yes but that it was like smoking air. The native tobacco is strong as sawdust. I was surprised to see that Aori passed the cigarette to the children, even to the four- and five-year-olds.

I gave the lollipops and chewing gum to the children, who reacted like children everywhere. I opened the bottle of perfume and let the women smell it. Then I dabbed on a little to show them how the liquid is used. When I passed the bottle to Aori she delightedly copied what I had done. Witar-ambat pulled the bottle from her hands, and soon everyone was pushing and shoving to have the next turn. Finally Virambat confiscated the bottle. He breathed the scent deeply and splashed most of the remaining perfume over his body without compromising his chiefly dignity, and then gave the bottle back to me. The younger children had been forgotten and were disappointed, so I let each of them have some too before putting the bottle away. This sharing of the perfume had the happy effect of breaking the ice, and the women were much more relaxed.

The lean-to was apparently the communal kitchen. I started naming the objects for which I knew the Big Nambas terms. This amused the women who joined in by giving me new vocabulary. Virambat wanted to play, too. He taught me how to make sentences. When I could not follow him, he explained in pidgin. That was the first time he had spoken pidgin with any of us. With his big toe, Willy made drawings on the ground. He was pouting. That was understandable. No one needed an interpreter at the moment.

Suddenly, like a child, Virambat became tired of the game. He got up, prepared to go, and made a royal declaration in Big Nambas. I was lost. I got some words, but not the meaning. Willy, happy to feel useful again, translated: *"Chief he tellum say you come long place here one time finish. Orright. Suppose you wannem come two time, three time, ten time. Orright. OK, OK, he good you come. Suppose you wannem go 'bout, you go 'bout witem Witar-ambat more Witar-ptarrn."*

I thanked Virambat. He smiled at me. Thanks to him, a whole new epoch with the Big Nambas was going to start for me.

I intended to return the following morning, but Virambat and Willy arrived early with other plans for us. The Meleun proposed a tour of the gardens. And if we wanted to take pictures or film, y pass! I didn't underestimate the importance of this invitation. As with the women, getting permission to do something once gives you the right to do it again and again. When a taboo is lifted, it stays that way.

Little by little Virambat was exonerating us from the taboos against outsiders. Now all we had to worry about were the native taboos. That was fine so long as we knew what they were.

Virambat was going to take us to the new gardens, and Willy explained to us that it was taboo to set foot in a new garden if

Women at work digging yams in one of the gardens. *Kal Muller*

you've eaten salt or meat during the day. If you have, the yams won't grow. We assured him that we had eaten nothing at all.

Willy obviously had other things to verify, but he was beating around the bush. At last, reddening deeply, he got to the point. Turning to me, he blurted out, "*You woman b'long who here? Tom? Zak? Kal?*"

"*Me woman b'long no man,*" I replied in surprise. "*Me woman b'long me no more.*"

Virambat and Willy exchanged some rapid words. Willy was very embarrassed but had to go on with his interrogation. We couldn't even help him, because we had no idea of what he was driving at. "*Suppose,*" he continued despite himself, "*one man he sleep witem woman . . . no sleep witem woman no more . . . sleep witem woman plus makem fak-fak . . .*"

There it was. Now that he'd said it I was sure he felt better. Pidgin is not very subtle on this subject. The only way to say "to make love" is *fak-fak.* I smothered a laugh.

Finally we understood and it was quite simple. If you have fak-fakked the night before, it's taboo to go into a new garden. We assured Willy we had done nothing of the kind. Not even a little. His natural color returned and we were off to the chief's new garden.

Two women were busy clearing the ground, pulling out weeds and huge roots with no other tools than pointed sticks and bare hands. Two other women arrived, hauling heavy loads on their backs, wood and wild cane. They were finishing the construction of the wall that surrounded three-quarters of the garden.

There was nothing surprising nor very secret there. I wondered why the gardens had been taboo for us—probably because of the spirits. If they didn't like us, they could hinder the yams from growing.

In this fertile country where even a broom handle could surely bud and flower, I noted that the manual labor in the garden is physically demanding. The sun is staggeringly hot and the rain doesn't make matters any easier. Willy told me that those last few weeks some women had been obliged to sleep on the land so that they could begin work at dawn.

Virambat's work consists of watching his wives work and giving an order from time to time, like a foreman who does not have to dirty his hands alongside his workers. I asked Willy if Virambat played this privileged role because he's the chief. No, corrected Willy, because he's a man. When wars were customary, the armed husband always stood guard over his wife or wives at work in the gardens and defended them in case of an attack. So, agriculture remains *business b'long woman.*

In a nearby garden the women, armed with their sticks, were busy digging up yams for the next meals. It's not an easy task when you realize that these tubers grow vertically, are tightly held by the earth, and are often over a yard long. When the women were loaded with fifty or a hundred pounds of yams on their backs and a child or bunch of bananas on their hips, Virambat said go—and they went.

I admired them. I knew I would not have been able to climb the steep hill that leads to the Big Nambas plateau with such a burden. But they scampered up like mountain goats without complaining. They jabbered away gaily, made jokes about I don't know what, and burst into laughter.

Virambat, of course, carried nothing—again, not because he is the chief, but because he is a man. Previously a man had always to have his hands free to protect his wife in case of ambush during the guerrilla wars. But today, war or peace, reasonable or not, it's still the rule: the men carry nothing.

That afternoon I followed the women home. I had the right. Willy, however, wanted to follow me. Did he simply want to be useful? Or did he want to become indispensable? Anyway I didn't care to have him around. I preferred to have language problems than be bothered by an official interpreter. When Willy insisted, I explained that I had no intention, for the moment, of asking the women for any precise information. I told him I just wanted to be with them and therefore I could manage quite well on my own. But Willy would not hear of it and continued to march on my heels. This made me angry. "Go complain to the Meleun, if you like," I cried. "But lay off!"

Willy was profoundly shocked. No woman had ever talked to him in such a tone of voice. Of course he couldn't complain to the Meleun, because Virambat had given me an official green light in front of Willy. But I immediately regretted having been so abrupt with him. It was simply that his need to feel important had finally provoked me. Smiling, I told him I would need him *too mass* very soon when I would want to ask questions, and I hoped very much he would help me. That made everything fine. The Melanesians, like the Orientals, must save face above all else. So, I went to the women's huts without a chaperon, which did create a precedent.

The women carrying yams, bananas, and children caught up to two other women struggling under bamboo trunks full of water. Each trunk must have weighed twenty-five pounds. They're hard to manage and the river is even farther away than the gardens. This was the water detail. There are no sources of water on the plateau, but the Big Nambas don't drink much anyway. They were always surprised to see us down quarts and quarts and still be thirsty an hour later. This was certainly a question of adapting to the climate.

Without ever hurrying, these women don't lose an instant. As soon as they're back, they get going with the cooking under the lean-to. Some of them sweep the clearing and the insides of the huts. Others settle under a banana tree to shred pandanus leaves, the first step in making nambas, skirts, and wigs.

It takes a long time to prepare the daily bread, laplap. Before starting, the women put a number of young yams on the fire. These cook quickly and hold off the hunger. Even though the Big Nambas women nibble cold yams (which taste something like unsalted potatoes boiled a week ago), bananas, and sugar cane all day long, they're always hungry. It's not only because they burn many calories, but also because their food has so little nutritional value they must eat a great deal to absorb a minimum of essential vitamins.

To make laplap, you peel the yams first, scraping away at them with the sharp edge of a shell. Then you grate them with a perforated banana spathe. I took a yam, found a spare grater hanging from a beam, and without saying a word I set to work like the others. The women howled with laughter. When they discovered that I wasn't very adept at my task, their laughter doubled. They weren't making fun of me. They were sincerely amused. When I went at the wrong ingredient, grating my thumb instead of the yam, they stopped laughing. They gathered around me in concern. The women were worried that a stranger might be too frag-

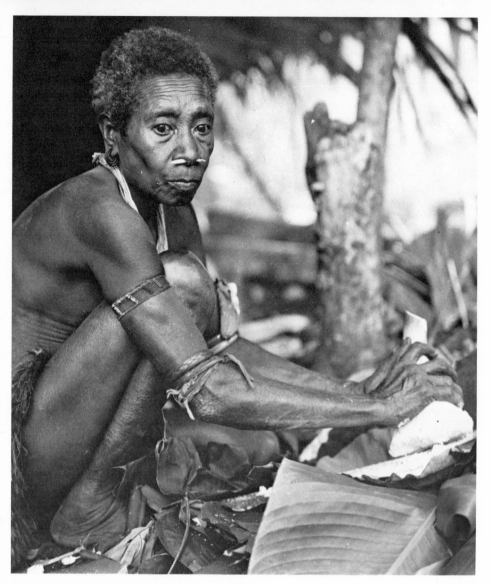

Preparation of the laplap. *Kal Muller*

ile. They felt responsible for me. I assured them it was nothing and continued to grate.

Afterwards, we worked the dough and made enormous fat pancakes which were covered with wild spinach leaves. Finally each laplap is wrapped in banana leaves and securely tied with lianas. The laplap is then cooked between two layers of heated rocks. I couldn't help thinking of Pierre Theuil's stories and the famous bed of stones.

For our palates, laplap lacks one thing above all else: salt. The Big Nambas do get small quantities of it from the coast, since salt is vital, but they do not waste it in cooking. They keep the large salt crystals, precious as diamonds, folded away in leaves and suck them like rock candy.

The two girls, Witar-ambat and Witar-ptarrn, help a little with the cooking, but their main task is to take charge of the small children. They play with them, keep them from hurting themselves, keep them out from under the women's feet, and shoo flies away from their cuts and sores. In this climate the least scratch gets infected, and the children develop a fair degree of immunity to these infections at a very early age. The same goes for diseases. Since the spirits are not always willing to heal the sick, despite the sorcerer's efforts, the weak die and the others become physically resistant.

During their free time, the mothers pluck out the lice that love to burrow in the children's hair. Then they take care of their own heads. Hunting lice is a daily routine. I've heard that "Europeans" (in the Melanesian sense) do not attract lice, and so far that seems to be true. The Big Nambas, who wash their bodies from time to time, never wash their heads.

Bringing up baby doesn't pose any problems or demand too many efforts. There's no need to dress and undress the small kids. They go naked. No need for diapers, with all of nature for a toilet and with a plentiful supply of leaves for a minimum of propriety. A runny nose? The child will wipe it away when it annoys him. The children get washed when they are so grimy that you can barely see their smooth brown skin under the black filth. Before that point, it's not worth the waste of water. Anyway it rains a lot. The kids play in the tropical rainstorms and take an effortless shower while they're at it. Their education is also painless. They mimic their parents and learn to deal with nature by themselves. I saw Mano, who is maybe seven years old, climb a palm some seventy feet tall to gather coconuts. He was faster than a squirrel. I saw Wyenpa, who is no more than three or four, take up a machete, its blade almost two feet long, to split open a coconut. He didn't make it, but he didn't cut himself either. A year or two from now, when he's strong enough, he'll be able to do the job far more efficiently than I.

I never saw a single spanking. Even a devilish child like Ulen was very receptive to a firm word from one of his elders. Moreover, I found that the Big Nambas women do not like tears. If a child wants to be cuddled in his mother's arms, even if she is busy or in a bad mood, all he has to do is start crying. And the men have the same reaction. I wasn't able to find a Big Nambas word for "tenderness," but they know what it is.

Child-rearing is nothing compared to swine-rearing. For women are also in charge of their husband's pigs—that is, the family bank account. As Virambat and Willy had explained to us, the value of a pig is measured by the curve of its teeth. The greater the curve, the more the pig is worth, but the more fragile the teeth become as well. And a pig with a broken tooth is like the ashes of a burned hundred-dollar bill. If the teeth are not preserved intact until the moment the animal is ritually sacrificed, all its value is lost. At a certain point, it becomes a game of chance. Should we wait and gamble for all or nothing, or should we pull our stakes out while the going is good and accept a modest gain?

It takes four years of growth without a single hitch for a tooth to form a complete circle. The Big Nambas are not gamblers by nature and rarely wait four years before cashing in their chips. Virambat was the only one who actually had a pig whose teeth had already gone around more than once.

The Meleun's wives considered that particular pig a bother. They had to survey the animal constantly, for fear he'd strike his precious hooks against something hard. If he bumps against the tree to which he is attached or against the ground or if a loose pig picks a fight with him, the women are responsible for any unhappy consequences. Virambat's wives will breathe a little more freely the day Still is sacrificed. But there will still be Kelia, Pouxel, and the youngest ones, whose teeth keep creeping along, little by little, day by day, reaching for that crucial point. The circle always begins again.

If the Meleun's wives can still manage to find a few free moments in their day, they weave mats or baskets, redo the weak sections of their roofs, or make more clothes. This last task demands a considerable amount of time. They must walk at least three hours toward the coast to find pandanus leaves, since the tree grows only at sea level. Then these leaves must be cut into strips, washed, and dried. At that point they are either braided or cut more finely. Next they are dyed with a root called *nesa* (I could never find the English or French equivalent for the plant), which also comes from the coast. The red-violet color, the sacred color, is extracted from nesa root. This is another regular activity for the women since the costumes do not last very long in the tropical humidity. If the color is too faded by the sun or the rain, the clothes must be replaced. Red is red, and redd*ish* is not sacred.

I understood why Virambat had entrusted me to his two oldest daughters instead of his wives. He must have thought that I would get bored with the latter since they are forever busy with their daily tasks—the life of these women is decidedly not one of leisure. The girls are freer. Witar-ambat and Witar-ptarrn help their father's wives, but they still don't have many personal responsibilities. They were very happy to accept me as their companion. At first they were simply available whenever I wanted something, but then the roles were reversed and I became available to them. They came to get me in our hut, in the gardens, anywhere and at any hour of the day. At first, I had trouble communicating with them, particularly since they didn't realize I was just beginning to learn their language. It was hard for them to conceive of anyone not speaking Big Nambas fluently. They asked questions with a vocabulary far beyond my own and waited for the answers. Or they would tell me stories in which they would get carried away by their enthusiasm and talk very fast. If I told them I did not understand, they repeated what they had said slowly and more loudly. I still didn't understand and they still didn't understand that I didn't understand. If I took the easy way out and exclaimed "ah . . ." as if I had understood, it would have complicated matters in the end. They would have assumed I knew all about things I had never heard of.

But all three of us made an effort. I studied the language as much as possible. And they began to understand that I needed to learn everything, starting from scratch, like a baby. So, they gave me lessons. They began with what was most natural for them and told me the names of all the plants in the jungle. Unfortunately, though I was able to learn the words, I was incapable of distinguishing among different trees, which looked exactly the same to me, and an hour later had forgotten the nuance which set them apart. There are thousands of plant varieties and hundreds that resemble one another.

Little by little we learned to communicate anyway. It would have been easier if I had accepted Willy's presence, but I would never have gotten to know the girls as informally and spontaneously as I did.

We didn't talk all the time. We laughed a lot, too. Every two or three days we went down to the stream to bathe. (It was the chief's stream, and it was okay because I was with his daughters.) They took off their wigs and pandanus skirts. Under the skirt they wear a small mat which covers only the lower abdomen. They never take this mat off, even for a bath. I followed their example, or almost—I kept my panties on.

The Big Nambas women are very modest according to the canons of their society. Walking around bare-breasted is an accepted practice for them, but they would die of shame rather than appear before a man without their wigs or skirts. The wig is the institutionalized symbol of feminine modesty. When a woman meets a man (except her husband, father, or one of certain other relatives) along a trail, she must crouch down and cover her face with the wig until the man has passed. Failure to do so is a crime, and its seriousness depends on the identity of the man. It is extremely grave if the man in question is her brother-in-law. One of the strictest taboos is against a woman looking at her brother-in-law.

Witar-ambat and Witar-ptarrn took a liking to our bathing parties. They had never gone so often before nor had it ever been so much fun. They liked it best when I brought my shampoo bottle. For them, the foam was magical.

On the way back, they picked up yams and bananas from the gardens. The bananas intrigued me. I had never known so many varieties existed. Green and pink as well as yellow bananas. Sweet and sugarless bananas. Bananas big as your forearm and small as your finger. I could identify ten species, but I'm sure there are others. I liked the banana trees, too. They made me think of sumptuous, turn-of-the-century French "salons" with their exotic potted plants. We nibbled on little "finger bananas" and sucked on long stalks of sugar cane before returning.

One day, Witar-ambat and Witar-ptarrn came to get me in our hut when I was writing a letter to my parents—a letter I would no doubt mail on the first snowy day in the tropics, but which I wanted to write nonetheless. I asked the girls to wait a few minutes. No, Sarrlin, no! They couldn't wait. They pulled the paper and pen out of my hands, their eyes alive with laughter. Witar-ambat pushed me. Witar-ptarrn pulled me. What mischief were they weaving? Since you just can't refuse an invitation like that, I followed them to the women's huts.

They had made a costume for me. A beautiful wig and a beautiful skirt in the richest red tone I had ever seen. The girls must have spent days making them. I was deeply moved.

"Y pass!" I cried and kissed them both. The Big Nambas do not kiss, and they found it a funny reaction. But they understood perfectly well the emotion. They were delighted to have pleased me.

The women were gathered all around us to see the show. Everyone was laughing. I thought the performance was over, but I realized it was just beginning. I not only had to accept the clothes; I also had to try them on. As soon as I started to undress, Witar-ambat grabbed my shorts and put them on and Witar-ptarrn snatched my t-shirt. They pushed my sneakers off my feet. Tennis shoes don't go with a Big Nambas costume. They helped me adjust the wig. And there I was, a true Melanesian! If I looked ridiculous, if they looked ridiculous, the one in shorts and a wig, the other in t-shirt and grass skirt, I didn't care, we didn't care, we were all having a good time.

I asked them why they hadn't made me a mat like the ones they wear under their skirts. Witar-ambat declared that I didn't need one because I have beautiful pink panties that are much nicer than their mats! I would have offered to exchange my panties for a mat, but I didn't want to encourage the idea that my clothes were better than theirs. So I scolded them gently saying that I preferred their mats, which is certainly true.

But I hadn't changed my mind since the day that Kal and Tom had decided they should wear nambas on the Big Nambas plateau. I still agreed with Jacques. I reclaimed my shorts and shirt, but the wig and skirt were mine to keep. I thanked the girls and the women again. We were already far from the time when the Big Nambas wanted to sell us a rotten yam for twenty-five dollars.

Witar-ambat and Witar-ptarrn considered me a little like their own private property, but property to be treated gently and kindly. I felt very close to them, too. Both of them are of an age to be my younger sisters. But Witar-ptarrn is still a little girl, while Witar-ambat and I found we were, in a sense, about the same age. This created a special bond between us. Even though we were separated by eight or nine years, I had the impression of having more in common with her than I would have had with a Big Nambas woman of my own age. Here, a girl becomes a woman rapidly and a woman gets old fast. At twenty-four a woman already has two or three children, has had miscarriages, stillbirths, and other babies who died in their first months of life. The infant mortality rate is very high. There is a complete lack of hygiene and care for the women. Many women die in childbirth, which takes place somewhere in the jungle, on the ground, in the presence of an old woman who is more sorcerer than midwife. When a woman dies this way, traditionally, the living child is buried with her. The custom is disappearing, but it has lasted longer than wars or cannibalism. No more than ten years ago, Virambat had a daughter buried with her dead mother. We know of the incident because a couple of Big Nambas talked about it to a missionary on the coast. Has this practice been carried out even more recently? Is it possible that the Big Nambas still perform this kind of infanticide? We have no way of knowing. If they do they surely hide the fact from the Europeans. For them, it is not an act of violence. The custom stems from the belief that a child cannot survive without his own mother's milk—even the milk of one of his father's other wives will not do—and that it is therefore more humane to kill the infant at once, as people sometimes drown newborn cats immediately, to avoid needless suffering.

A healthy twenty-four-year-old Big Nambas woman has already thickened around the waist, and her breasts hang low and flat.

I was surprised to see how much Witar-ambat resembled a Western teen-ager. She played the role of a woman, reprimanding her little brothers and sisters or caressing them maternally. She played the little girl, sulking because she didn't want to work, laughing with the little kids for reasons incomprehensible to adults. When I offered candy to the children and cigarettes to the women, she wasn't sure which she preferred. She wanted to be a girl and a woman at the same time. She told me she didn't like men and that she didn't want to get married. But she was always very flattered when men, Big Nambas as well as Jacques or Tom, paid attention to her.

Whether or not she liked the idea, Witar-ambat's marriage was a current topic in the tribe. For the Big Nambas, marriage is generally not a complicated affair. A girl is the property of her father, who sells her to the future husband, the price being paid in pigs. If the husband is not content with his wife, if he finds she's not a good worker, he can always send her back and get reimbursed. The father is morally obliged to pay but has the right to keep one or two pigs as indemnity since his daugher is now a used woman and will be sold for less the second time around. If a husband dies, his brother inherits all his wealth, including his wife. Usually, however, the wife dies before the husband. But this is no occasion for great mourning by the husband, who replaces his wife with another as soon as possible. This doesn't mean that there isn't affection between a man and his wife. Marriage is simply a business deal and not a question of will, desire, or love.

Witar-ambat's case was very complicated. Willy and Virambat explained it to me since I was interested in the girl. When she was four or five years old, her father had betrothed her to the son of another chief, an oppressive number of pigs having been settled upon. The future husband died before the marriage could be consummated. Normally, his brother would have replaced him as the future husband, but the brother had left the tribe to work on the European plantations. So, Virambat was forced to return the pigs paid for his daughter. (He kept a few anyway since, after all, this lamentable situation was not his fault.) But he found it very difficult to replace the fiancé. There was not another man in all of north Malekula rich enough in pigs to pay for Daughter-Number-One of Virambat, Chief of Chiefs. Now, if he insists on the asking price he is courting risks since, princess or not, at about eighteen a Big Nambas girl is already an old maid and her value drops considerably. But if he lowers the price too much too soon, his honor is compromised.

One afternoon, Virambat announced a meeting during which his daughter's fate would be determined. I was anxious to see how the problem would be debated and told Witar-ambat to hurry up, that we would go together. Her mother, Virambat's first wife, Aori, was amused. Strangers are so naïve! You can't go there, she explained. I can't go. Witar-ambat can't go. Taboo! It's *business b'long man.*

Jacques and Tom, who had the right to be present at the meeting, told me that after hours of talk nothing definite had been decided. Witar-ambat wasn't eager to hear the news. She seemed to worry very little about these decisions that concerned her future. She seemed to think, what will be will be and I'll know about it soon enough.

At night I often thought of the two girls, and mostly of the women. Are they happy? But the question had no significance. Around there happiness does not exist in the abstract. You're happy to eat meat; you're unhappy to be sick.

I didn't jump to conclusions. I simply tried to sort out my impressions. Virambat's wives seemed to like their husband very much. They were always glad to see him and showed a respect not lacking in affection. Virambat was kind to them. He treated them "normally," which is to say according to the norms of the only society he knows. It is certain that they were exploited, but among the Big Nambas the chief is an ideal husband.

I began to understand better when I realized that love between a man and a woman, as we understand it, doesn't exist in Amok. Sexual relations are sexual relations and not "physical love." The nature of marriage and the rapport between the sexes also explain why there is no jealousy among Virambat's wives. The idea of exclusive emotions does not exist. If the husband is going to take another wife, there will be more to share the work. Virambat's wives lead a communal life, carry on like sisters. Aori, the first wife, is a big sister to all the others.

It was clear to me that a Big Nambas woman is not an individual. But it took me a great deal of effort at first to understand or perhaps to accept the striking corollary: they don't have the least desire to be individuals. If they are missing the joys and cares of a

"European," they have an emotional tranquillity that is rarely found in modern society. The Big Nambas woman isn't bothered by "traditional" feminine worries—what will I wear? what will I make for dinner?—nor by more fundamental problems—what will I do with my life? No, such questions have never robbed a Big Nambas woman of a good night's sleep.

According to the missionaries (who at least in this case would have a common cause with certain members of women's liberation movements) these women are unhappy without knowing it. I must admit that the logic behind this point of view escapes me. If you don't know you are unhappy, are you?

Jacques and Tom had been accepted by the men as much as I had been by the women. We saw little of one another during the day. Evenings I was always in the hut, because the women go to sleep early. But Jacques and Tom went to drink kava three or four nights a week. In principle, kava is drunk to communicate with the spirits. But I was convinced that the opposite was also true. Communicating with the spirits is an excuse for getting high on kava.

It wasn't too hard for Jacques and Tom to follow the men's activities for the simple reason that there are practically no activities to follow. Previously war and its associated work had been the full-time occupation of the Big Nambas men, while the women did the day-to-day work necessary to run the society. The women's lot has not changed. But the men, *big-fella* warriors deprived of wars, are not ready to change roles and will never be ready to share, even a little, the women's responsibilities.

They don't seem to be too unhappy with all the free time. They take peaceful promenades: to see that the pigs are doing well; to be sure that the women aren't lying down on the job. They smoke their clay pipes and savor their slices of laplap. The old men, no doubt absorbed by their thoughts, while away the hours watching the flies. Willy told us that they are very busy during the ceremonial period—that is, about once a year, if not less frequently.

The only other institution that the men have kept going is the war council—in a modified form of course. The matters at hand are still pretty much the same: woman troubles or pig troubles. But the outcome of a council is no longer a potential declaration of war. Disputes are resolved, if possible, with fines. If not, they just aren't resolved. The pleasure of exchanging opinions in public seems to be an end in itself. The Big Nambas are orators.

These councils are large gatherings of all the men of one or several villages, taboo to women except in exceptional cases. Big Nambas now call them by the pidgin word *miting*. The first miting during our stay in Amok was the one concerning Witar-ambat's marriage. Nothing was decided because of the lack of a serious buyer.

The second miting concerned a pig. A man from Brenway, a man-salt-water village, had killed a pig belonging to Virambat that had been on Brenway territory. This man had no right to kill someone else's pig, but the pig had no right to wander far from his owner's land. He could have damaged the coastal village gardens. Virambat thought he should be compensated nonetheless. Before, he would have won hands down, because the man-salt-water would have found that one pig was not worth a war with the Amok Big Nambas. But now, this menace gone, the Brenway men stood their ground and refused to pay. After three days of miting there was no general agreement and therefore no decision. Virambat's only possible recourse was to bring the case before European justice represented by the Condominium Delegate.

But the indigenous justice continues to hold its own in local affairs on the Big Nambas plateau. The third miting concerned a woman, so other women, for once, were allowed to attend as well. But I was the only "other woman" who went. Even Witar-ambat didn't want to come with me.

At noon we gathered in a corner of the ceremonial ground. Everyone sat on the earth at random except for Virambat, who sat directly opposite the defendant and her husband.

Before the discussion began, we asked Willy to tell us quickly what it was all about. One woman had killed another a while ago, he explained, and now the matter had to be settled. I asked him what "a while ago" meant—a few days? a few weeks? a few months? "*Me think-think,*" said Willy imperturbably, "*woman 'kil-lem woman dead finish he got now . . . seventeen, eighteen year, no more.*"

We stayed through the entire miting, which lasted about five hours. Everyone was angry and excited. Everyone talked fast and loud except Virambat, who hardly uttered a word. He calmly asked a question from time to time and his face didn't show the slightest emotion.

I spent my time studying the participants. The accused looked about forty years old but was probably thirty, considering the rapid aging process of Big Nambas women. She defended herself vehemently. Her husband, who had seemed shy, composed himself and strutted around before speaking. His verbal torrents were less aggressive, less emotional, than his wife's.

The chief's male relatives enjoyed a manifest prestige. They were listened to silently, respectfully. The Terrible Hermaphrodite seemed to have even more prestige than the others. He never hesitated to interrupt anyone, with his characteristic shrill voice, when he wanted to express an opinion, which was often.

At last, Virambat took the floor. Five minutes and a few thousand chiefly words later, the miting was adjourned. We swooped down on Willy to find out who had won and all the details.

About eighteen years ago, a girl, whom we can call Peterlip (the defendant), killed a girl called Tnupah. (Willy had to consult with Virambat in order to name them. Should we say so-and-so's daughter or woman of such-and-such village? In any event, one can easily understand the confusion created by the existence of nameless women.) Peterlip apparently had killed Tnupah with *"hand no more."* Could it have been an accident? Willy waved his arm to say that that was an irrelevant question. Whether it was intentional or not, she killed her and that's what counted.

Both girls had already been bought by future husbands. Peterlip belonged to Kalmendu. Tnupah was Pita's fiancée. The wrong to be compensated was not only Tnupah's death but also, and probably more important, the loss of the future husband's investment! A wife is an expensive acquisition and Pita had paid, without bargaining, in cash. Peterlip could have been put to death for her crime. Kalmendu, undoubtedly just to protect his investment, took the initiative in settling the affair amicably. He promised to give Pita the first daughter he had by Peterlip. That way, Pita would have a daughter to sell to a future husband, would get back his money, and, since the cost of living is always rising, could even realize some profits. Pita accepted the offer.

However, after having had only sons with Peterlip, Kalmendu

died. There was no brother to inherit his wife. Peterlip then married a certain Wilton, who refused to honor his predecessor's promise. When Wilton and Peterlip had a daughter Pita claimed her. Thus, this miting.

Pita lost. Kalmendu's promise was made informally, without witnesses. (Thus, witnesses count in Big Nambas justice, too.) Peterlip was aware of the promise but hadn't told Wilton about it before their marriage. And since a daughter is her father's property and not her mother's, the obligation to Pita was judged to be invalid after Kalmendu's death. Wilton had nothing to do with the whole situation.

I might as well be frank. There were times when my morale just gave out, when I had to use all my energy just to camouflage my depression. It certainly wasn't because of the Big Nambas. Everything was getting better and better on that score. Maybe it was that I was beyond the first stage of adapting to a new place, beyond the initial excitement, beyond the early intense curiosity, expectations, and hopes. We had adapted to the Big Nambas slow rhythm, as slow as the earth, as slow as the passage of centuries. It had been raining for three days straight, and we spent the whole time lying down, sitting up, and pacing back and forth in our hut. The inconveniences of Amok life, which hadn't bothered me before, began to weigh me down.

I'd had enough of waking up each morning with my waist and legs swollen with hundreds of flea bites. Unlike lice, fleas seem to adore the flesh of "Europeans." Even if we had had insecticides, they would have been useless. (The people who had made them evidently weren't familiar with the beasts you find around there.) I wondered if the wretched red blotches that covered my body would ever disappear.

I had also had my fill of the rats who came out of their holes and grew bolder every night. They had even stopped making detours to avoid us. Several had climbed right over our legs. I slept hiding my head under the blanket, afraid they might decide to cross over that end of the bamboo bed. Eventually I learned that the rats gnaw at the natives' feet. New Hebrideans develop a thick layer of callouses on their soles. The first time I saw a Big

Nambas walk on fire I was horrified. Then I realized that he really didn't feel a thing. Walking barefoot all your life has more benefits than one. However, the rats like to sharpen their teeth on your callouses. A Big Nambas doesn't even wake up till blood has been drawn. By that time there's a hole almost an inch deep bored into his foot. The risk of infection is very high. After absorbing this information I panicked. I never slept without my shoes on again.

I was fed up with tropical infections, too. You don't even notice the tiniest insect bite or the slightest scratch until it's already infected. If you cover the wound with a bandage, it never heals. If you leave it uncovered so it can dry, the flies cover it *quick-time* and hang on with all six legs. Even the adult Big Nambas were no more immune than us. Some of them had untended infections that really worried me. Almost every day we took out our elementary first-aid kit and set up a most primitive hospital. But we didn't know much, didn't have much, and couldn't do much. Before long we had to economize on disinfectant. We had hardly any left. I had thought one large bottle would be more than enough. Next time, I'll bring several.

Fortunately, there weren't any mosquitoes on the plateau. But as soon as we went down to the river, there were swarms of them. We didn't know it at the time, but we had already caught malaria despite the quinine we took regularly.

I was sick to death of yams three times a day. Boiled yams for breakfast, roasted yams for lunch, yam laplap for dinner. The result of such a diet is a rapid loss of appetite. We had almost no canned food left with which to garnish the monotonous daily fare. The Big Nambas don't seem to need a varied diet. Most of them who tried our canned goods didn't appreciate them and went straight back to their yams. I noted that they get very little protein. Pork is reserved for ceremonies. There were a few chickens roaming about, but it appeared they were very seldom eaten. The natives don't eat eggs. Willy told us that the men hunt wild fowl from time to time, rather infrequently. Their diet does include a variety of nuts. And when they go toward the coast they eat coconuts. So apparently they're not undernourished or underfed, but I, being rather spoiled, believed I was both. I had visions of filet mignon and took to ogling the pigs and the chickens, imagining them in another form, expertly prepared, swimming in sauce. I had the impression a good meal would boost my spirits.

Jacques was always even-tempered, kind, and smiling. But Tom, at times, became absolutely unbearable. Tom is a much more complicated person than I had thought at first. He had obviously been pleased when Kal decided to leave us. He immediately appointed himself acting chief of the expedition, tucking our communal cash box into his knapsack, stepping forth as spokesman on our behalf in dealing with the Big Nambas elite. Jacques and I didn't mind. But after a while he started giving us suggestions as to what we should or should not do, suggestions that sounded like orders. Sometimes Tom seemed to resent us, sometimes he was perfectly charming.

Although I had trouble understanding Tom, I came to see one thing that created a gulf between us and that was perhaps the basic problem. Our attitudes toward the Big Nambas were altogether different. Tom idealized them. To him, the members of a "primitive" culture are by nature superior to us Western degenerates. For Jacques and myself, the question was much more relative. There were some Big Nambas we liked, and some we didn't like at all.

Tom arrived at the hut one evening with Ari, clapping him on the back and exclaiming, "This is my buddy!" Ari asked him if we had a flashlight, implying he wanted to borrow one. Yes, of course, said Tom, handing him his own. Ari is sneaky. He didn't want to borrow the flashlight at all, he wanted to keep it. We pointed this out to Tom, who said we were dreadful cynics. The next day Tom went to reclaim his "loan" but Ari had already hidden it away.

For all Tom's admiration, he didn't know the Big Nambas as well as we did. He spent hours talking with them, but it was he who did most of the talking. He liked to explain America to them. He talked about superhighways, people living in gigantic huts one on top of the other. He tried to make them understand what trains were, long boats that go *"quick-time too mass"* over the land. For the Big Nambas, it was all very abstract. The world of whites is like the world of spirits to them: incomprehensible. But Tom believed he was communicating and was always in a good mood after one of these discussions.

Even though man-salt-water are more used to modern technol-

Ari. *Kal Muller*

ogy, they don't understand it much better than man-bush. I heard
Willy comment when he saw Jacques cleaning a camera, "It must
be expensive to make a film!"

"Why's that?" asked Jacques.

"All those people who get killed!"

Willy had gone to the Norsup plantation movie house where mostly old Westerns are shown. He didn't know what an actor was. He thought that all those people had really been killed, so their families had to be paid a compensation, as Big Nambas law would dictate.

Kal sent us a message. It had been radioed to the coastal mission, and one of the men there had been kind enough to climb to Amok to find us. Kal had rescheduled our getting back together in Santo two weeks later than planned. He hadn't had any luck in the interior or on the north of Santo. He was going to south Malekula to do a little more prospecting. No details. We'd just have to wait until we saw him to know more.

The same night someone got very sick in Amok. A man developed a high fever, malarial most likely, and had an epileptic fit as well. The Big Nambas treated the epilepsy like a joke, viewing the sick man like a madman. They laughed and sat on him to stop his writhing on the ground. We asked if the "poison-man," the sorcerer, couldn't help. Willy assured us it was nothing, that the man was often like this because *"head b'long him no good."* After the crisis was over, the man still looked as though he was in very bad shape, and we suggested that he ought to be taken to the infirmary on the plantation. Since we were to stay at Amok longer than we had planned, Jacques proposed that we make the round trip to Norsup, too. A brief change of air might give us a new perspective on things, and we would also be able to pick up some more provisions. I said fine. Tom said no. He preferred to stay.

Jacques asked Virambat what he would like for a present from the Norsup store. We never could have guessed his answer. Boots, he said, without hesitating. Boots? Indeed. Canvas and rubber boots like ours.

Tom asked for a flashlight to replace the one Ari had "lost." Since he was now our treasurer, I asked him for some money. He wanted to know what I intended to buy besides the boots and light. I told him I didn't know exactly, some canned food, a few odds and ends. I'd have to see when I got there. Clutching his knapsack, he advised me not to be extravagant.

We left very early the next morning with Willy, Ari, and the sick man, whose name was Tina. I was thrilled to find that the trek seemed easier to me than the first time. Now I was relaxed. I saw the natural surroundings for the first time. When we had climbed to Amok, I had been much too preoccupied to appreciate the scenery.

Beyond the village of Aori, deep in the jungle which extends from the beach to the plantation, Willy and Ari both heard something. Jacques and I didn't hear anything, and Tina was still only half aware. Willy dropped the machete and package he was carrying. His eyes were literally bulging out of his head. I asked what was going on. He didn't answer but dragged me by an arm to a tree he had quickly chosen and barked, *"You go you go you climb. Quick-quick! You CLIMB!"*

I was scared. I could sense Willy's panic. "But I can't!" I cried. "What's going on?"

Ari let me use his back as a step, and Willy, forgetting his habitual embarrassment, shoved my backside. I managed to clamber up the smooth trunk. "Higher!" growled Willy. I went higher. I caught a branch, twisted my wrist, almost lost my balance, but I ended up securely perched some ten feet off the ground.

Jacques, Tina, and Ari were already at the same level. Willy didn't waste any time getting himself upstairs as well. He left his package on the ground. Ari had left his, too, but held on to his machete.

I didn't have to wonder much longer what was going on. From high on my branch I heard a muffled, scratchy sound, like horses galloping through a thicket. A moment later I heard frantic howling and perceived yellow blotches struggling through the foliage. I was sure there were no wild animals in the islands. At the very most, maybe a few wild pigs. But there they were, hair bristling, teeth bared, eyes crazed: dogs. Five medium-size, emaciated wild dogs. They paced around and around the trees like caged animals. Frustrated at not being able to get at us, the dogs continued to moan and growl, their front paws clawing high up the tree trunks. I shivered at the thought that they could possibly jump as high as my branch.

"They're rabid!" cried Jacques, perched in a tree a few yards away. "Get up higher!"

I trembled. I was terrified that I would fall into the howling pack. I couldn't move.

Willy tried to reassure us all. *"Dog he no savvy kaï-kaï you-fella. He no savvy jump."* But his voice was choked and hardly reassured us.

"It's okay," Jacques called bravely, trying to bolster my courage. "Just don't move. He's right, we don't have anything to worry about up here. Shit, if only I had a gun!"

But Ari had other thoughts. He was a few yards from me, straddling a branch slightly higher than mine. With his machete he had cut off a long bough and several yards of lianas. I watched him bind the machete to the pole. I understood. I was more afraid than ever when Ari stood up. He steadied himself with his left hand and brandished his lance with the other.

The dogs understood, too. They drew back, wailing still more frantically, leaping up and down, though at a respectful distance, their ferocious eyes never leaving us. They had sensed the danger and were even more excited than before. Savagery unfurled. One dog got imprudently close. Swift as an arrow, the makeshift lance nailed him to the ground. The dog struggled to his feet, yelping, and tried to work free from the blade that impaled him. But Ari, having held the end of the liana, had already pulled out the lance and thrust it home a second time. The beast rattled, floundering in pools of blood. The other dogs reached a peak of frenzy. They arched their backs high, like cats. I was seized with vertigo at the thought that the dogs could have attacked us in an open space, on the beach. Ari and Willy shouted for joy. A long mournful moan answered their cry. Another dog that had been harpooned had managed to get away and, licking his wounded flank, had skipped into a nearby copse. It was over.

To my amazement, the dogs disappeared as fast as they had arrived. I heard the resounding crackling of branches already far away. Little by little, the dogs' barks were absorbed by the jungle thickness. Then nothing, except the gaping hole of silence. I was drenched in sweat. My t-shirt stuck to my skin along with dust, spider webs, leaves, moss, and grass. I had an absurd but intense craving for an ice-cold Coke. Willy and Ari had climbed down from their trees and were talking triumphantly about the adventure while they turned the dead dog's body over with the end of a stick.

"They may come back," I cried to Jacques. "Don't go down yet!"

But Willy had understood my fear and called to me with his most beautiful half-moon smile. *"Sarrlin! You come down now! Dog he no savvy come again. Dog he go finish."*

The only thing that comforted me as I descended was that we were in the middle of the forest. At any given moment, in a few seconds, I could fly back to a dizzying perch ten feet off the ground or more. My strength would be adrenaline-doubled. From every direction branches would reach out to save me.

Willy became my protector. *"Me savvy hear longway too mass,"* he assured me.

We hadn't much choice. We had to trust their sharp senses and instincts in the virgin forest.

When we were very close to the plantation, Willy made us stop. Five minutes' rest, he said—curious, because the three of them certainly didn't need a break. But Ari and Tina disappeared into the jungle with the package Ari had been carrying. They returned a few minutes later, dressed in filthy shorts and shirts. The parcel, wrapped in new leaves now, contained the nambas and bark belts. They didn't dare go onto the plantation in traditional dress. I hated to look at them that way. They had lost their proud Big Nambas bearing. They neither walked the same nor looked the same, particularly Ari, who is usually so sure of himself. It wouldn't have surprised me if he had started to call us "mastah" and "missis."

This time the most disagreeable part of the walk was crossing the plantation under the blinding, burning, dehydrating sun. We got to the Figas' at the end of the morning. The last quarter mile, climbing the hill to their pretty colonial house, was rough. Claudie was home. She was used to these walks, not that she had taken so many herself, but she was island-born. She told Jacques and me to take off our shoes. And before we were even finished doing that she brought us cold beers. I asked if we could offer some to Willy, Ari, and Tina, too, that I would replace them in the afternoon, but Willy refused. He said he ought to take Tina straight to the infirmary. I don't think they were very comfortable in the company of Europeans. Even Willy was strikingly ill at ease, despite his having worked on the plantation a few years earlier.

We found it deliciously cool in the house. We went into the living room where there was a low round table surrounded by chairs made of braided plastic, washable red and blue rattan. In one of these Pacific-style armchairs sat a small gentleman who held a whiskey in his left hand and was already extending the other for us to pump. Claudie introduced us to Dr. Potte. She told us diplomatically that we had come at a good time since the doctor would very much like to visit the Big Nambas. Perhaps we could offer him some suggestions.

Before either of us had a chance to say anything, Potte started in. "I am fifty-five years old and I live in Paris," he announced. "I am a surgeon by profession but a traveler by vocation! I have gone around the world seventeen times. And not like a tourist either! I've lived with the Jivaros, the Eskimos, the Mau-Mau, and the Blue Indians."

"That's very interesting," began Jacques, but Potte wasn't finished.

"I know the Pacific well. And I've been hearing about the Big Nambas for a long time now. So, I told myself I had to get up there this time. The next time I may be too old for such a rough journey. Maybe I'd even have to be carried, ha ha! But you don't have to worry about that. For the moment I'm still tough. I walk better than a man of thirty!"

What a character! Jacques looked at me, amusement sparkling in his eyes. We agreed. We offered to take him with us the following morning.

"That's just what I had hoped you'd say," he confided. "Will you have some Scotch?"

We were out of shape for drinking and eating. Claudie served a roast at noon. Robert brought out a good bottle of wine. At the end of the meal, Jacques and I were half under the table. We had been living too long on yams, bananas, and water.

In the early afternoon, we took naps. Later I went down to the plantation store to do the shopping—more canned food, candy for the children, disinfectants. I noticed there was canned New Zealand butter. I didn't know if it would be very good, but I took some just the same. It might help the yams go down. Of course I got the boots for Virambat—and socks—as well as the light for Tom. For Willy I bought a blanket. I was sure he'd be pleased. But I didn't have the faintest idea what to buy for the women. I didn't want to create needs for them, especially after their reactions to my clothes. I got them tobacco sticks, since whenever the

European smokes run out they can always go back to their own. But beyond that, I really had no idea at all. I decided I would bring them some jams and canned meat and try to think of a better gift for next time. Yes, I was already sure there would be a next time.

Toward the end of the afternoon, when it was a little cooler, Jacques and I took a walk along the beach. After having been closed in by the jungle for so long, we appreciated the sea's sights and smells. We watched the sunset before returning.

To celebrate our return to "civilization," Claudie cooked us tons of crayfish. In the New Hebrides that's not even a luxury. There are crayfish coasts and oyster coasts throughout the islands. The natives eat neither but they do catch both and sell them very cheaply to the Europeans. That night Jacques and I were in fine shape. We didn't even think of yams. If we had come down to the coast for a new perspective, it had worked. It was good for both of us.

Willy and Ari came to get us around six o'clock the following morning. Tina had to stay on for a few days. Dr. Potte was ready. He had two porters for himself whom he had hired among the plantation workers. But what could he possibly be carrying to need two porters? One of them had a big, bulging, handsome red bag. The doctor couldn't resist any longer. He wanted to show us what he had brought: a fully equipped bar. Two bottles of Scotch, a bottle of vermouth, a bottle of Perrier, red wine, glasses. And in a special refrigerated compartment, he told us proudly, he had ice cubes. I wondered if he had traveled around the world seventeen times like this.

As promised, he was an excellent walker. We lost no time on the trail. Ari let us get ahead of him so he could put his nambas back on, but he caught up easily. I was always thirsty, and when we arrived at the first stream I fairly dove for the water. I was already on my hands and knees along the bank when Dr. Potte's voice froze me still. "Stop!" he commanded. "Mademoiselle! Don't move!" Panicked, I wondered if he had seen a snake, or even a crocodile, next to me. Theoretically, there are no crocodiles in Malekula. There are snakes, however. My back was stiff and my hair on end. But the time it took him to reach the bank was enough for me to look all around and find nothing.

"You're not going to drink that water, are you?" exclaimed the doctor.

I had calmed down seeing there was no immediate danger. But the doctor's question threw me off. "Why not?"

"Because you'll catch every illness under the sun!" he pronounced. "Hold on, I'll give you a glass and a pill that kill the germs."

I didn't really know anything about it, but I had never seen water purer than the Malekula stream water. But maybe I was wrong. Who knows? He's the doctor.

Jacques, smiling devilishly, reminded Dr. Potte that the natives drank nothing else and that none were the worse for it. And of course, he added, it's ideally hygienic next to kava. You'll see!

"Kava!" growled Potte, his face suddenly flushed. "Imbecile! You're not going to tell me you drink that crap! Half of the old men must be tubercular, and they spit in it! And then there are all the other diseases. You must want to die young, don't you?"

Jacques, who had always found kava pretty disgusting but never thought of the problem of tuberculosis, stopped laughing. After a moment of silence, he shrugged his shoulders. "Yeah, there's a risk all right, but what do you want me to do? It's an honor to be invited by the chief to drink kava. We couldn't turn him down. We might as well have stayed home if we wanted to be like that!"

"I," the doctor announced theatrically, "would rather shoot a bullet through my head. It's faster and cleaner."

We got to Amok just before sunset. Virambat received Potte graciously, because of us. Without delay, the doctor offered everybody a drink. But Virambat, a generous host, was not about to be outdone by his guest. He announced, for that very night, a special kava session in Dr. Potte's honor. Dr. Potte did not, of course, wish to attend.

"Listen," said Jacques firmly, "you take risks in France every time you get in your car. You know the driving accident statistics? And even if you stay comfortably at home, you can always electrocute yourself or fall down the stairs."

"Yes, but——"

"No buts! I invited you to join us in good faith. I even invited you because I knew it meant a lot to you to come. I have recommended you personally to the chief. And now you're not going to ruin everything for us by refusing this invitation. Maybe you hadn't realized that kava is not meant for getting drunk, it's sacred!"

The sweat was falling from Potte's face in large drops. But he went. Very early the next morning, though, Potte left for the coast, in a big hurry. He had had enough of the Big Nambas. No doubt he was going to close his eighteenth tour of the world recuperating in a good Tahitian hotel.

Virambat loved his boots. He didn't care about the socks. He gave them to his brother Molinma. Although I picked out the right size for him, his feet were not proportioned for European shoes. They fit in the width, and I put some cotton in at the heels to make the length right. The Meleun still impressed me. Even booted and bare-assed, he didn't look ridiculous. However, he didn't wear the boots very long. They were beautiful, he said, but they didn't let him walk freely.

Our last days at Amok went by quickly. We had shared as much as possible the daily life of the Big Nambas. But we hadn't even seen their ceremonial life, which is equally important, maybe more so—and certainly more dramatic. But it was the wrong time. Virambat told us that we were invited to the next ceremony, which would be very important, and in honor of his oldest son, Nisaï. We tried to find out approximately when it would be held, but Virambat couldn't tell us any more than "*longway little bit.*" It depended on a lot of things: the yam crop, the "man-poison's" attitude, and so on. It would be necessary for us to return, perhaps several times, to keep in touch.

The evening before we left, I asked Tom if he had hired porters. "Not yet," he said, looking at me strangely. But I didn't think anything of it. I was used to his moods. "We'll have to do it tomorrow morning then," I said. "How many do you think we'll need?"

"Three!"

"Three?" I repeated. "We had just enough with nine when we came. Even without the presents and provisions, we'll need more than six people to climb down."

"Too bad. We'll have three porters and no more. We only have six pounds left. We'll have to go to the bank in Santo."

"Six pounds! We must have twenty or twenty-five!" A suspicion crossed my mind. "What have you done with the money?"

Tom went into the back of the hut and got the copra bag in which we had brought our supplies to Amok. "I wanted to have a few souvenirs from the Big Nambas. I don't think I'll be coming back again with you."

He emptied the bag. It was filled with some of the junkiest things I had ever seen in Amok: a pig's jaw with teeth just beginning to curve; two warrior clubs that had never been used, made of white wood artificially aged by smoke; another club intended for pigs but that couldn't have hurt a fly; four or five poorly sculpted combs; a few women's bead necklaces, but the crudest ones.

We left the Big Nambas the following morning with three porters. We were all loaded down like mules, even having left some things in Amok to pick up the next time.

Luckily the Figas were there to greet us in Norsup, and fortunately we had bought round-trip tickets when we left Santo.

4

Four Men in a Boat

A T this point I could draw at least one conclusion about the trip: making plans was a waste of time. A week before, Virambat had asked me where I would be going next. I said to another tribe in south Malekula or the interior of another island. I was already gearing myself for other jungle treks, perhaps more difficult than the one up to the Big Nambas plateau. But I had to change gears rapidly; there I was, off the coast of Santo, far from inland trails, squeezed between coils of rope on a fairly decrepit skiff called the *Tangoa*. We were headed toward the Banks Islands at the northern end of the New Hebrides, following the traces of the first explorers. Instead of ethnological notes or vocabulary lists, on my knees I held the ship's logs of Queiros, Bougainville, and Cook.

We had met Kal in Santo, as planned, at the Ravons'. After he had left us at Amok, he had gone first to the Sakau villages in the north of Espiritu Santo. The Sakau tribes are different from all others, even physically. They're larger and darker than most New Hebrideans. Their customs are also different. The men are the only ones in the archipelago who duel with heavy sticks. The Sakau women are the only ones who wear no clothes at all. But, said Kal, all that's over, dead. All the Sakau are under the missionary influences at present and are totally "pasteurized" (pastorized), as the islanders say. Their traditions belong to history now.

So Kal went off to meet the central island dwellers, the "man-Santo," and was pleased to find that they have conserved many of their traditions. Inconveniently, however, they are under the protection of the Na-Griamel, the native movement directed by Jimmy Stephens, the sharp mestizo we had met at the beginning of our stay in the islands. Jimmy Stephens had decreed that all dealings with the man-Santo must pass through him. Kal concluded that the results might not merit getting involved in dubious politics.

From there he went to south Malekula, far from European domains and New Hebridean politicians. From the minute he got to the man-salt-water villages, Kal had the feeling that the traditional Melanesia, unchanged by outside influences, the Melanesia he had been looking for since Mrawe, did still exist. The Christianized coastal men spoke of "mountain savages" who lived in the interior. Kal asked if you can go there. *"No! Him no-good too mass! Him savvy killem man dead finish!"* This didn't discourage Kal in the least. On the contrary, he succeeded in hiring a guide on the coast and they penetrated as far as the first mountain villages. The walk was difficult, even for Kal, who is a practiced hiker. The trail follows neither crest nor valley. It climbs and falls constantly. Up and down steep hills, slippery and muddy. But Kal was full of hope. The people he met attracted him in a totally different way from the Big Nambas. He felt he was at the door of a truly isolated culture. His guide told him these people weren't the "savage" men, that those were even deeper into the mountains. He said that the walk got even more difficult, that it could become dangerous, as the "savages" were capable of shooting at strangers, and, above all else, that there was no guarantee of being received at the end of the journey by the inhabitants of the distant mountains.

Kal acted on instinct and decided not to go any further. For the first contacts with such a people you have to be prepared. You should arrive with presents, with enough food supplies (you shouldn't count on being offered any), and, in Kal's case, with camera equipment and Jacques ready to use it. Those people certainly wouldn't have any ideas like "one photo, one pound," and there may be things to photograph from the very beginning. Though Kal felt the need of such precautions, he was under no illusions. He knew there might not be anything at the end of that difficult road, but he felt it was worth finding out at all costs. He returned to the coast with a light heart and waited impatiently for a boat to Santo. In Santo, he waited impatiently for our arrival from the Big Nambas.

Tom had already decided to leave the team, to continue his trip in the Pacific alone, on his personal search. Kal, who had taken Tom for a faithful sailor in his little boat, was surprised. I wasn't. I was sure Tom wouldn't want to be back in Kal's shadow after his first taste of autonomy and self-confidence with the Big Nambas. Being a geologist, he didn't have a well-defined role in the crew and felt he was too much everybody's assistant. I understood that.

Jacques, however, was eager to join Kal for the expedition into south Malekula. It seemed best for me to separate from them for a while. Kal presented me with the difficulties of the voyage and the uncertainty of success. He suggested that if everything went well, I could always join them later. Had there not been other things I wanted to do, I would surely have insisted on going along. But there *was* something I wanted to do which didn't interest Kal in the slightest. I wanted to see the islands in general, meet the Christianized natives and the New Hebridean Europeans as well as the man-bush. For me, it was all part of the same whole. For Kal, only the traditional Melanesians existed: everything else was a waste of time. So I agreed to go my own way. The time was ripe for me to face the world alone.

How does one go about such a thing? In Santo there are always possibilities. At the Marine bar one stormy night I met a certain Monsieur Bob, a little man with a limp, who put on gentleman-adventurer airs. He had had to dock his boat at the Roseraie, a small Santo port, and cursed the bad weather, as he doubtless would have celebrated the good weather, with numerous rounds of Scotch on the rocks at the Ravons'. He was a superb story-teller, always on the lookout for uninitiated ears. He told any one of probably a thousand anecdotes like an accomplished actor who recites well-known monologues as if he were improvising. Since he obviously doesn't like to waste his talents, he is also something of a snob when it comes to choosing his public. I was a prime choice, not because he particularly appreciated me or even found me attractive, but simply because he liked the idea of impressing a young American woman. "In the United States, you cannot know . . ." and so on. I didn't have to be forced into the arena. I found the little man amusing.

Monsieur Bob, according to Monsieur Bob, is not only a navigator but also a one-time boxer, trapeze artist in an Australian circus, football player, crocodile hunter in the Solomons, photographer in Tahiti, and pearl diver in the Torres Straits. At the moment, he was a copra maker and trader, which is to say, more prosaically, the plantation manager on Mota Lava in the Banks and director of several tiny trading posts scattered throughout those northern islands, for the Sewald Company. Two days after our meeting he was to return to the Banks, taking with him a Sewald accountant who was supposed to verify the accounts and inventory all the trading posts. Monsieur Bob offered me passage on the *Tangoa* for this trip, which would last about ten days. I accepted immediately. The Banks are hard to get to. Even though the natives have lost almost all their traditions because of the powerful missionary influence, they've held on to their mythology, based on a man-god called Qat. So, I was off to the Banks to seek out Qat.

Before our departure—without even waiting until my back was turned—Elsa Ravon took the opportunity to make her favorite kind of joke. "The American," she kept informing anyone who listened, is more afraid of the natives than of a womanizer like old Bobbie. . . . She didn't get to me that time. But I knew the limits of my patience and already saw that I was bound to have it out with Madame Ravon one of these days.

Leaning on the rail, I watched the blue green Santo jungle. There were some six hundred yards of turquoise sea between us and the shore. There was no wind. The wooden bridge of the boat, impregnated with the bittersweet smell of copra, was baking in the tropical solar furnace.

The north of Santo Island is in the form of a backward J. The little arm is the Cape Queiros. The now deserted bright sandy beaches are fringed by coral. When Queiros passed by this coast in 1606, he saw on the beach the tall silhouettes of Sakau warriors waving their weapons and he heard the rumble of their tom-toms. One of the sailors signaled me to look far to the northeast, directly over the bow, and he repeated "Merelav! Merelav!" I knew that was the volcanic cone christened Star Peak by Bougainville. But I couldn't see anything. Over beyond the heights of Cape Queiros, very far to the west, in that bank of dark clouds, I could vaguely make out the mountains of Cape Cumberland, named by Captain Cook. Between the two peninsulas yawned the Bay of Saint Philip and Saint James, a veritable inland sea, modestly called Big Bay by everyone since the beginning of the century. I had the same feeling I get in front of a historic monument in Europe. But there was no monument, only the timeless sea and immemorial islands of Oceania. Yet there, where the *Tangoa* gently rocked, the caravels and frigates of three of the greatest Pacific explorers did sail again and again.

How can today's moon explorers be compared to yesterday's earth explorers? The astronauts have been as courageous as their seagoing predecessors, but they have accomplished their feats as highly trained, well-paid representatives of modern science who generally knew what to expect. And furthermore they are replaceable. If Armstrong at the last moment had told NASA that he was staying home, we'd be talking about a Jones or a Kennedy who would have done the same thing on the same day.

Pedro Fernandez de Queiros had no more than a dream. Although there were probably others at the time who had similar dreams, he was the only one ready to persist enough to make his come true—not over hell and high water (as he wasn't too concerned with the former and knew all about the latter), but despite church and state. He had been a member of Mendana's 1595 expedition. The extremely physically taxing and very dangerous voyage had resulted in the discovery of the Solomon Islands. The Portuguese Queiros, working for the Spaniards' profit, was a sensitive young man and determined to the point of obsession. He returned to Europe, his dream still intact. The discovery of an archipelago wasn't his dream. Queiros wanted to discover a continent. In Spain he went back to his erudite papers and books. He was sure that the austral continent did exist, all the more certain as the science of his day projected the existence of such a continent to balance the world. Mendana didn't find it. Queiros would!

The decision made, Queiros set to writing petitions with youthful confidence, never suspecting he would have to write thousands of them during his life, mostly useless papers that would be more taxing than his future explorations. He had little trouble obtaining official letters and encouragement from Pope Clement VIII. Why not? The Church had nothing to lose and maybe millions of souls to gain. It was harder to get boats from Philip III of Spain, who had accepted Queiros's daily petitions months before granting him the absolute minimum to attempt such an expedition. Queiros was elated. A minimum was better than nothing. And he finally left Spain, in true conquistador style, burning with eagerness.

Soon, however, Quieros's pride would be deflated. He lost sixty men in an ambush at Guadeloupe and half his boats during a storm, and he was shipwrecked. With great difficulty he arrived at Panama, where his royal and papal letters counted for nothing. All that mattered was that he had no money. He went to Peru and started again a series of daily petitions addressed, this time, to the viceroy. More than two and a half years after leaving Spain, he succeeded in obtaining three boats, the *Capitana*, the *Almiranta*, and *Los Tres Reyes*. He could finally continue his quest, tempt fate again. He was still accompanied by the Spanish poet Bermudez. His second in command on leaving Peru was Admiral Luis Vaez de Torres, who was to become an explorer of the Pacific in his own right.

Queiros had everything going for him. He had become the conquistador again. Starting with a grandiose gesture, he rebaptized the entire Pacific "Golfe de Notre-Dame de Loretto." At last he would be able to prove himself.

Now that Queiros really had his chance, his major failing as an explorer became clear: he could not control his men. He was a dreamer and a navigator, but he was also a weak man, a limited person, with no grasp of human nature and no desire to understand anything except his own desires. The little fleet sailed toward the southwest. The sea was rough and the crew protested. Why go so far south during the winter? The captain's regulations on board didn't help the sailors' morale: obligatory prayers and no swearing or cursing; sailors guilty of infractions sentenced to one day without food; and no gambling! That was pretty hard for men who adored the excitement of wagering everything down to their underclothes, if they possessed any, and who had no other distractions. What was needed aboard was an arm of steel at the helm. Queiros's arm was made of cotton. Inches from having a mutiny on his hands, he changed course and sailed to the northwest. If he had continued south he would have discovered New Zealand and maybe Antarctica.

As it was, Queiros was headed right for the New Hebrides, or just a little off. He missed the southern and central islands but arrived at the Banks Islands at the crucial moment, when everyone had lost hopes of finding land. From the distance he could see the volcanic peak, Merelav. The boats dropped anchor in front of Gaua, which Queiros named Santa Maria in thanks to the Virgin for having led him that far. A few canoes of unarmed natives— bones through their noses, tattooed, adorned with their most beautiful feathers and shells—paddled out to welcome the frigates. They offered coconuts to the strangers in a gesture of friendship. The first contact between two civilizations happened like a scene out of a play from the Golden Age of Spanish theater. Queiros surveyed the scene, dressed as if he were about to receive Philip III himself. When the first, the boldest, native set foot on board, Queiros embraced him in an ecstasy of sacred joy, with tears in his eyes.

This drama, this misunderstanding, would have consequences for centuries to come. The Portuguese believed he was embracing a savage, a son of God whose soul was to be saved. The Melanesian believed he was embracing a spirit.

Queiros as a psychologist was as poor with the island people as he was with the members of his own crew. He established rules that were destined to create problems: Weigh the natives down with cheap presents but don't hesitate to take chiefs and important men as hostages. Treat them in general like children who cannot distinguish good from evil. Do whatever is good for them, even against their own sinful wishes.

Queiros took two prisoners at Gaua "for their own good." He didn't let them go until he had had their heads and beards shaven and had dressed them in luxurious silk clothing. His mistake was that on Gaua abundant hair and beard were signs of a man's honor. Moreover, a man's head and chin were considered sacred.

The captain didn't waste much time on Santa Maria, which was only an island. He took off toward Big Bay, which he baptized the Bay of Saint Philip and Saint James. Never at a loss for pretty Catholic names, he called the land Australia del Espiritu Santo (Southern Land of the Holy Ghost) because he was convinced that it was the promised land, the austral continent. If he had followed the coast a little farther, he would have discovered only a small chain of islands.

The first contacts on Santo were also peaceful, but that didn't last very long. Seeing the natives winding their way through the jungle beyond the beach, the sailors believed it was an attack, took up their harquebuses, and shot just above treetop level to scare them. However, one of the sailors forgot his orders and fired low, killing a native. The sailors thought it was unfortunate but decided to make a lesson of it nonetheless. With their swords they cut off the head and the feet of the dead man and hung the body in a tree as a warning to the others.

During the next skirmish, they killed a chief.

Since the natives, under these circumstances, offered them no more food, and since they had to eat in any event, a party of Spaniards led by Torres penetrated the jungle as far as the first village and pillaged it. To make the maneuver really profitable, they took everything they found—yams, taros, fruit. And all the pigs.

The peace which Queiros sincerely hoped for was already impossible between the natives and the Spaniards. Maybe the white men were spirits, but they were spirits who killed and mutilated the bodies of their victims. They even killed chiefs! The natives might be cannibals, but they never mangled a corpse, and even during wars, a chief is sacred, not to be harmed. The white men probably were spirits, but spirits who violated and dared to steal pigs! It was inconceivable. They must be spirits, because human beings would never do such things. But they were obviously evil spirits, pernicious beings. They had to be defeated or all was lost. If Queiros had known what the "poor pagans" whose souls he wanted to save were thinking . . . but he didn't know anything, didn't care to know. He had a clear conscience and a lot of work to do for his king and his God.

He assembled all his men and delivered a long sermon on their noble task. He announced the creation of a new order, "The Knights of the Holy Ghost." Every sailor became a member. Solemnly, he distributed to each the insignia of this poor proud disinherited Spanish order, a blue cross.

He created an administration. Admiral Torres was in charge of establishing a capital, a "city" that would be called New Jerusalem. He set right to work on building a fortress out of branches and disposed four small cannons with which to protect it. Since this was to be a proper municipality, civil servants would be needed. Queiros called on-the-spot elections for judges, senators, a secretary general, a minister of finance, and of course a minister of mines, since the Spaniards expected to find gold. The six friars who were in charge of the crew's spiritual health erected an altar which could be considered the first church of the New Hebrides, Notre-Dame de Lorette. Bermudez composed a pious poem for the occasion.

The possession-taking ceremony was theatrical. On the beach the men paraded up and down with an orangewood cross. Pedro Fernandez de Queiros, in the name of the Holy Trinity and in the name of the King of Spain, proclaimed Spanish all the discovered land and all the lands to be discovered as far as the South Pole. Four masses were said, one after the other. Prayers were recited for the souls of the pagans. Banners were planted in the sand. There was firing of the guns. "Long live the Faith of Christ!"

The native resistance became relentless the day Queiros and his men kidnapped three boys, the oldest of whom was eight years old. The parents were incensed, outraged, desperate. The sailors made them believe they would exchange the children for pigs. A native arrived in a canoe with a magnificent pig, the best on the island no doubt. A member of the crew accepted the offering and mocked the giver, saying that all the pigs in the country couldn't buy back the children, who were destined to become Spaniards and Christians. The children on the bridge, already dressed in silks and wearing enormous crosses around their necks, cried to their fathers on the beach and wept, heartbroken, when their fathers, seeing that there was nothing to be done, went away. The oldest of the boys, baptized Pablo, implored his kidnappers to let them go ashore. Queiros, inflamed by his mission, told him to be quiet. "You know not what you ask. You will be better with us, in the love of God, than with your pagan parents." The three children stayed on the frigate and all died, surely of grief, before ever having set foot in Spain.

After this abduction, all relations with the natives were impossible. New Jerusalem was attacked repeatedly. Despite their beautiful blue crosses and their noble functions, the crew members complained. The conditions of life were hard, and they felt it was time to see their families again and to rediscover the amenities of the Old World. Queiros himself, who had never exerted enough authority with his men, fell ill. It may have been malaria or the result of the poison found in certain fish. Whatever it was, though he was still captain, he was no longer master. One evening while he was sleeping, his boat, the *Capitana*, cast off without even signaling the *Almiranta*, commanded by Torres. This happened only fifty days after the Spaniards had arrived at Santo.

Queiros was to die, old and poor, still writing daily petitions to the king. He never got another chance as an explorer. Torres, a determined man, went on to discover the straits between Australia and New Guinea. And the phantom city of New Jerusalem, at the mouth of the Melanesian jungle, beyond some lonely beach, was lost, reabsorbed by the land. No one even knows exactly where it was. A Santo Australian recently claimed to have stumbled upon the site, but he had found only the remnants of a nineteenth-century trading post.

For 162 years, the outside world forgot the land Queiros had discovered. Over eight generations, the arrival of the white spirits in giant canoes with sails became a legend. The natives never suspected the historic reality of Queiros, Torres, and company. The next time they would have a chance to see a white spirit it would be an eighteenth-century man and a Frenchman. The representatives of the Spanish Golden Age and the French Enlightenment resembled each other about as much as the spirit of the moon and the spirit of the sun.

May 21, 1768. Louis Antoine de Bougainville, on board the *Boudeuse*, surveyed behind him his second ship, the *Etoile*, which was unable to make headway in the calm. Dusk. In front of him on the western horizon he observed a patch of gray clouds. Could they be the kind of clouds that form over land? He fervently hoped so. Tahiti was no more than a marvelous memory by then. It was Bougainville who named it New Cythera and made it known in Europe as a veritable terrestrial paradise, a reputation that lives on even today. But since leaving Polynesia he had had nothing but troubles. No wind. Food and fresh water supplies exhausted. Scurvy. Bougainville himself became prey to this deficiency. At dawn came the good news. Land ahead! Two lands, in fact. Two islands. Given the day and the hour, Bougainville called them Pentecost and Aurora. Far off he could see a third land, which seemed to be a mountain surging out of the sea. He called it Star Peak.

The wind picked up. The *Boudeuse* and the *Etoile* sailed between Pentecost and Aurora without being able to land. They headed directly for another island where they found a suitable mooring. They had no choice but to cast their anchor. At all costs they had to find water, food, and wood. The natives were hostile. Bougainville offered them lengths of red cloth. Without knowing it, his choice of color was perfect, for red is the sacred color there. Thus, he was able to obtain wood, water, and some fruit. But all the same, the Frenchmen scurried back to their ships under a shower of arrows. Despite their red presents, they were surely taken for evil spirits. Bougainville, somewhat embittered and having noticed an illness among the islands which he took for leprosy, baptized their island "Leper's Island" and took to the open sea. The sailors had been forced to respond to the arrows with musket fire, but the captain was disgusted. We cannot permit ourselves, he said, to abuse our superior strength. We are so strong that we cannot punish these peoples. For this reason, and also because they were too physically exhausted to make the effort, the French never again set foot on land in the archipelago.

Fortunately, there had been an incident in Tahiti that had amused the entire crew and was still the source of excellent jokes that boosted the morale. There was a botanist on board, Philibert de Commerçon, a renowned scientist who could, according to Harrisson, identify at a glance the sex of even the rarest plants. Commerçon had a young assistant, Baret, who had been such a help in Paris that he was already well provided for in his employer's will. During the entire voyage Baret was a veritable beast of burden, carrying on his shoulders all of Commerçon's heavy botanical equipment and doing all the thankless tasks without a word of complaint. They liked each other well and on board shared the same cabin. During their stay in Tahiti, on the bridge of the ship, a native had circled around Baret, excited, waving his arms wildly, exclaiming, "Wahine! Wahine!" Commerçon and Bougainville didn't know the word, but it didn't take them long to guess the meaning. Woman. A sailor took the liberty of confirming with one well-placed hand what the Tahitian had known instinctively. No doubt about it. The full name of Commerçon's assistant was Jeanne Baret. Disguised as a boy, she had succeeded in tricking everyone for the two years since they had left France. Commerçon might have been quick when it came to the subject of the sex of plants, but he didn't have the slightest suspicion that he was sharing his cabin with a female assistant. He was highly embarrassed, to the overwhelming amusement of the crew. Jeanne Baret thus became the first woman to travel around the world.

Bougainville spent many more days navigating among the islands, looking for moorings, always hoping to be able to get provisions. But the wind and currents were against him, and he was haunted by the fear of crashing on the reefs, especially at night and during the storms that made maneuvering so difficult. Moreover, every beach where he could land was rapidly covered with bands of aggressive natives.

The French explorer was sure he had found the Southern Land of the Holy Ghost. After proving that the land was only an archipelago, he put an end to any remaining belief in Queiros's continent. He bestowed on the group a lovely name: Great Cyclades. The name was perhaps too literary for Captain Cook, who would arrive in those parts six years later and debaptize the same islands without a second thought. But the straits between Espiritu Santo and Malekula still carry, on English as well as French maps, the name of Bougainville. Yet this important navigator, whose name also remains for one of the large islands he discovered afterwards in the Solomons, lives on in the memory of the peoples of the Pacific above all else in a beautiful red and violet bush, now call bougainvillea.

Captain James Cook was also an eighteenth-century man, not

simply by accident of birth but in spirit as well. Quite unlike Bougainville, there was nothing aristocratic about him. He must have barely known that a man called Shakespeare had existed. His father was a farm hand who had ambitions for his son and found him a situation as an apprentice to a country merchant. For the family, this represented a step up in society. But young Cook had a dream. He was attracted to the sea as if by a lover. Where did that strange yearning come from? No one in Cook's family had ever been a sailor. Maybe that was it, maybe he longed for liberty on the high seas just because his family had always been prisoners of the soil. He abandoned commerce with no regrets. At seventeen he became a cabin boy on a boat that transported coal up and down the Thames. At forty-five he set out to trace Bougainville's route in the Pacific, having already become the greatest English navigator of his time.

It was his second important Pacific exploration. As on the first voyage, he brought famous wealthy and influential scientists with him. They were lucky enough to have obtained a copy of Bougainville's logs and some of his men as well. Joseph Banks, the rich botanist who had financed much of the expedition, was inspired by Commerçon's experience and hired on Madeira a female "valet."

Cook arrived in the area from the north and became the first to explore the entire archipelago all the way to the southernmost islands. He was also the first to draw precise maps of the group. He baptized it the New Hebrides, although he never gave his reasons for this choice. Perhaps during the austral summer of 1774 it rained a great deal, as it does in the north of Scotland.

Cook didn't have Bougainville's problems about provisions because he didn't hesitate to take the initiative in contacts with the natives, despite the danger. He always searched out the chiefs. He wasn't content to invite them in relative safety on board, where the Europeans could control the situation, but advanced onto the beaches to meet them. This attitude led to a number of squabbles, even though Cook was against violence. The English were forced to defend themselves, although it was never too hard, not with firearms against spears and clubs. However, Cook did his best to avoid these incidents and willingly put his life in danger before risking the lives of any of his sailors.

To Cook these savage islands were as beautiful as Tahiti, but he found the New Hebrideans the ugliest and most badly proportioned people he had ever seen. He didn't hold this against them, though. He was convinced that if they stayed long enough, the English would get along well with "this simian nation." Cook didn't unleash such adjectives with the intention of insulting the islanders. Quite simply, like Bougainville, his conception of beauty was conditioned by his own society. His "most beautiful" people were those who most resembled Europeans. Thus, the Polynesians were more beautiful than the Melanesians.

After the New Hebrides, Cook went on to discover New Caledonia. And a few years later, during this third voyage, he met his death in Hawaii because he was taken for a god and because he did not want to be the aggressor. On the beach of Kealakekua Bay on the island of Hawaii, Cook was stoned, pierced with spears, and finished off with clubs. The natives had nothing against him; they wanted only to affirm their power against a supernatural being. Cook faced the Hawaiians, speaking softly and reasonably, and never lifted his rifle. His last gesture was an order to his crew: hold your fire.

Queiros, Bougainville, and Cook were not, in fact, the first explorers of the archipelago, as they are commonly believed to have been. They were only the first European explorers. The real discoverers of the islands came from the south of China some three thousand years before the Christian era.

This fact is fairly astonishing when we get away from scientific texts and just look at the Melanesians, who have nothing visibly Asiatic about them and who strongly resemble certain African peoples. Seeing the color of their skin, their hair, their facial features, their chants, their dances and diverse customs, you are tempted to consider them emigrants from distant Africa. But it isn't true. The Melanesians don't have the slightest connection with the Africans. This black race of the Pacific comes from Asia, as do the Polynesians and Micronesians, despite the theories of Thor Heyerdahl and his followers, who believe in an American stock. The domain of agriculture offers irrefutable evidence for the Asiatic origin of these populations. The methods of farming and the varieties of tubers, pigs, and chickens found in Oceania come from Southeast Asia. But the definitive proof seems to be linguistic. The Pacific tongues are part of the group called Malayo-Polynesian. The Melanesian languages have nothing in common with those of Africa. Their roots are in Asia.

The Pacific peoples go back to an ancient cross between Caucasoids, Negroids, and Mongoloids. In the case of the Melanesians, the Negroid influence dominates. The New Hebrides were surely discovered and populated by successive waves of migrants. Probably the first inhabitants were pushed to the interior of the islands by more aggressive people who arrived later in greater numbers. It is important to note that the mountain peoples of central Santo and Malekula are generally smaller and darker than the coastal people of these islands and that there still is antagonism between the man-bush and the man-salt-water. We really don't know anything about these earliest peoples. In certain islands there is an evident Polynesian influence and more crossbreeding, which probably occurred between 1300 and 1400.

There were probably never any mass migrations. Limited groups of people set out on the seas with their pigs, chickens, and stocks of yams in large canoes. One or two canoes would have been enough to populate an island. They must have been daring to undertake such voyages, across thousands of miles of water, aided only by distant stars and gods. But they dared to do it, and succeeded. We can only imagine how many canoes must have been lost at sea during these attempts. Thousands of people must have gone astray, starved to death or drowned. These Pacific peoples may have been the greatest navigators of all time.

And there he was, the last of the great white navigators, master of the *Tangoa*, who seemed to have taken Long John Silver for his model rather than Bougainville or Cook. Right in front of me, strutting on the bridge with his exaggerated limp, a bandana knotted around his head turban-style, a dagger slipped into his pareu. The only item that was missing was the black patch over one eye. Brandishing a flask of whiskey, he let loose torrents of curses at the native crew, presenting formal excuses to me after each outburst, like a real gentleman-pirate.

So far as I was concerned, Monsieur Bob was a paragon of politeness. He was most attentive: are you thirsty, are you hungry, are you cold? He congratulated me energetically for not being seasick. I congratulated myself even more. Having never been on a boat before, I was a little worried about this possibility. Kal, despite the experience of his journey across the Pacific in a sailboat, is still prone to this malady.

But our good captain was distinctly less amiable with Xavier Bernard, the Sewald Company accountant. Xavier was a lanky young man, freshly arrived in the New Hebrides from the Paris suburbs. He had never left France before, but he knew the sea, he told me, to convince himself no doubt, because he had spent his family vacation for years on the beaches of the Sables-d'Olonne. This is something like calling yourself an oceanographer for having spent countless summers at Coney Island. Instead of a dagger, he kept Polaroid pictures of his wife and two young children close at hand. Monsieur Bob did everything he could to intimidate this nice boy and succeeded easily.

Before nightfall we could no longer see Santo behind us. The bleak clouds above us grew more and more threatening, and the waves went wild. Our poor *Tangoa* pitched and reeled crazily. Xavier wasn't seasick, but he admitted to me that he was particularly conscious of the existence of his stomach. The captain, twirling the ends of his little moustache into an urbane smile, offered us gin and tonics. "No thanks, captain," I said, "I'm fine." Thereupon he placed his chubby little hand on mine.

"My name's Bob," he confessed. "But please call me Bobbie. All my English friends do." He launched into anecdotes, speaking of himself as if he were the classic adventure hero of some novel, the eternal intelligent and moral bad boy, the good swindler who triumphs over all stupid established authority.

"The day I realized that missionaries were making more money than me," began one of his typical stories, "I became a missionary. I mean, I got myself a black suit and a little white collar and cruised around the islands, passing for a priest, selling masses to the natives. At first, I was a little worried since of course I didn't know how to say mass. I hadn't set foot in a church for years and I remembered very little of what went on. But I said to myself, hell, what does that matter? The natives know even less than I do. All I had to do was put on a serious face and talk in a booming voice, like in a play. You can say anything as long as you repeat the names of the Father, the Son, and the

Holy Ghost often enough. Well, it worked. I was earning a lot of bread. Until the day I ran into a difficult village . . ."

He waited for some signs of encouragement before continuing. We gave him what he wanted.

"In this particular village—it was on Maewo Island—the men didn't want to buy a mass. It was the first time anyone had said no and I was raving mad. They didn't even offer me any presents, nothing at all. They wanted me to leave, just like that, with nothing! Can you imagine? I didn't have a revolver with me, luckily, or I would have done something disastrous. I didn't have any weapon at all! So I racked my brain to find some way, quickly, of saving face. Then—I don't know how I got this idea, it came all at once, a real brainstorm—on the beach, before all the assembled men, I invoked the wrath of I don't know what god, the god of the Condominium probably. And I made a prophecy: that because of their lack of faith, each of their women would bear triplets, one for the French, one for the English, and one for me! Their eyes popped out of their heads. And I was happy. I had my revenge. Back on board I forgot all about the incident.

"Then the next day on the radio I learned the police were looking for me. Those imbeciles in the village had actually called the Catholic mission in Santo by radio, saying that a white priest had come to get all the women of the island pregnant and was that normal. Talk about a loose interpretation! Well, I threw my costume overboard right away. And a little bit later a Condominium boat came up alongside me with two policemen on deck. They asked me if I had encountered an unknown priest who wanted to rape the Maewo women. You see the way a story gets exaggerated? I would have liked to explain the joke, but I had a feeling they wouldn't have found it very funny. So I promised to report immediately any suspicious priest in the area. Unfortunately, due to the circumstances, I was forced to give up that line of work."

"What did you do then, captain?" asked Xavier, naïve as the Maewo men in the story. Bobbie eyed him kindly.

"Well," he continued, "for the moment I had had enough of the New Hebrides. I went down to Noumea and made myself a pretty bundle by parachuting. I had never even seen a parachute before. But that's nothing. So I spent a few days in the bistros meeting new people and old friends. And I said to everyone, I said, what would you bet that I'll go to Tontouta Airport and take the first available plane and jump, without any training, without knowing a thing about it, nothing at all? They were fantastic bar bets. Everyone was pretty well smashed, and they were all sure that I'd back down. Then I did it. And they were men of their words and they all paid up. Some of them had bet as much as fifty pounds! I did the rounds again real quick, one more time, before everyone had heard about it. But it wasn't a line of work that could last very long. Noumea isn't big enough. So then I felt like traveling a bit, taking a vacation. So I went and bought myself a secondhand camera and had some 'French Television, Producer' cards printed up and I invented a show. I took the plane to Tahiti where I told everyone I was making a tourist film on Polynesia. All the hotel and restaurant managers were fighting over me to get me into their places. I made them happy by taking some shots from time to time—no film in the camera, of course. I wasn't about to waste money buying rolls of film! So that's how I got a whole month's vacation, all expenses paid, on Tahiti."

The captain poured himself a glassful of gin, disdaining the bottles of tonic. I didn't know if his stories were completely true, but my feeling was, if he was making them up, he had missed his calling. With such imagination, he could have made a real fortune, even if he couldn't write, in selling his ideas to Hollywood. All of a sudden he manufactured a real pirate's laugh and scowled at Xavier.

"Listen, Monsieur Xavier," he said, tapping his stiffened finger on the young man's shoulder, "I want you to know that I've already had some encounters with your kind. The last time an accountant tried to make trouble for me, I knew he was taking a boat to go see the accounts of a Malekula plantation. I went up along next to the boat that was taking him there and boarded it with my *bosco*, my first mate. I hadn't forgotten my revolver that time, and my friend was armed with a bull's pizzle. So, I *invited* this accountant to my cabin to settle the problem we had. And you know, after a quarter of an hour together, we had no problem whatsoever! He found my accounts absolutely perfect! I'm telling you all this just to warn you that in the New Hebrides business is often settled rather brutally. And don't think that the Condominium would bail you out, either. When such 'incidents' occur, the government closes its eyes. So you understand, mistakes can be deadly around here, Monsieur Xavier. Therefore watch your step! You are not in France!"

Xavier got the message. He may be naïve, but the threat wasn't subtle. And I took it most seriously, too, far more than the batty stories. I felt intuitively that Monsieur Bob did have a violent side. I was convinced that his attraction for revolvers, whips, and daggers, even if he used them as props, was completely real.

Bob started rubbing his deformed foot. I asked him if it was painful.

"Oh, yeah, it hurts like the dickens, especially when the barometer drops. That's the worst. The pain cripples me more than the limp. No doubt about it, I'm just not the same man since this goddamn accident."

I hadn't wanted to question him before on this possibly delicate subject. But now that he clearly invited my curiosity, I asked. The accident happened while he was hunting crocodiles in the Solomons. Because of a malfunctioning revolver, he shot himself in the foot.

"Crap! Excuse my language, but how can you talk politely about the bloody irony of life? You kill hundreds of bloody crocodiles, and you end up like this because of a bloody gun that goes off when it bloody well shouldn't. I was working with an Englishman, Ron, who had been a professional hunter for fifteen years. He was known in all the Australian canneries. An incredible guy! When he shot a crocodile, it wasn't an animal he saw at the end of his rifle, it was a fifty-pound note! I did it mostly for the sport. We worked well together."

Xavier asked exactly how they did it, and Bob was only too happy to explain. During the night they went in a canoe to swampy bays which they had already mapped out. The crocodiles were caught by a spotlight, which hypnotized them. The men then had to approach fairly close in order to break the nose with ax blows, so that the animals would stay on the surface in order to breathe. Then, the reptiles were finished off with a revolver shot into the bump on the top of the head. The greatest danger was the tail. If you're struck by a crocodile's tail, you're either maimed for life or dead.

Xavier, carried away by his enthusiasm, punctuated Bob's story with "darnits" and "goshes." At the end, the swinging-tail part, he couldn't contain himself any longer and unfurled a "shit" full of admiration.

One of the crew served us rice garnished with chunks of a tuna which had been caught off Santo with a line that trailed behind the stern of the boat. I was as hungry as a Malekula wild dog. Bob was still thirsty. Xavier nibbled a few grains of rice. The rolling boat and the captain's character hadn't given him much of an appetite. Bob offered me his minuscule cabin, insisting that he preferred to sleep on the bridge in the open air. Indeed, there wasn't much air inside. I fell asleep wondering where Jacques could be spending the night, hoping that everything was going well for him and Kal in south Malekula.

Land straight ahead! I thought of Queiros, who had headed toward the same island—Santa Maria or Gaua, as you wish. I barely distinguished the small, fine outline on the horizon, a little more blue than the sky, a little less blue than the sea. The sailors had spotted it a while before. I didn't have a trained eye. Slowly the silhouette of the island became clearer. I had the impression we would get there quickly. I was wrong. The shape stayed blue, vague, and distant longer than I would have imagined possible.

Drinking lukewarm coffee on the bridge of the *Tangoa*, I watched the blue of the island transform by degrees into a deep green. The coconut palms were the first trees whose shapes stood out from the mass of vegetation. We moored in a calm little bay. A few men, women, and children waited for us on the beach, just as their ancestors had been there to greet Cook. Only these people were neither nude nor armed. They had simply come to the coast for a little entertainment, having deserted their gardening, cooking, and other daily tasks. Boats do not arrive very often in the Banks Islands.

I followed Bob and Xavier to the Sewald "store," a corrugated steel shack about as big as a garage for a Volkswagon, a few hundred yards behind the shore. It would take them until the end of the afternoon for their bookkeeping and inventory. Bob asked the natives who were surrounding us to take care of me, and I went off to the nearest village, called Ver. The islanders had said there was an old man there who could tell me some good stories.

It was true. I saw that in the Banks even the children can talk about Qat as easily as an American youngster can tell you all you want to know about Cinderella or Baby Jesus.

We continued our trip in this manner, from mooring to mooring. Bob and Xavier spent their days in the stores. I spent mine in the villages. The Banks have a fairy-tale beauty. Mota emerges from the sea like an oriental temple, Mota Lava like a mythic kingdom. The Vanua Lava mountains are always enveloped by a fog which unveils, from time to time, for a few seconds, the gracious forms of the peaks. It's a dreamworld. Perhaps the most striking island is Ureparapara, at the northern end of the archipelago. It is the summit of an ancient volcano, one side having been caved in by the relentless onslaught of the ocean. The crater walls now frame an immense horseshoe bay. When you enter this haven, you barely notice a few tiny light spots in the greenery at the back of the gulf. Just a few huts, the infinitesimal impact of humanity on this majestic nature. Ureparapara is Bligh's island, which he discovered during his remarkable and involuntary 1789 voyage. As a result of a mutiny, Lieutenant William Bligh, commander of the famous *Bounty*, was thrown onto a sloop and abandoned in the middle of the ocean. In this small open boat he crossed almost four thousand miles of sea to arrive safe and sound, and a bit miraculously, at Timor. On the way, he passed by these islands which he named the Banks after Joseph Banks, Captain Cook's botanist.

It is unbelievably hot in those parts, and the relative humidity must be close to 100 percent. The sumptuous vegetation, with no tropical breeze to animate it, gives the effect of theater decor, too perfectly drawn to be credible.

The village, too, seems unanimated. The people are calm and speak softly. They certainly don't laugh in the unbridled manner of the Santo and Malekula islanders. Their rich traditions of art, dance, chant, and ritual are a distant memory at most. All this cultural wealth seems completely forgotten, for these people are Christians now and have abandoned all their former pagan practices. Unfortunately, in space and in spirit they are as far from the Christian world as from their ancient Melanesian world, so there isn't much left for them. I sensed right away, in these villages, the sadness of nothingness, of a life without goals or traditional con-

text. The natives know all about God now, and they still remember Qat and the other *vui*, the spirits, but neither of these
ideals is able to shake them out of their profound lethargy.

Qat hasn't always existed. He has nothing to do with the vague
beginnings of time. Although he was "born," his birth was unlike
everybody else's since his mother was a rock which split in two to
bear him. That rock still exists on Vanua Lava. It is called
Qatgoro, which is also the name of Qat's mother. He didn't have a
father. He had eleven brothers, who were all named Tangaro.
The first was Tangaro the Wise; the second Tangaro the Simple;
and the other nine were named after trees in the jungle.

Qat also had a companion, Marawa, a wood spirit who often
took the form of a spider and whom he met in a most extraordinary fashion. Qat had cut down an enormous tree to make a beautiful canoe and began carving it that very day. The next day he
found all his work undone. All the chips of wood had returned to
their original places and the tree was intact. This happened again
and again, for many days. One evening, instead of going home,
Qat made himself very small and hid under a large sliver of wood.
He saw an old man with long white hair who put each piece of
wood back in place. That was Marawa. Qat left his hiding place
and intended to strike Marawa down with a shell ax. Marawa
implored Qat not to kill him, promising to make good all the
ruined work and finish the canoe quickly. And so he did, working
faster with his fingernails than Qat with his ax. (The first time the
Banks natives saw nails, they called them "Marawa's fingernails,"
pismarawa, and the word lives on in their language.)

It was Qat who made men and women. He shaped them out of
dragonwood, meticulously sculpting all the parts of the body, at-
taching one to the other, at the end adding the eyes and ears. This
work took him six days, and he gave himself six more days to give
life to his creatures.

He danced in front of them. When he saw them begin to stir he
played the drum for them, and they stirred even more. Thus,
little by little, Qat charmed them with his music and his dances
until they became living men and women. There were three men
and three women. Qat quickly divided them into married couples.

Marawa, to reclaim the upper hand as vui-creator, also sculpted human bodies, but out of the wood of another tree, the *tavisoviso*. He assembled all the parts of the body. He danced and played the drum to give them life just as Qat had. But when they began to budge, Marawa, who was contrary by nature, dug out a hole and buried the creatures for six days. When he finally retrieved them, he found the bodies decomposing, definitively deprived of life. And that was the origin of death.

Among other things, Qat also created plants, animals, the seasons, and the winds. It is said that he was like a child. Whenever he was bored he amused himself by constructing this or fabricating that. There was one exception, an element of nature that Qat didn't create but rather imported. One day he returned from a voyage to the Torres Islands, north of the Banks, bringing mysterious objects with him: a long piece of bamboo plugged up at both ends by leaves, a tightly knit pandanus fiber sack, and a piece of red obsidian. He gathered all the inhabitants of Vanua Lava together and uncorked the bamboo trunk. Immediately, a black mantle covered the sky and the earth. Qat had unleashed Night. Before, the Banks Islands had known only Day and daytime light. Qat taught the people how to sleep and that darkness was good. After a few hours, he untied the sack and let out a rooster who started to crow immediately. Qat then took the red obsidian and cut the night along a straight line at the horizon so that dawn could enter. The memory of this event lives on in expression in the language. To say daybreak, the Banks Islanders say that morning has been cut.

Innumerable adventures of Qat are known. His ever-jealous brothers tried constantly to kill him or steal his canoe or his wife, Iro Lei, a beautiful woman-spirit. Bad spirits were always laying traps for him. Qat always walked away the winner. If his supernatural strength wasn't enough against the strong evil vui, he was always the craftier.

He left the Banks Islands in an enormous canoe which he constructed in the center of Gaua Island, the prow of his boat cutting a long canal right to the sea. The people say that when Qat left, he took with him in his canoe most of the good things that had existed before in the islands. But he was supposed to return with all those things; he promised he would. Thus, when the first whites

arrived in the Banks, it's not at all surprising that they presumed
it was the long-awaited return of Qat. But they realized quickly
that it wasn't so.

How odd it is that despite the disappearance of traditional life,
this mythology is still so alive. Do the Banks Islanders, deep in
their hearts, despite the missions, still await—even today—the return of the vui?

That evening on the *Tangoa* I discussed these legends with Xavier. Bob cared as little about Qat as I did about his commercial
accounting. Besides, the captain was becoming more and more
nervous. I concluded that he was simply anxious to get home,
having been gone for several weeks.

We arrived in front of Rana, his plantation, at the end of a rainy
afternoon. We advanced into a black and white world, like black
and white film. The mooring was protected and Bob dropped
anchor not far from the coast where the water still seemed to be
deep. We could see the layout of the plantation very well. A few
wood and sheet-metal houses, a few huts, all grouped in half
moons behind the black sand beach. A little farther on a faded red
sailboat was in dry dock on a scaffolding where it had undoubtedly been for a long time. Not a very gay picture. The Rana people who came to the shore to welcome their boss did not seem
very gay either. Getting off the boat, Bob scrutinized the welcoming committee. His piercing eyes darted everywhere. He
seemed to be looking for someone. When he didn't find what he
wanted, his face grew grave. He spied an old woman who was
trying to camouflage herself among the others. "Josephine!"
shouted the captain. "You come! You come here now!"

She came, dragging her feet. She looked terrified.

*"Flora he stop where here? Bloody hell! Where he stop, woman b'long
me?"*

"Mastah," said the shriveled old grandmother in a quavering
voice, *"Flora go. Flora go finish."*

"Wamem, he go? He go? He go where here? Goddamn you!" If the
old woman was trembling in fear, he was already trembling with
anger.

"He go witem brother long mama long him. Long village veraman."
Josephine recoiled as she said the awful words, undoubtedly expecting to be hit. But Bob paid no more attention to her. He

turned to a hardy young native and commanded him to get his horse ready.

"Come on," he said to Xavier and me. We had been watching him nervously. He brought us to a pandanus and bamboo kiosk just behind the beach. It was his dining room and living room, nicely arranged in the native style with furniture conceived for the comfort of Europeans. A table and chairs on one side of the room, a bamboo bar and easy chairs around a low table on the other. Bob mastered his emotions to play the cordial host.

"Make yourselves at home. Serve yourselves at the bar. You'll be comfortable here because there's lots of air. Please excuse me, but I have to leave you for a while. I hope to be back for dinner. If I'm not, Josephine will serve you. And she'll show you your room, too."

"There's no serious trouble, is there?" I asked timidly.

"Nothing I can't fix," he said.

From behind the bar he took several revolvers, each wrapped in oilcloth. Like an actor who never turns his back to the audience, Bob placed himself so that none of his movements would be hidden from us. He picked out two big guns, slipping one under his belt, holding the other in his right hand. Xavier, very tense, stared at the weapons.

"The bastards stole my woman," he told us gruffly. "But they'll regret it before I get through with them!"

After this pronouncement he stalked out of the kiosk, kicking the screen door open and letting it slam. The muscular young native was holding the horse and got on behind his master. They galloped into the night. I felt like I was living a cowboy movie.

Both Xavier and I had some ideas about what was going on, but we didn't discuss it. Josephine, while serving us some soup a little later, confirmed that Flora was the boss's wife.

During the night we heard distant gunfire several times.

The following morning, Xavier came to the kiosk a few minutes after me. The table had been set for three. A pretty *metis* came in with a coffeepot, a pitcher of hot milk, and a platter of hot toast. Her skin was light copper color, and she had long hair tied in a ponytail. She was very visibly pregnant. She couldn't have been more than sixteen years old. I already knew it, but I asked anyway as gently as possible if her name was Flora.

"Yes, missis."

She didn't dare look at us. She seemed thoroughly miserable. And she disappeared before I could say another word. Bob came to join us. He served himself a large cup of black coffee and lit a Gauloise, asking us amiably if we had slept well.

Xavier couldn't restrain himself. He fidgeted in his chair and finally decided he had to speak up. "Excuse me, Bob," he said, "I really don't mean to pry into your life. But why don't you tell your wife to join us for breakfast?"

"You don't understand," said Bob with a small wicked laugh. He sighed deeply. "That's not my wife. That's the maid." A heavy and embarrassing silence filled the room. Bob lit another cigarette and sighed again.

"Okay," he declared, "since you're here and since you've already formed certain opinions, let me explain."

"You don't have to . . . I'm not asking——" babbled Xavier.

"Shut up, sweetie pie," Bob said sardonically. "You're not even a man, you're just a newborn babe and you don't understand anything about anything."

Xavier turned red and obviously would have liked to disappear. Bob began his tale lightheartedly. Flora is the daughter of an Australian sailor and a native woman from a nearby village, Veraman. Bob didn't exactly kidnap Flora, he said, snickering, but he let it be known that she pleased him. Manorial rights still seem to function beautifully in these distant islands where a single European can make the law. So Flora, about fourteen years old, came to live with him.

Bob was ignoring Xavier now. He wanted to justify himself to me.

"You've got to understand," he said, "I've done everything for her. I would even have married her. I wanted to make her a European. She's a good-looking woman, and she could have done better in life than making laplaps with the other *ponoches*. You know that word—native women. I bought her pretty dresses and it took me months to convince her to wear them instead of those ugly missionary dresses. I tried to teach her French. All she remembers now is hello and good-bye. I insisted that she eat at the table with me, really like a wife. But it was a fiasco. She looked at her plate and never touched a thing. I asked Josephine what Flora would like for a present. Josephine told me a record player. So I brought one back from Santo. No show of enthusiasm, no thanks. But I know she's happy with it because whenever I'm not here she uses it. I found records scattered everywhere. The only time she reacts to me at all is when I get angry. So, I get angry regularly. Fear is better than indifference."

He waited for me to say something. I didn't hesitate. "Maybe she would be happier as a Melanesian than as a European," I suggested.

"No, you're wrong. I'm convinced that she is really very happy to stay with me. It gives her a certain superiority over the others. The bitch takes advantage of it, too. She's tougher on my workers than I am. But I was expecting a move from her family when I left for Santo. I was sure they were going to try to get her back . . . because she's pregnant. They figure they've got more rights over the child than I do."

"Did they really kidnap Flora? Did she want to come back with you last night?"

"Good God, who knows what she wants, after it's all said and done. She didn't protest and she came back meekly. It's her uncle who yelled and screamed. But I'm going to keep that child, you know. It's very important to me. It may be the only one I'll ever have. And no goddamn native is going to take it from me!"

Bob and Xavier worked for several days. I roamed around the island and the villages behind the plantation. At mealtimes we all met in the kiosk. Bob (I could never get used to calling him "Bobbie," as he would have liked) had changed his attitude toward Xavier. He tried less to intimidate him directly. He settled for harassing and mocking the young man by calling him "darling-baby" and "my precious," treating him like a homosexual or an imbecile. Now, our accountant friend was basically a good guy who had no sense whatsoever of repartee. Bob could surely tell that I found his jokes rather gross, but I kept quiet. Xavier was big enough to defend himself. I just waited for Bob to address the least impolite word to me. But he never did.

Bob was always finding excuses for displaying his revolvers. We were having dinner when he decided to give Xavier some lessons on firearms. Xavier held the rod as if it were white-hot. Bob grabbed it back and, without pausing, fired. We were all shaken by the blow. Bull's-eye. The barometer that hung on the opposite wall, thirty feet away, now had a big hole in the middle. Xavier and I looked at Bob as if he were crazy. The gun had gone off just in front of my face and had left me momentarily deaf.

"No harm!" cried Bob. "That barometer never did work right, anyhow!"

The same evening we heard "Pow! Pow! Pow!" coming from the kitchen area. Bob burst into the kiosk afterwards, furious, screaming, "The idiot! The goddamn lousy idiot!" He calmed down after half a glass of whiskey and looked us in the eye sadly.

"It's all ruined," he said. "I wanted to give you a surprise. I had sent out a whole crew to go fishing and two boys to trap crayfish. I made you a delicious fish stew that's been simmering in a large kettle since early this morning. So now! Lord Jesus, a real disaster! Justin, the boy who helps Josephine with the housework, gave my soup to the pigs! To the pigs! I caught him and almost killed him for it. But I above all wanted to know why, *why*, he had the diabolical idea of giving my soup to the pigs! And you know what he said?"

Bob stopped to light a cigarette and to be sure that we were listening.

" 'Mastah,' he says to me, 'I didn't do it on purpose. I didn't know. I thought it was the leftovers, with dirty water on top.' Dirty water, he said! All day long, I'd been going to smell it and it smelled really good. And he calls it dirty water! Can you believe it? But how can you kill such a moron, who doesn't even know what he's doing, so I let him run away."

Once Bob exchanged his revolvers for a rifle, informing us that a few crocodiles had come down to the mouth of the river not far from the plantation. Being cautious, he felt he should suppress them right away.

"You can come with me if you like. There won't be any danger, not with me. I have enough crocodiles under my belt. Unless Xavier's afraid," he added threateningly. "You afraid, boo-boo? Well, you can always stay home."

All three of us set out in Bob's motorboat. At the first view of the river I couldn't believe my eyes. The water is gold-colored and transparent. Gold! Bob explained that the surprising tint came from a sulfur spring near the source.

No crocodiles at the mouth. We went up the river for about half an hour, but it was hard going. Shallow and rocky. Still no crocodiles. Bob seemed disappointed not to be able to use his handsome rifle and to have to return empty-handed.

Apart from these tales of gunshot and folly, there was the book-keeping, which didn't seem to be going too well. Xavier was in a hurry to finish. He had promised his wife he'd be back on Santo by the end of the week. But the work was apparently very compli-cated. Bob wanted to persuade the accountant to drop it. He of-fered to finish it off alone during the following week and to bring the results down to Santo.

Now, even though Xavier was shy in general, when it came to his job he was like a sergeant totally committed to carrying out the captain's order. He and Bob argued some, and Bob returned to direct threats. Nothing doing. Xavier studied lovingly the photo of his dear wife but wasn't about to give an inch. He decided to work longer and longer hours and, since Bob couldn't leave him alone, he was forced to do the same. The jokes continued, but more and more I felt a coldness between the two men.

Everything was completed by Thursday at about noon, so we took to the sea in the early afternoon. With good weather the *Tangoa* needs about eighteen hours to arrive in Santo. Since the wind was against us, it took us somewhat longer. We tied up to the Santo pier at about eleven o'clock, Friday. Xavier was happy. He hadn't lied to his wife. He did make it home for the weekend.

Bob, in a burst of good humor, insisted that we all drink to our safe arrival at the Marine. And the drinks were on him, he yelled. Okay, we accepted. Xavier warned us, however, that he was game but wanted to join his family for lunch. I teased him gaily. What a model husband! He was flattered.

I asked Bob if we could stop at the post office on the way. Sev-eral letters were waiting for me, from my parents and friends, from my brother. Every one except the one I had most hoped to find, the one from Jacques. He had promised to send a note. No news, I said to myself, probably just means that there hasn't been a boat from south Malekula in the last two weeks. Nevertheless, I was disappointed. Could he have quite simply forgotten?

All the pillars of the Marine were there, boosting the place up as usual. And they welcomed us warmly with laughs and shouts and rounds of drinks. Elsa Ravon shook my hand from behind a mask of friendliness. She would have been really pleased only if I had arrived in tears, saying she had been right. Since I had no horror stories to offer, she lost no time in suggesting—overtly, but behind my back, of course—that I had to be Bobbie's mistress. Moreover, in the months to come she was to proclaim that I was the mistress of just about every man in the land between the ages of twenty and sixty. Jean Ravon, on the other hand, though rather high, was perfectly charming. I was particularly happy to see Ernst Lamberty again—Ernie, the great big Dutch captain of the *Konanda*. He had always given me the impression of being an interesting man who enjoyed life and had his heart in the right place.

While Bob was ordering yet another round for everybody, one of the planters yelled at Xavier: "Hey, there, Mr. Accountant! There wasn't too much cash missing, was there?"

Xavier replied with a giggle. When it came to professional matters, his lips were sealed.

The conversation turned to other subjects. It seemed there were some Americans who were buying up a lot of land in the New Hebrides. It was all very vague, but everyone had his theory. They're going to build Hiltons. They're going to establish some industry. They're going to install military bases . . .

Round after round, in quick succession. I had several full glasses lined up in front of me.

Mr. Thibault, the planter who admired Pierre Benoit so much, asked me how things had worked out in the Banks. I told him everything. He was highly amused. He placed Monsieur Bob somewhere between a would-be Groucho Marx and Jesse James. Would-be, meaning a loser. Then he told me something more precise about the man.

"You know why he's like that? His father was a colonel, a worthy man, who really did succeed in life. So Bobbie, who just isn't of the same caliber, always tried to revolt against his father's authority. He's always tried to be the black sheep."

Mr. Thibault considers all of Bob's apparently well-known anecdotes as just a lot of hot air. Even though I didn't like Monsieur Bob, speaking frankly, I felt an obligation to defend him. I fell back on the only thing in his stories that seemed true to me, the crocodile hunting and his terrible accident in the Solomons. Mr. Thibault laughed outright.

"You poor dear," he cooed, "you are unbelievably naïve. That's very charming, but really I can't leave you in such a state of ignorant bliss. Bobbie has never killed a crocodile in his life! And the first time he tried, the first time, mind you, the only thing he was capable of hitting was his own foot. He was a clumsy novice, that's all. His stories of being a heroic crocodile hunter, the hundreds of crocodile skins, the hair-raising adventures, all that is just pure—pardon the expression, mademoiselle—shit! There's not a word of truth in it."

At the other end of the bar, I saw that a planter had gotten hold of Xavier again. "Come on now," he said to the young accountant, "among friends you can tell the truth. I'll bet there were at least ten thousand dollars missing, huh?"

Xavier, who wasn't used to drinking so much and who was pretty far gone, burst into laughter. "No, my friend," he hiccupped, "you lose your bet. Only three thousand dollars and not a penny more are gone with the wind. I'm not implying that the money was stolen! Oh, no! Our friend Bobbie could have made a little error in his arithmetic. How can you ever be sure, ha ha? Right, Monsieur Bob?"

Xavier tumbled toward his neighbor on the next stool. He was completely drunk. Bob gave him a somber look. He undoubtedly regretted that he hadn't brought his revolvers along.

5

The Spirits Are Out
to Get You!

FRIDAY, December 13. Eight A.M. The rain came down in
sheets. Before me lay the dismal prospect of being a Marine tearoom prisoner all day long. What can you do in Santo in that kind
of weather? Settle into another café and get drenched on the way?
It's not worth it. I couldn't even go back to my room, the beach
cabana about a hundred yards from the Marine which was our
headquarters. The large window was no more than a gaping hole
in the wall. I had pushed my bed to the opposite wall where the
rain reached it less and come to have coffee in the Marine.

Jean and Elsa were both discreetly tense. They were already on
strong drinks, Jean downing his overtly, Elsa hiding her glass
behind a vase filled with hibiscus at a corner of the bar. They
didn't talk.

Outside the garden window there was a curtain of water
through which everything was blurred. You couldn't even see the
raindrops. It was a continual flow. That's what it takes to produce
the exuberant island vegetation, but it has the opposite effect on
human beings. I had about as much resiliency as a piece of soggy
bread. Even your bones seem to go soft in that humidity. I was
huddled up in a rattan armchair in the most withdrawn corner of
the café, the gusts of wind and rain blasting in through the win-

dows without panes and the four entrances without doors. I didn't take off my cheap Chinese raincoat, which, after all, turned out not to be very rainproof.

Jean started playing with the short-wave radio and tuned in Noumea. Despite the crackling, the tenor voice of Schuyler Hamilton singing an aria from *The Marriage of Figaro* came through.

I had hoped to go spend a few days in Port-Vila, the tiny capital of the archipelago, but all flights had been canceled because of the bad weather, and the boat captains preferred to remain in port instead of confronting a wild sea. Nothing's ever hurried in the New Hebrides. You can always wait for better weather. The only one to cast off was Ernst Lamberty, two days before, for a two-week run to Ambrym and Pentecost. I was tempted to ask him for a place on board the *Konanda* but I didn't dare leave for so long. I was persuaded that Jacques and Kal would be coming back soon even though I still had not received a letter from them.

Five or ten minutes to nine, before the news, the Noumea station was interrupted by a special announcement of particular interest to us. A cyclone, which had changed course, was headed right for the New Hebrides and, for the moment, point-blank toward Santo. Unless it changed course again, it would reach us in the evening.

A cyclone! The man said a cyclone. The rain didn't bother me any more. All my senses woke up. I was as full of curiosity and excitement as apprehension. A cyclone.

Jean snapped off the radio and pounded his drink against the table. "I knew it," he cried. "I could feel it."

"All right," said Elsa, "but let's not lose any time. Go get the boards."

"Boards? For what? This cabin was built to resist cyclones, and you know it," said Jean.

"Yes, Jean, I know. But it would be safer to nail up some boards on the doors and windows anyway. Come on. All you have to do is go get them now, and then we won't have to think about it anymore."

Vivid colors rose to his face, and anger rose in his throat. "I said we don't need boards." His voice cracked, though he tried to control it.

"Yes, but Jean, you know very well——"

"Shut up!" he screamed.

I would have liked to melt into my chair. I wanted them to forget my presence. Elsa didn't let go and didn't change her whining, condescending, and distinctly provocative tone of voice.

"But if we don't put up the boards, you know——"

"That's enough! I don't need you to tell me what has to be done. Lay off, will you? Get the hell out of here if you can't keep your trap shut!"

"But, Jean——"

He got up from the table in a rage, knocking over his chair. He caught her fatty arm and squeezing it tightly led her to the door. Elsa never stopped protesting, but her feet followed, one after the other, like a mechanical doll. He threw her brutally out the door. Right afterwards, over the sound of the rain, I heard the jeep starting up.

Once she was gone, Jean Ravon turned his attention to me and began a light, courteous conversation, as if the weather were fine, as if Elsa had simply gone off to do her shopping. A planter arrived. Then two others. What the hell, the rain doesn't quench our thirst, they proclaimed. Jean was affability incarnate. The customers didn't stay long anyway. With such weather, they had a lot to do. One of them mentioned in leaving that he had to rush home to board up his windows. Jean gave a little start, but never stopped smiling. It was almost noon, when we heard the arrival of the jeep, that his mask changed again. He welcomed his wife suspiciously, ready to jump on Elsa if she said the slightest thing. But this time she contained herself. She silently began to set the table for lunch. We ate together. One or the other of them answered me when I spoke, but neither of them addressed a word to the other. Finally I stopped talking, too. I was the only one who was embarrassed.

A truce doesn't last very long at the Ravons'. I should already have known that. While we were having our coffee, Elsa said something about the velocity of the wind. Jean did not agree. It took no more to set them off again. And, perhaps for lack of other ideas, they repeated their morning performance. Elsa was shown to the door a second time and drove away in her noisy jeep.

The afternoon stretched out before me like a vast dead plain.

I had a visitor, Alan Snowsill, the young airline agent, who came to confirm the definitive cancellation of all flights in the archipelago. Far out, I replied. Sensing my low spirits, he kindly asked me if I didn't have any shopping to do in town. I jumped at the opportunity to get away, even briefly. Alan took me to Burns-Philp, the large Australian department store where he had his office. He told me to take my time choosing whatever I needed. I really didn't need anything, but I joyfully spent over an hour selecting a few paperbacks. Then I had no more excuses for dawdling, and he brought me back to the Marine in his car.

I noticed the difference right away. All the windows and three of the four entrances were boarded up. When I entered, Jean said nothing. He was listening to the four o'clock news. The cyclone had not changed course for the moment. It wasn't hot, what with the wind and rain, but Jean was in a sweat. Suddenly, I had an intuition. He was afraid! He was afraid of the cyclone and that was the reason for his bizarre behavior since the morning.

The comings and goings continued. Elsa returned. Jean wanted to throw her out again. She tried to reason, all her belongings were there, where did he want her to go, and so on. In the end it was Jean who stormed out. The only thing he lacked was a door to slam. I watched him disappear into the beating rain.

At sunset the wind began to take on a new force, and its moaning drowned out the water sounds. The rain no longer fell straight down but was carried off horizontally. I heard sinister creakings, something caving in, branches breaking. Uprooted bushes were thrust against the walls of the Marine.

It was my turn to be tense. I didn't know which of the cyclones I was more afraid of, the real one, or the one that Jean would surely let loose when he came home. For the time being, Jean was probably drowning his sorrows in another one of the town bistros, but I feared he would come back angry and aggressive. I didn't have the least desire to get mixed up in their personal business, but my very presence threw me into the situation despite myself. While Elsa was setting out soup bowls for us, I talked to her about her husband. For a woman who had drunk such a large number of generous Scotches during the day, she was in remarkable control of herself. Was she really as calm as she seemed, or was it an alcoholic stupefaction? In any event, she tried to reassure me about

Jean. When he got into such a mood, she told me, the best solution for him was precisely to go have some drinks with his friends. He always came back tranquilized. Since I had the impression that she liked those violent scenes, that she actively provoked them, I wasn't exactly reassured by her soothing words.

Suddenly in the night we heard the jeep's horn, a few short little bleeps at first, then the doleful cry that didn't stop. I was petrified.

"I wonder what that could be?" Elsa asked indifferently. "Oh. It's probably Jean. I'll go look."

Calmly, she dragged her heavy body toward the door. On an impulse, I wanted to plead with her not to go out. But I didn't. He's her husband. After their years of such a life together, my advice would have been superfluous and probably unwelcome. The horn stopped. I heard a few dull thuds. I tried not to imagine what they were.

A few minutes later she came back just the way she had left, dragging her feet. I thought that under the thick layer of makeup she wore her face was whiter than it had been.

"It's nothing," she breathed. "Something was stuck. Must have been the wind."

The wind. Sure.

There was no way I could go to sleep in our sweet little cabana. Not only because of the lack of windowpanes or any kind of closing, but because if the cyclone was to do any damage in the night, our cabana would be the first to go. I was ready to spend the night on two chairs in a corner of the café, but Elsa told me that wouldn't be necessary. I could sleep in the bedroom next to theirs.

Then Jean stormed into the cabin, called his wife every name in the book, and proceeded to push her around.

"But Jean," she wailed, "we're not alone."

Exactly what the lady shouldn't have said. Damn her, I thought, she has a knack for instigating trouble. At that instant I saw that Jean was strongly tempted to hit me. His anger reached a frightful peak.

"Not alone? What the hell are you saying? We're not alone! I don't give a shit about others! I don't give a shit about anybody! Especially you! And if you stay here, I'm leaving!"

He went into the bedroom and found a raincoat, which he

threw over his soaked shorts and shirt. He plunged into the night.

I hoped, given the hour and weather, that he wouldn't come back before morning. I even had a spare hope; maybe if he did come back tonight, I would be asleep and wouldn't hear him.

Elsa showed me a pile of our clean laundry in a corner of the kitchen. I pulled out a nightgown and went immediately to bed. Jean was back before I even had time to think, worse than before. He was stark raving mad. I heard him screaming and hitting his wife. How can such a rage keep growing? There's got to be a limit. It couldn't continue. Something had to give, and I was terrified at the thought of what might happen.

I was tempted to charge into the bar and help Elsa—two against one—but then I realized that Elsa wasn't even trying to defend herself, that she was actually doing her best to egg him on. My intervention couldn't possibly help her, it could only send Jean's furor momentarily in my direction.

Until then I had not been concerned about my own safety. My fear was disinterested, abstract, and certainly egoistic in a sense. He was going to kill her one of these days, but please, God, let it be when I'm not around. Now, all of a sudden, stretched out on the bed, listening to them a few yards away, I began to think how crazy I was not to be afraid myself. In his boundless rage, he was entirely capable of attacking anyone. I remembered that he kept a loaded rifle at his bedside. Elsa had pointed it out to me. At the same time, I was aware of the storm, whose violence was mounting also. Was the cyclone already battering this house? I wondered if the Marine would stand up to it.

I also began to wonder what I would do if Jean came into my room aggressively. I searched among the shadows for objects with which I could knock him out. But he's strong and I'm a coward, so I knew I couldn't do much against him if ever he decided to attack me. I started to panic.

I heard his angry footsteps. I saw him through the grillework of the bedroom door. He went into the room. Was he going to get the gun? He crossed back to the kitchen, in front of my door, and returned to the bistro. I couldn't see whether or not he had the gun, but I was at my wits' end. I had to get out of there. I had to leave. I threw on my raincoat over my nightgown and slipped through the door at the back of the kitchen.

The wind knocked me down right away. It was an incredible

struggle, but I finally managed to get back on my feet and continue. It was hard to stand up and almost impossible to walk. I missed not having a flashlight, but at least I was familiar with the path that led to our cabana and could grope my way by feeling out the plants with my feet. Almost swimming through the torrential rains, I didn't proceed too fast. Besides, I was racked by the fear of being alone, in the night, outdoors, with a cyclone as an adversary. I heard coconuts fall all around me with enough force to kill a person instantly. I heard the trees groan as they were snapped in two. You live an easy life, and you never realize how fragile you are.

Arriving like a castaway at the cabana, I knew at once that I couldn't stay there. The storm was raging inside my room and my bed was already saturated with water. Worse still, I heard part of the house collapse while I was entering the room. I forced myself back into the night once again. I had to go back to the Ravons'. Against Jean, there's always a chance of coming out all right; against the cyclone, not much.

About fifty yards behind the trail which leads from our cabana to the Marine, there's a new house where three young geologists live. I knew them only by sight, and I hadn't thought of going there before. Now that I noticed the light in their window, I didn't hesitate. Not finding the path that led to their house, I headed straight for the light, tearing my legs on the brambles.

One of the geologists opened the door. All three of them were there, alone with a young woman who teaches in the local elementary school. They were playing cards. They invited me in graciously, as if I were paying a cordial call one sunny afternoon. I collapsed into a chair and explained to them what was going on at the Ravons'.

There were four of them, couldn't they do something? I insisted, saying that Jean was capable at that moment of killing his wife.

But the geologists took it all in stride. "They're always that way," remarked one of them. "Don't worry about it. He won't kill her."

"If I had a wife like that," added another, "I would have killed her ages ago!"

I asked if nonetheless they might be so kind as to go get the police. What? Bother the police in weather like this? they exclaimed. And at night! Just because of a quarrel between the Ravons? What a funny idea.

There was nothing to do. I dropped it. One of them invited me to join in their card game. I said I didn't know how to play. However, no one thought to offer me any dry clothes. I huddled in the easy chair, shivering, without taking off my raincoat, since all I had on under it was one very drenched short nightgown.

The cyclone was in full swing. I finally fell asleep listening to the sounds of happy card players.

The next day, under a blazing sun, I saw that there were a few uprooted trees, a few damaged houses, but on the whole less destruction than everyone had feared. The cyclone had skimmed by Santo and was headed directly for south Malekula, where Jacques and Kal were. According to the weatherman, it was going to ravage the area. I was afraid for my friends.

Jean Ravon hadn't killed his wife during the night. He hadn't even wounded her seriously. She swore that morning that she would leave her husband, though she knew she could never do so. He swore off drinking, a promise he was to keep for only a few days.

I finally got word from Jacques and Kal. But it was René Romero and not I who got the letter. There was a little P.S. for me: "Can you let Charlene know what's happening?" I was a little annoyed. Jacques could have sent a more personal word for me. They had survived the cyclone. Kal was staying in Malekula. Jacques was making a round trip to Santo on the next trip of the *Windua*, the small cutter that belongs to the Southwest Bay plantation. The *Windua* is the only more or less regular link between southwest Malekula and Espiritu Santo. Since they didn't have a radio on board, they couldn't announce their arrival. And though I regularly watched the Segond Channel, I wasn't on the pier when it landed.

Jacques found me in town in front of the Burns-Philp department store. I almost didn't recognize him. Thin would be an understatement. Skin and bones, perhaps. Hollow, hollow cheeks. A phantom really. A wave of emotions welled up in me. I felt joy at seeing him and pain at seeing him in such a state. I had already

forgotten my numerous visits to the post office without ever finding a word from him. But besides the rings, which weren't there
before, his eyes hadn't changed. His smile proclaimed his greeting
as he shook both my hands.

"You got my letter okay?" he asked, sure of a positive response.
He couldn't believe I hadn't gotten it. He was downcast. "I entrusted it to Kailuan, one of the coastal village elders. He swore
he'd get it on the next *Windua*. Wait until I see that guy again!"

"But what did you say in the letter?"

"Come on, let's get off the street and I'll tell you." We found
shelter from the sun in the Tahitian café, Chez Mao. We picked
out the farthest table, just in front of the open windows facing the
sea.

"Okay, Jacques, the letter—what did you say?"

"I told you, among other things, that I love you. Darling, I
realized it as soon as I left you."

I was aware of the blood flowing through my veins, and I listened with buzzing ears. I didn't say a thing.

"You're not saying anything," he affirmed softly. "Is it because
you don't love me?"

"No." I finally was able to say in a voice that sounded foreign to
me. "Yes. I love you."

We spent much of the afternoon and much of the evening re-
peating it to each other. And much of the night tenderly demon-
strating it to one another in the dark garden of the Marine.

Love had priority for the moment, but there were other things,
too. Jacques had exciting news for me. The inhabitants of the
mountain villages where he and Kal had been staying since their
departure had never seen a "European"! Not a missionary, not a
Delegate. No one had ever ventured that far. And they never
went down to the sea. The only outside influences were a few
scraps of cloth and a few knives which they had gotten trading
with natives who lived closer to the coast. No more. Apart from
that, they live as they have for hundreds, indeed thousands, of
years. Jacques and Kal had named them "Mbotogote," after the
word they use to designate their language, which doesn't resemble
in the slightest the other Malekula languages.

The Europeans, if they knew these people, would call them
simply Small Nambas, which is what they call all the non–Big

Nambas tribes of the island. This generalization is based on the fact that they all wear relatively small penis sheaths compared to the big tufts worn by Virambat and his kind. However, the Small Nambas do not form a single group but several, and the Mbotogotes are surely one of the groups that stand alone.

Jacques was to stay in Santo only briefly, just long enough to send off some rolls of film and most of all to pick up a parcel of new film, which must have been waiting for him at the customs office for a while. He was counting on returning by the same boat in a day or two. He couldn't be late because there was going to be a Mbotogote ceremony.

I wanted to know just one thing. "Can I go there, too?"

"Yes, but listen," started Jacques. "I have a proposition to make. The Mbotogote ceremony ought to take place at about the same time as the Big Nambas one, from what we've gathered. But no one has fixed any dates yet. And we know that the Big Nambas dates are flexible, to say the least. Now, I can't risk missing the ritual in the south. We'll be the first strangers to see their ceremonies and I absolutely have to film them. But it would be a shame to miss Virambat's ritual if it's just before or after the other one. If the two *do* go on at the same time, it would be good if at least one of us were there and took some pictures. So, if you want to, you can go to Amok alone and see if Virambat has set a date and then you can come down to the south to join us."

"And how will I 'come down'?"

Jacques laughed, guessing my thought. "No, not on foot. That's impossible. It's at least thirty miles of really impenetrable jungle. No, you'll hire a boat at Norsup and go down as far as Lawa, a village at Southwest Bay. There you'll ask for a guide and a porter or two to take you up to the village of Lendombwey. Don't carry anything if you can avoid it because the walk is very hard. I'm warning you. It even took it out of Kal and me. So, what do you think? Will you do it?"

"Well, of course. But I hope I'm strong enough."

"Don't worry about it," Jacques reassured, taking my hand. "You'll get there just fine. And I'll be waiting anxiously."

We talked about the cyclone. "Metak, whom you'll meet," said Jacques, "announced it well in advance. *'Big-fella wind he come!'* I was pleased. I was hoping to get some spectacular shots. But when it hit us—Jesus Christ, what a blast!—I didn't think any-more about filming. I thought more about saving the camera and most of all saving my own skin! Half of the hut we were in was crushed by a tree trunk as big as a cathedral pillar. Luckily we were all on the other side of the hut."

Before leaving each other we spoke of marriage. Jacques wanted to marry me and protested that this was the first time he ever wanted such a thing. I teased him a little. "What about the Mex-ican girl? And that Japanese beauty who still writes to you?"

We had already shared some past secrets about ourselves, but he assured me this was different. It could have never lasted with the others. I stopped joking because I wasn't at all sure it could last with us either. Were we living a dream in that enchanted world? If we had met in New York or Paris under more ordinary circumstances, would we have fallen in love? I was afraid he wasn't made to be a married man. A confirmed rolling stone, in-cessantly bound for one of the four corners of the earth, alone and independent. Wouldn't a woman get in his way—or in this case, the same woman all the time?

But I didn't make any decisions. I basked in the moment's joy. If it was a dream, I hoped I wouldn't wake up.

We left Santo together on board the *Windua*, a tacky, over-grown rowboat, half-roofed, powered by an ancient motor.

The captain stopped to let me off at Aori and, without losing any time, continued on his route south. A number of people from Aori came down to the beach. The sight of a boat is always an event, even if it doesn't stay. I found Willy, who agreed to come with me up to Amok.

We had our conference with Virambat. The ceremony would be *"c'losup little bit."* Last time it was *"longway little bit."* I tried to find out more precisely in terms of suns or moons, but the Meleun could not say. No one had started preparations. I concluded it would be several weeks if not several months.

Since nothing was going on in Amok, I was eager to get down south as fast as I could. Willy came with me as far as Norsup. Even though I was beginning to know the trail, I had a vivid memory of the dogs and didn't want to venture out alone. With the help of the Figas, it still took me two days to find a boat. Next to the one I found, which didn't even have a name, the *Windua* was a luxury yacht. The Fijian captain didn't exactly inspire confidence either. I strongly suspected that his always handy thermos contained a liquid stronger than water. But my distrust dissolved quickly in the sun's heat. One of the two crew members gave me native "coffee": in a cup of boiling water, add a pinch of instant coffee and at least three heaping teaspoons of sugar. Leaning over the rail I lazily watched the flying fish who usually jumped in groups of three and separated into pretty fleur-de-lis in the air. The farther south we went, the more wild and mountainous became the coast of Malekula. Once in a while there was a village or mission, but they were rare.

We had been at sea several hours when a jolt, accompanied by a frightening crack, knocked me off my feet. We had hit a reef. In the same instant I thought of my belongings, the camera, and, most of all, the sharks. The captain rushed into the hold, reappeared at once, and confirmed my suspicion.

"We're sinking!" he cried.

The two sailors bounded onto the roof of the boat to detach the outrigger canoe, the only lifeboat we had on board, barely large enough for two people. I gathered my things together and jumped with another sailor down into the canoe, now floating in the water. The captain handed us the radio, his thermos, and a little bag. He and the other sailor dived into the water without ceremony and swam behind us. The boat slowly but implacably settled into the sea. A sad show. With a final glug-glug it disappeared forever.

In a coastal village a little farther on, I found a motorboat I could hire for the rest of the trip. This time I was lucky. Only the outboard motor broke down. That made us lose a few hours, but we arrived safely in Lawa, Southwest Bay.

Lawa is pretty much like Aori. They are typical man-salt-water villages. Kailuan, who hadn't sent off my letter and was perhaps still keeping it as a souvenir, came to meet me. He was a lame old man with shifty eyes. Next to him, Willy was angelic. He discouraged my going to join the others in the mountains, graciously inviting me to wait for them in Lawa. He explained that the walk was too difficult for a woman. I protested that I could manage the walk, that my friends were expecting me in Lendombwey, and that I had every intention of going. *Orright,* he replied, but you will not find a guide or porters; the coastal men do not like to go up to the "savages' " territory. Well, how did Jacques and Kal find porters? They paid a lot of money. Okay, I too will pay a lot of money. No, no good, no one wants to go right now. Wait a little. But I'm in a hurry, I exclaimed.

Wait a little. He gave me a hut. I waited. I had no choice.

That evening a man came to tell me that if I could find no one else, he would go with me as guide and porter. Only, he added, if I could find someone else, that would be better, because *"me fright too mass."*

"B'long wannem you fright?"

He didn't want to say. I insisted. He finally showed me his right hand, which lacked two fingers.

"Wannem him-here? B'long wannem finger b'long you he no stop?"

"Man-bush him he shootem musket long me!" Then he pulled back his shirt to show me the scar on his shoulder, the result of another gunshot.

"Who-here man-bush? B'long wannem he shoot?"

Hesitantly, rather embarrassed, he told me his story. His name was Kamensump. He himself was a one-time man-bush from Len-dombwey. The son of a chief and the black sheep of the family, he had committed adultery with three village women and the hus-bands had sworn to kill him. A year before they had almost suc-ceeded. Kamensump, who had run away to the coast, was return-ing home with a small pig in his arms to offer to one of the wronged husbands. He was ambushed on the way, and it was the pig tight against his breast that took the fatal bullet. Kamensump went back to the coast as fast as he could. Since then, he had been longing to return to Lendombwey but hadn't dared another at-tempt. And he thought I might present the ideal opportunity. Maybe they wouldn't shoot if he hid behind a woman.

Not possible, I tried to tell him as gently as I could. First, I didn't want him to expose himself to such a danger using me as a pretext. Second, I had no desire to walk behind a target.

I talked with the villagers, trying to find a guide on my own. No success. They needed the approval of the village elders. Kai-luan pulled the strings. I began to wonder if I wouldn't need Kamensump after all.

Two days later Kailuan sent me three men, one of whom knew

the way to Lendombwey. The others wanted to be hired as porters. The price for each man, payable in advance: six pounds,
about fifteen dollars, or two and a half times what they would
earn at hard plantation work. I pointed out that I didn't need
three men, one or two would do. But the choice was three or
none. I chose the three and paid up. I had just enough cash left to
do so. Kailuan's aim, of course, was precisely to take all I had.
But he thought I had more. He insisted that I buy provisions in
their cooperative general store. When I told him I didn't have
another nickel, he was disappointed. But that didn't get him down
for long. For me, he announced, they would make an exception,
they'd let me have credit. I wasn't keen on the idea. But yes, it's
necessary! objected Kailuan. If I didn't take some provisions what
would the third man carry? It was useless to say that I hadn't
asked for three men. I let myself be led to the store. Kailuan took
care of choosing the menu for his three delegates since he had ne-
glected to tell me that the porters wouldn't eat just anything. I
bought everything he wanted, hoping that Jacques and Kal still
had some money.

Learning my companions' names cheered me up. The guide, a
man of thirty-five or so, was called Peony, a native name. I was
amused to confirm that there was nothing flowerlike about this
muscular, well-built man. The first porter said his name was
Chumwul Yam. It took me a good few minutes to realize that he
was saying, with his thick island accent, "John William," his bap-
tismal name bestowed by a native "teacher" of the Presbyterian
mission. The second porter was called Snow, another native
word.

We set out at dawn. The sky was overcast, menacing. We
didn't see it for very long. We disappeared under the trees just
behind the village. And we started to climb. Already a steep
climb! I repeated to myself that the first half hour was always the
hardest, but that time I didn't really believe it. It started to
drizzle. The clayey earth became more and more slippery. Up
and down continually. And I knew it would be that way throughout the two-day trek. Jacques had warned me the Lendombwey
trail followed neither crest nor valley. You plod up one side of a
mountain and slide down the other. Mostly, we climbed. The
drizzle became a penetrating rain. We walked in ankle-deep mud.

The village of Lendombwey, in the mountains of Malekula. *Kal Muller*

Even the porters slipped, but they caught themselves with their toes more nimbly than I could in any way. I had lost my beginner's anxiety. Now I simply wondered if I had enough strength to continue like that for two days.

We got to the top of a cliff. Below there was a river. Nawaybuss, first lookout. We couldn't see the water. From the top of this chasm, the gorge on the way to Amok seemed like a bird's nest. We started down the sheer drop on a narrow muddy trail. To our left, the precipice, with nothing to stop a fall. I proceeded slowly, leaning to the right, toward the vertical face of the cliff. What a sense of powerlessness when you feel your two feet sliding uncontrollably in opposite directions. I tried to hold onto the roots and lianas that surfaced out of the earth. They weren't solid. From time to time there was a small tree on the path toward which I aimed myself like a novice skater who heads desperately toward the rail around the rink. I had an insane desire to let myself go, to roll all the way to the bottom of the gorge.

Reaching the bottom was one of the unforgettable moments of joy in my life. My heart pounded and my muscles trembled. We crossed the river. The water was knee-high, but Peony told me that often it's up to the shoulders. A few minutes of rest on the other bank. I closed my eyes. I calmed down. I was happy. If I had gotten this far, I could do anything. Then Peony pointed out the enormous mountain upriver which burst out of the earth.

"Now you-me climb on top!"

I lost my confidence again. The climb was hard and seemed to go on forever. But all the same I preferred it to those vertiginous descents. The view from the summit was spectacular. We could see the ocean, and I was happy that it looked so far away. Toward the interior, where we were headed, green-covered mountains extended, one after the other. Peony indicated the distant blue summits, saying that Lendombwey was over there.

The rain stopped, but the sky remained cloudy. We came to a small deserted village, Meleundua, where the porters wanted to stop for lunch. They could have eaten raw pigs and swallowed the tusks whole. I wasn't hungry, but I was thirsty. Fortunately, getting wise, I had anticipated my thirst. With the cans of corned beef and sardines which I had bought for the porters, I had included two cans of pineapple juice for me. Chumwul Yam was the kindest of the three men. (Peony was too brusque and Snow never said a word.) He passed me a cracker with corned beef spread generously over it.

"You kaï-kaï. Suppose you no kaï-kaï, you no savvy go go go long-way!"

He was right, of course. I made the effort to eat something. We didn't lose any time before going back to the trail.

I was too tired to be careful and fell a number of times. The porters laughed, not maliciously, and cried gaily, "Oh! Sorry! Oh! Sorry!" I was almost in a total daze when we came out into a cultivated valley, like a deep bowl full of vegetables. It was the Thepbaramen garden. This first village of the mountain peoples was Peony's birthplace. From far off we heard a woman's singsong voice. It struck me that there was something Oriental about that tone. Peony answered. I saw no one. She called again, Peony answered again. A whole conversation was going on.

"Him-here mama b'long me," explained Peony.

"Why doesn't she come out to see you?" I asked.

She doesn't want to, was the reply.

We didn't go to the village because it wasn't on our way. We stopped in front of an uninhabited hut where the porters told me we would spend the night. I collapsed. Chumwul Yam and Peony went to fetch water, bananas, and water taros, a kind of riverbed tuber. Snow built a fire. I noticed with pleasure that the men seemed tired, too. They were in as much of a hurry as I was to go to sleep.

Before dawn I heard the rain, coming down harder than the day before. Six o'clock, seven o'clock, eight o'clock. We waited for it to let up a little before taking to the road. Peony was getting nervous. He wanted to go. The others, like me, wanted to wait. Chumwul Yam told me that Peony was in a rush because he wanted to come back to Thepbaramen before nightfall. Peony threatened me. If we don't leave right away we won't get to Lendombwey today. Chumwul Yam's glance told me otherwise and I held my ground. We wait! At about ten o'clock the rain turned to drizzle and we set off.

An hour later, while we were climbing a steep hill—yet another—the rain started up again treacherously. I almost wanted to go back to Thepbaramen, but I never would have said so. I persuaded myself that we had to push on to the point of no return. Since I didn't know the distances, it wasn't easy to convince myself. That day I had no second wind. Without compunctions, I asked for a break whenever I needed one. Peony grumbled. Chumwul Yam was still kind. It's okay, he said, for a woman. I was *"strong little bit."* Chin up!

After hours of walking, we stopped for five minutes before a difficult incline. I again asked Peony if Lendombwey was *"c'losup now."* No, still *"longway."* I did wonder if we would get there before nightfall. A half-hour later we came to several rows of banana trees. We were evidently at the entrance to some village, but it hardly encouraged me since the villages in that area are never near one another. So, Lendombwey must still be pretty far. Depressed, I asked Peony where we were.

"Lendombwey!" he announced mockingly.

The bastard! He had lied to me, undoubtedly to encourage me to go on. But I didn't want to kill him. On the contrary, it was a wonderfully unexpected surprise. I wanted to kiss him and kiss the ground and shout my joy. My fatigue was wiped away by my enthusiasm at having arrived. Peony told me to talk with the porters. He hastened his steps and disappeared, taking another little trail, probably to let the villagers know.

Jacques and Kal, surrounded by men, women, and children, probably all the inhabitants of Lendombwey, were waiting for me in a little clearing in front of the first hut. I immediately sensed a difference between the Big Nambas and the Mbotogote. These people were excited, amused, disconcerted to see me. Jacques told me that no one had believed I would come. They talked quickly among themselves. They laughed. They shoved and pushed for a touch of my clothes, skin, hair. I let them examine me. I smiled at everybody, at the shy children most of all. Jacques told me to take out the barrette which held my bun. When my hair fell onto my shoulders, it was as if I had accomplished a magician's trick. Oooh! Exclamations of enchantment, more laughing, pushing, and shoving to see if the locks were really attached to the head.

Ilabnambenpen, the chief, who had kept to the side until this moment, forced his way through the crowd and shook my hand. He was about sixty years old, had lively eyes and the kind of smile that makes you want to whip out your camera and snap the

Chief Ilabnambenpen. *Kal Muller*

shutter quickly. Jacques had spoken of him. He has never in his life been to the coast. Even from the summit of a distant mountain he didn't dare look at the sea. He said it would give him a headache. The Mbotogote have numerous taboos meant to discourage all contact with the coast. What could have been the origin of such taboos? Jacques had noticed that there are no mosquitoes in the mountains, whereas the Lawa region is overrun with malaria.

Perhaps, long ago, the Mbotogote noticed that each time they went down to the coast they got sick. Not knowing that the mosquitoes were the fever carriers, they must have attributed the disease to the spirits. And perhaps, also, long ago, there were hostile tribes on the coast.

I very quickly discovered that, though the name may be technically inexact, "Small Nambas" is nonetheless descriptive. Unlike the Big Nambas, the Mbotogote men wear nothing but a single leaf wrapped around the penis and held in place by the bark belt. That's all, except for bones through their noses. The Big Nambas women, with their wigs and long skirts, seem to be in formal attire next to the Mbotogote women, who wear raffia miniskirts and nothing more, except, like the men, a bone or a stick through the nasal septum.

Kal and Jacques had brought a large jar of instant coffee and I followed them home for a cup. "Home" was a small hut, rather a lean-to, open in front. They didn't have the right to sleep in the nakamal, the men's hut, which is strictly reserved for initiated men. But in Lendombwey we were as far from the Big Nambas as we were from European influences, and I would not sleep in their lean-to. Mbotogote men and women never sleep together. It's taboo. All the village women sleep together in a large communal hut.

The sun set behind Lawa. Metak, Ilabnambenpen's right-hand man, the only person in the village who spoke a little pidgin, having spent some time in the villages closer to the coast, brought Kal and Jacques their laplap. He told me mine was waiting for me in the women's hut. Limbois, the chief's wife (and the women's chief, it seemed), came to take me there. I said ta-ta to Jacques and Kal and left. I would have liked to stay a bit longer with Jacques, but I did also want to see how the women lived.

It was a good thing I saw their hut, for I never could have imagined it. They share their home not only with the children and a few dogs, but also with the pigs, who live at the back of the hut, separated only by a little bamboo fence. As soon as I was inside, Limbois closed the door—that is, she pulled a wooden panel across the only opening in the hut. In the middle of the hut, there was a fire whose smoke already had begun to sting my eyes. The women were friendly and still excited by my presence. They pressed around me to offer me laplap. We ate together. I felt I was in summer camp, in one of the girls' cabins. Unfortunately, all the time I had spent learning Big Nambas was worthless here. The two tongues, of the same island, had nothing in common.

But we didn't need to understand each other verbally in order to be able to communicate. Two women sat down in front of me, an old woman with scars covering a good part of her body, whose right arm was maimed, useless, and a woman about thirty whose left breast was mutilated, festering with recent wounds. Burns. Both of them. They wanted me to heal them. Since I was an extraordinary-looking stranger, they presumed I was endowed with supernatural powers, that I was a sorceress. The other women explained, by gestures and words whose meaning I could only guess, how the accidents occurred. At night it's cold. The women gather around the fire to sleep on their banana-leaf beds. They roll over and get up, half-asleep, blinded by the smoke. They often burn themselves. I saw other women who also had more or less serious burn scars. I was uncomfortable. They were waiting for me to do things I couldn't do, and I couldn't even explain that I was neither a witch nor a doctor. I applied an antibiotic ointment to the young woman's breast. That could protect it against infection, but unfortunately the breast tissue was already destroyed. For the old woman there was nothing I could do. I gave her two doses of quinine, thinking that couldn't hurt her, anyway.

Perhaps to insure me against such dangers, or perhaps because it was the place of honor, they made me a bed, two banana leaves on the ground, at the back of the hut, next to the indoor pigpen. They were proud to set me up and happy because I seemed pleased. Exhausted as I was, I told myself I could sleep anywhere. That's optimism for you. My first night at Lendombwey was as sleepless as they come. For hours I couldn't even keep my eyes closed. A yard from me the pigs grunted. A baby cried, a child whined, the women tossed, coughed, and breathed heavily. The smoke hurt my eyes and throat. It wasn't hot, but the atmosphere was stifling. I didn't dare go out despite my desire for fresh air. I was afraid to wake the others in removing the heavy panel blocking the door. I was choking. At two or three in the morning I began to doze. Without knowing whether it was a dream or reality I became conscious that someone was shaking me. I woke up.

There was no one. I was still being shaken. It was the earth trembling beneath me. The women got up, laughing. They're used to earthquakes. They took the children in their arms and left the hut, chattering gaily. Limbois came to take my hand, to be sure I followed them. From the yard, we watched the hut shiver like a living being. We all seemed to be dancing on the quavering ground. The children screamed. The women laughed. They could already tell it wasn't a very big earthquake. In a few minutes it was over. A little slice of cold laplap for everybody before going back to bed. I got back to the concert of women, children, and pig music and listened to it all through the wee morning hours.

Whereas we had been completely at ease on the Big Nambas plateau, in Lendombwey I had the impression of having slipped into a mysterious world, peopled with disturbing spirits. The Mbotogote had seemed carefree and outgoing since my arrival, but it was an exception. Usually they do not talk loudly and they do not burst into laughter. You'd say they were holding themselves back in order not to attract the attention of a malevolent eye. They're fearful. A broken taboo, a poorly accomplished rite, any little sin can provoke the anger of the spirits. Although the wars are over, as in the north, there is still the dread of an unnatural death which might be caused by the ancestors' souls or by the sorcerers or even by an ordinary man with a vengeance to satisfy. Death itself is not to be feared. The only danger is the possibility of being expedited into the beyond without being prepared for the voyage. And the result of this apprehension is a tense atmosphere.

We observed a trial, in a clearing near Lendombwey, under the shadow of a funerary platform on which the body of a nine-year-old girl, Yausnetaonassua, lay. She had died a few days before, without any warning, without any apparent illness. Even in the open air, the odor of the small decomposing body was overpowering. An old sorcerer, Bialo, was accused of having poisoned her. It may indeed have been true since poisoning is a common sorcerer's technique in Lendombwey, and Bialo himself was known for having delved into such matters. But that time there was a basic prejudice against Bialo, whether he was innocent or guilty.

According to the Mbotogote, and according to the beliefs of a fair number of traditional tribes, a natural death is inconceivable

Mbotogote woman in ceremonial headdress. *Kal Muller*

except for old people. The death of a child cannot be natural. It has to be a case of sorcery. Therefore, to solve the crime, you simply have to pinpoint the guilty sorcerer. Or any available scapegoat.

Yausnetaonassua's father, whose name is Kabangalamandrou (we scribbled down these names right away, as we could hardly pronounce them, let alone remember them), played the roles of prosecutor and principal witness for the prosecution. He had seen Bialo murmuring magic words and throwing poison leaves against his daughter's chest. A week later she died. How could he know that the leaves were poisoned, that it was Bialo's sorcery that killed his daughter? He had used the finger test. Metak explained to us that it is a method of communicating with the spirits who are omnipresent and omniscient. You must ask a yes or no question. You pull successively on the index and middle fingers. If the cracking of the index finger is louder, the answer is positive. If the cracking of the middle finger is louder, the answer is negative.

Kabangalamandrou presented his case dramatically, capitalizing on his expressive hands and eyes. We couldn't understand the words, but the sarcastic tone was clear. Bialo defended himself calmly. He possessed no poisonous plants, and he wasn't familiar with their use. The general opinion seemed to be against him. After a particularly sharp verbal attack, Bialo collapsed. He dragged himself across several yards of earth toward the fire. No one helped him. He succeeded in getting back to his feet and his defense became impassioned. Ilabnambenpen gave his point of view. The judgment was rendered. Bialo was guilty and sentenced to pay a fine of two tusked pigs. The chief placed two coconut palm branches wrapped in leaves called *nowulgaï*, symbols of the pig debt, in Kabangalamandrou's hands. Ilabnambenpen insisted that Bialo shake the winner's hand, which he did, reluctantly. After that, Bialo left, shouting to the entire group that everyone would some day regret this miscarriage of justice.

Metak, who was responsible for us because of his knowledge of pidgin, told us that this kind of trial was fairly common.

If Mbotogote life is less relaxed than Big Nambas life, it is also in a sense better balanced. The Mbotogote men are not inactive. Obviously, like their northern neighbors, they are all retired warriors, but now they occupy their time shooting at pigeons and flying foxes instead of shooting at men. At least, in general (incidents like Kamensump's being an exception). And though they do not take advantage of the riches of the sea, the jungle rivers and streams hold no secrets from them. Their daily laplap is often enriched with shrimps or morsels of eel. Eating with the women, I learned to appreciate the laplap I had detested for so long in Amok. Garnished with shrimp, it is definitely better. The pigeons were succulent. The flying foxes were disgusting, but I must admit that I was probably the victim of my own prejudices. When I had seen these animals in a cage in Santo, with such sweet expressions on their faces, I couldn't imagine eating them. But now it was no longer the face that bothered me; it was the repugnant smell of these giant bats who perch upside-down and marinate in their own urine. If they were steeped in wine or whiskey for a day or two, they would probably make a good wild-game dish. But the Mbotogote just throw them into the fire, with hair, innards and stench intact. However, with a certain admiration I confirmed that this tribe, more "primitive" than the Big Nambas, if you can say such a thing, has a much richer and more diversified die:.

In this fecund land, where no one has ever gone hungry, the men don't have to consecrate their energy to the basic necessity of providing food. Consequently, they have time for religion, for art, for *"something b'long custom,"* and the Lendombwey men spend a great deal of their time behind a banana-tree fence. The area is sacrosanct, *"taboo too mass."* The village huts are scattered throughout the jungle. In the middle is the ceremonial ground, adorned with five sculpted drums. This ground is so sacred that no woman may set foot upon it and live to tell the tale. I was permitted to look at this place from a respectful distance. The human heads carved on three of the drums planted vertically in the earth stared me down. The drums are also sacred. Jacques and Kal learned that they are now made with knives obtained by trading with the natives nearer the coast. But traditionally they were sculpted with the arm and leg bones of a killed and eaten enemy. Decorative bushes brighten the border of the clearing.

On one side I noticed a funerary platform among the trees, in front of which stood a large black statue. All around the catafalque clay pigeons and flying foxes were hung in the trees like props for a play. I couldn't see very well, and I didn't have the right to approach. Jacques told me that there was indeed a cadaver on the platform and that it was wrapped in a shroud of leaves. The black statue was made from the trunk of a tree fern. It had been made on command. A spirit had visited a man of the tribe one night and made him understand that his sculpting services were desired by the dwellers in the beyond.

There is one single coconut palm in view. Jacques, having asked for a coconut, discovered that it is a sacred tree. No one touches its fruit.

The art objects, the dazzling sun, the multicolored plants, and the majestic trees on all sides did nothing to dissipate the ominous air of mystery that emanated from the ceremonial ground. At the rear left there is a row of banana trees. Several rows of banana trees, in fact, a vegetal wall constructed to hide what is going on behind it. Two stalks of wild cane, stuck into the earth at either end, serve as a warning that only those who have the right may pass. Kal and Jacques could wander freely over the ceremonial ground, but they were not allowed to cross the banana barrier under any circumstances. However, it wasn't taboo to know what was behind the fence, and we knew: the nakamal, the men's sacred hut, in front of which there is an equally sacred small yard. We wondered exactly what could be going on there for the area to be so formally forbidden. Men bustled back and forth and always seemed preoccupied. They stayed there for hours. The wind would bring us the sound of their conversations. Metak told us that among other things, it was there that they prepared the rites and ceremonies and made the sacred objects, the sculptures. He left "other things" purposefully vague, but Kal asked anyway. Metak smiled like Mona Lisa's brother and answered succinctly, *"Business b'long me-fella."*

One thing was certain. They didn't spend their time inside drinking kava. This drink, primordial in the life of the Big Nambas—less than forty miles away—is unknown to the Mbotogote. The same plant grows on Lendombwey land, but the people don't know that their northern neighbors make a beverage from it. This suggests, of course, that there has never been any contact between the tribes.

I was used to taboos against women and had consequently learned to control my curiosity, but Kal and Jacques went out of their minds. It was too much for them. They were dying to know what was behind the Banana Curtain, as we called it. Were there strange rites? Were there still cannibal feasts? The men leaving the enclosure always wore the most bizarre expressions. Kal started to talk nonsense. He wanted to order from the United States, without delay, a balloon that could float him and Jacques over the taboo place. They both became obsessed. The only thing they wanted to eat was the forbidden fruit.

We also knew there were things going on that would have been very exciting for us, but from which we were excluded. Metak came to tell us one day that that evening we must not leave our huts. If we heard tom-toms, we had to ignore them. Kal and Jacques were beside themselves. They pleaded with Metak to at least tell them what was being planned, even if they couldn't see it. Taboo! answered Metak. He couldn't say a thing until the following day, after the fact.

Very late at night we heard not only drums but also howls of pain and fear. We were not even sure if they were a man's or a woman's screams.

As it turned out, they were children's. The next morning I went to see Jacques and Kal very early and learned that Metak had already come to explain the events of the previous night. He hadn't wanted to make them wait any longer than necessary and had told them all he could.

"Come and see," Jacques said to me.

He led me along a path I didn't know. We came to a small hut surrounded by a cane fence about three feet high. It was close to Kal's and Jacques's hut, but it was concealed by the thick vegetation. On the other side of the fence there were five boys between, I'd say, eight and eleven years old, who looked at us sadly, like little prisoners. Their bodies were covered with ashes. On their heads they wore banana-leaf caps. Around the penis they wore not only small nambas, but also a packet of leaves bound like a bandage. The nocturnal ceremony, Jacques told me, had been their circumcision, effected with the aid of bamboo knives, in hands that were undoubtedly brutal. Thus the howling. These little boys, gentle as fawns and on the verge of bursting into tears, were becoming men. The initiation period was to last one year, and during that time the initiates would be confined to this hut, behind the fence. Their mothers were allowed to bring food but not to stay. Their fathers and uncles were going to submit them to other trials, in order to liberate them definitively from childhood.

Several days later, Jacques and Kal were given the right to witness one of these rites. They were awakened in the night and abruptly invited to attend a taboo ceremony in the forest. About ten Lendombwey men were singing, hidden behind thickets vaguely illuminated by reed torches. They sang in measure to the beat they tapped out on coconut shells. The five circumcised boys with their strange miterlike headdresses were sitting in the background, in the grass and among the branches. Metak informed Jacques and Kal, in his limited pidgin, that this ritual was part of the cycle of initiation ceremonies, that the boys had been brought here to be frightened and that it's a very serious matter, since every step of the ceremony is monitored by the spirits. Ilabnambenpen, in front of the men, led the choir. The children, whom Jacques and Kal could barely see, didn't seem to be frightened at all. But they seemed quite unhappy, huddled up in the damp grass, shivering with the cold and the lack of sleep. The ceremony was to have lasted all night. There were several songs, refrains really, which were translated for us the following day:

"The serpent sits inside the *Nabanga* tree. Someone whispers in his ear, 'Come here.' The sun glistens on the rock before disappearing."

"Girl . . . Star . . . The girl walks in your garden. She scratches her head all the time."

"The devil comes. He comes from the bush. He comes here. Come here! Come here! Fly! He runs toward the salt water."

"The head of the cyclone thrusts, and the name of the cyclone is Lending. Red parrot, two times red, come here!"

"Little girl, come here! On the inside of her thighs is much hair. Look, and want her. And serve yourself, little man, with your switch."

We were in the ceremonial period, which had begun with the circumcisions. Behind the Banana Curtain there was constant activity. No one would tell us what was happening. For us: taboo. Even the knowledge of their current events, this time, was forbidden. Kal and Jacques were bothered by being kept so strictly apart, but we were all impressed at the same time by the seriousness of things and the secret, magic, exciting atmosphere that hung over Lendombwey. The women were excited, too. I went with them to the gardens to transport huge baskets of taros and yams. All ordinary business had ceased. The men didn't even go hunting. The women spent many long hours doing nothing inside their hut. They seemed to be waiting.

Ilabnambenpen, Metak, and their wives, Limbois and Woshuk, respectively, never failed to let us know when we had the right to see something that was happening. As we learned by successive experiences with the Mbotogote, each wait was justified by a final surprise that surpassed our every hope.

One day we were summoned to the ceremonial ground with no explanation other than the fact that it wasn't exactly for a ceremony. The tom-tom players were at their places and began to beat the tall wooden drums. What followed was, for us, a surrealistic parade. The men arrived, one by one, from behind the banana-tree wall, like actors coming onstage. Each one carried a bizarre figurine, a puppet about three feet tall. On a wooden frame a human form had been fashioned in clay and painted with beautiful vegetable dyes, red, white, and black. The arms were lifted to an angle of 120 degrees, and the fingers were spread apart. The head, crowned with feathers, had exaggerated, grotesque features. A curved pig's tooth protruded from each corner of the mouth. The statues were sculpted as far as the waist, below which was the naked, pointed support-pole for driving the object into the ground. Twenty-nine of these figurines followed one another around the ceremonial ground in the arms of respectful carriers. We learned that they are called *Temes Nevimbur*, but we couldn't learn much more. What did they represent? Why the parade? Is it to consecrate them or just to take them out for an airing? Or for another reason?

The answers to our questions were vague. Metak admitted that they could represent different people. It depended. Apparently our guesses weren't too far off. The parade was indeed a kind of consecration of these objects, but it was also quite simply an occasion for them to walk about the ceremonial ground on a bright, sunny afternoon.

I believed I knew something about it. In 1925 a brilliant young Englishman came to the New Hebrides. Arthur Bernard Deacon was a classics student at Cambridge and an amateur ethnologist. At twenty-two he was too young to take his doctoral exams, so he went to the islands to roam among peoples totally unknown or known to be hostile. At twenty-four he died a miserable death on the south Malekula coast of blackwater fever, one of the worst forms of malaria, which attacks the kidneys. You know you've got it when your urine turns black, but at that point you also know you're going to die from it. Although Deacon never penetrated so far into the island's interior, at that time the people closer to the coast weren't Christians and hadn't yet abandoned their Melanesian customs.

One of the Temes Nevimbur being made. *Kal Muller*

In his posthumously published notes, Deacon talks about figurines which very likely were Temes Nevimbur like those we saw. What he said about them is fairly extraordinary. He saw a veritable jungle theater. The figurines appeared on a stage made of branches and were used as puppets to act out plays. They represented legendary figures. The central theme was the confrontation between good and evil. Evil was incarnated in certain puppets and wiped out at the end of the plays. Not symbolically. The evil Temes Nevimbur were killed. Some were stabbed with spears and their "blood"—the red sap of a certain plant—flowed. Others were burned. Deacon saw hundreds of these figurines go up in flames.

We asked Metak about these performances. He was shocked that we knew about them. Indeed, he finally admitted, it is something *"b'long custom."* Is it the custom here? Has it been done always? No, no, no, Metak said. But we didn't know whether that was a negative response or whether he simply did not want to answer us. He wasn't loquacious. Little by little his tongue would loosen with us, but we would always have trouble drawing out information.

However, Metak was inclined to be agreeable at the moment, and seeing that we were excited by the strange objects, he consulted with Ilabnambenpen on the other side of the ceremonial ground. We could tell they were talking about us. They came to a decision and crossed over to announce it to us. Metak slapped Jacques and Kal on the back, a sign of friendship. While they were about it, they were going to show us some other objects besides the Temes Nevimbur. Then the two Mbotogote threw me a severe look, as the New Hebrideans often eye women. *She*, they said without talking directly to me, she can watch at first, but afterwards she must leave. Okay, I was happy just to see a little. I gave them my biggest smile and they smiled, too. No problem. "She" knows her place.

From behind the Banana Curtain they then took out the most unimaginable treasures of primitive art. Their nakamal must be a museum. Heads with snail eyes sculpted at one end of a stake. Double-faced conical masks, both sides adorned with pigs' teeth. Everything was drawn precisely and painted with vivid natural dyes. A ceremonial shield with three small faces in relief. Two fantastic dog statuettes. A painted white round disk about seven feet in diameter with a grimacing face modeled in the middle. That one intrigued us because of the form and lack of colors. What is it? The sun.

Then it was time for me to leave. The rest was taboo for women. But I returned to the hut enchanted, happy. Such artists! They must have dozens of marvels tucked away in their forbidden hut! Of course I wondered what Jacques and Kal were seeing at that moment, but I wasn't dissatisfied to have been sent away. It is precisely the sacred character of these objects that keeps the Mbotogote art alive. Naturally that won't stop me, I thought, from asking my friends as soon as possible what they got to see when I left.

But I didn't think about it any longer, because Metak's and Woshuk's four-year-old son, Sian, was sick. Woshuk is an endearing woman, about twenty-five, shy. She took my hand and led me to her little boy, who was lying perfectly still on some banana leaves in the rear of the hut. His golden skin had turned a sickly

The representation of the sun. *Kal Muller*

greenish tint. His cheeks and the whites of his eyes were red. His forehead burned my hand. Woshuk was filled with concern and maternal tenderness. Her eyes implored me. I couldn't really say what it was. Malaria? Some other tropical fever? Woshuk and I made him swallow aspirin and quinine. I really couldn't do any more. I covered his small body with my blanket. He moaned. He seemed to be too weak to cry. I was afraid, but I reassured the mother. If it did turn out to be malaria, the quinine would work. Woshuk picked up a slice of laplap, explaining to me by her gestures that the child didn't want to eat. Then she chewed small pieces of the laplap and fed little Sian mouth to mouth. Her other son, Tasong, a chubby baby about a year old, clung to her skirt. She caressed him and spoke absently to him, but she never stopped taking care of Sian.

We watched over him together. I didn't dare go away, even though I wanted to go see Jacques and Kal before nightfall and ask them what had happened with the art objects. Although I couldn't help Sian any more, my presence seemed to soothe Woshuk. We gave the child more aspirin. The other women were eating, and they brought us slices of hot laplap. In the beginning of the evening Sian began to toss and cry. He became cranky, wanted to be in his mother's arms. I touched his forehead. His fever had dropped. Woshuk knew that he was better, the knowledge radiating from her. If the Mbotogote were familiar with the gesture, she would have kissed me. She communicated her warm feelings by squeezing my hand and letting loose a stream of words I didn't understand, but whose meaning was easy enough to guess. I didn't know whether the quinine and aspirin had done very much or if it was simply time that had brought the child past the crisis. But I felt concerned in any case.

I also felt exhausted. I still didn't sleep well in the hut. The smoke bothered me less, my eyes and lungs had begun to adapt to it, but I couldn't get used to the cacophonous concerts of pigs, dogs, and children. And, moreover, that night I knew I'd be cold. I had given my blanket to Sian.

Metak came to visit Woshuk in the night. Not having a Big Nambas–style tradition of an individual hut for each wife, the couples get together in the communal hut. Since under these circumstances the clandestine is excluded, illicit meetings must occur somewhere in the jungle. It appears that adultery is not rare, probably because there are more men than women in this community. Moreover, pig-wealthy old men often buy the youngest and prettiest women. The young men can choose to accept their frustration, to borrow the wives of others, or to go find a wife near the coast. The last solution is not even considered if the young man adheres to the traditional life. No Christianized coastal native will marry a pagan. The tribesman must become a Christian, disavow his tribe, abandon his village and his parents. In Lendombwey there are actually several single men between twenty and thirty years old but not an available single woman. We can also understand why adultery is a serious crime. The husbands want to protect their valuables.

Metak and Woshuk were discreet, as were the other women if they were not asleep. I did wonder what this aspect of Mbotogote life was like, but I was careful not to peer over secretly. It wouldn't be right, I said to myself. All I can say is that it's quick and quiet.

"Okay. Tell me what Metak and Ilabnambenpen showed you after I left."

"Their dead ancestors," replied Jacques.

"What? What are you talking about?"

"I don't know if I should explain it to you or not. It may be taboo."

"Don't you put me on! Spill it, right now, or I'll tell Metak you told me everything and even drew a picture!"

Jacques and Kal pretended to debate. They decided I had been very good the afternoon before, leaving obediently and not spying from behind a tree. So they explained. They had seen ancestors' skulls, not preserved in a natural state as in Amok, but fixed to the ends of poles, modeled with clay, and painted. Jacques and Kal thus met many Mbotogote who were no longer able to introduce themselves in flesh and blood, notably Kaiapamban, Ilabnamben-pen's late father, dead for some twenty years. He had been an awesome warrior. Enemy arrows and spears couldn't harm him. Favored by the spirits, he had magical powers. During battle, the other warriors lined up behind him to benefit from his immunity. Kaiapamban still looks out for his son and tries to protect the village against malevolent spirits.

That evening I went back to my friends' lean-to. Moonlight over Lendombwey. Even the trees on distant mountains were illuminated. Every star of the southern hemisphere twinkled "Present!" Jacques reminisced. "A year ago," he said, "I was in Paris. Two years ago I was in another jungle, the Amazon jungle, and the Campus Indians and I were feasting on giant snails. Three years ago I was in Hong Kong on a French destroyer, the *Amiral-Charner*. . . ."

We had lit all our last candles to create a little holiday spirit. It was Christmas Eve.

The end result of this ceremonial period would be an important rite which we would be allowed to observe.

The *Nimangki* is at the heart of traditional life in the New Hebrides. It is at the base of religion, politics, economy, and art. It is a society within the society and it is strictly hierarchical, somewhat like the army back home. Each man has a grade. He can be promoted to higher grades by paying pigs and organizing ceremonies. A man who thus rises in rank acquires prestige and power in life. Moreover, since the Melanesians are farsighted, he assures himself a more privileged position in the beyond as well. The higher his grade, the more powerful his spirit will be after death. Nimangki is the name of this hierarchical society and also the name of the grade-taking ceremony. We were going to see a Nimangki ceremony.

In Lendombwey, as in all of the tribes except the Big Nambas, there is no hereditary chieftainship. Ilabnambenpen is the chief because he is the man with the highest Nimangki grade. He hasn't any living sons. If he did, he could leave them his pigs, thus giving them more facility to pay for ceremonies and raise their grade. But there is no guarantee whatsoever that the son of a chief can become chief himself. On the contrary, a man who has no heritage can earn pigs in doing service for others or in having daughters to sell to future husbands or by still other means. There are even men who climb the grades thanks to borrowed pigs. They repay them later, with interest. If you lend me a pig whose teeth have begun to curve, in two years I will repay you a pig with teeth up to three-quarters of a circle. New Hebrideans are capitalists.

This time the ceremony was in honor of Sinmormara, a man of about twenty-six, who was taking the grade of *Namarimba*, the sixth of nineteen possible Mbotogote ranks. For this honor, he had paid two pigs of the *iraringue* class, the third category of eight, which means "the teeth approach the skin," between three-fifths and three-quarters of a circle. (It is less rare in the Mbotogote village than in the Big Nambas village to see pigs' teeth that form a circle, a circle and a half, even more. The norms are higher in Lendombwey than in Amok.) One of these two pigs is destined for the chief, Ilabnambenpen, the other for Mbatiklao, an old and powerful tribesman. In return, Mbatiklao would offer Sinmormara a *marimba*, the sculpture associated with the grade of Namarimba. It is a red pole, about ten feet high, decorated with leaves, at the base of which is sculpted a human form painted in white, black, and red. In this village, each grade is associated with an art object.

Sinmormara must also pay one pig for each ornament he would wear during the ceremony. Prestige and power are expensive.

On the nights before the rite, not a single man came to visit his wife. It is taboo for males to sap their physical powers in relations with their mates.

The morning of the big day, I was told it would be best to stay in the hut. Anyway, I could not go to Jacques's and Kal's lean-to since the path I would have to take passes by the ceremonial ground, which women aren't allowed to look at before the start of a rite. The men were busy clearing the area, sweeping it with leafy branches and pulling out the weeds all around. Woshuk told me they were also doing *nelangalanga,* shaping a triangle with her hands to explain. Though she multiplied her gestures, I still couldn't understand.

It was raining. No one cared. The Mbotogote would not cancel a rite because of the weather unless they expected a cyclone. They have an advantage over us; in the warm tropical climate skin dries quickly, while clothes stay wet, get cold, and mildew.

As soon as we heard the tom-toms we could go. In fact, we had to go right away. The women gathered the children and walked rapidly. We all arrived together and stayed on one side of the ceremonial ground. Nelangalanga. I understood Woshuk's explanation. A V-shaped enclosure, built with leafy branches, mostly croton branches with their yellow, white, red, and green leaves, planted in the earth. This decorative enclosure, which was about three feet tall, opened toward the Banana Curtain. Across the two arms of the V, the marimba was supported horizontally, a bit higher than the enclosure, by two forked sticks. Was the structure supposed to resemble a catafalque? The sculpted human figure at the bottom of the marimba was stretched out, facing the sky, as a cadaver would be.

The drums that had convoked us continued to pound their engaging rhythms energetically. They resounded in my body. The five musicians were the only men on the ground besides Jacques and Kal, who were installed in a corner, busy taking readings in every direction with diverse light meters.

The rain had become a fine drizzle. The atmosphere was luminous. Without sunlight the colors had an otherworldly quality, pale and brilliant at the same time. I imagined the work of a painter who would try to reproduce those so subtle tones. Kal came and asked me to do the background tape recording. With the powerful microphone we had, it would be possible to record the ceremony, even from the distance I had to maintain. He would take back the machine later and approach the participants. The taboos against women impeded me from being very helpful to my friends. From where I was, on the side, there was no way of taking good photographs.

A dozen men came from behind the Banana Curtain and grouped themselves at the edge of the ceremonial ground. They were all wearing new nambas, the leaves still green, as well as all the ornaments they owned. There were innumerable pigs' teeth and bead armlets on display. They were all armed, with sculpted clubs or with bows and arrows. With the cycas branches they had tucked under the backs of their bark belts and with their proud bearing as well they looked like human roosters. The drums crescendoed and then stopped altogether, on a penetrating note. A man began singing in a rich and powerful voice. The others joined in after a few minutes. I suddenly realized that these people did come from south China. Although I'm not a music specialist, I still recognized the Asiatic sonority of their chants. There was a sorrowful quality in those sounds which sent shivers up my back.

On a sign, the group headed slowly toward the drums, which they encircled, still singing. The drums started up again. The men's steps became rhythmic. They weren't walking around the drums any more, they were dancing. The tempo of the accompaniment accelerated, as did the chants and the movements. Ilabnambenpen detached himself from the circle with small, rapid steps and gestured in every direction, his arms extended, his body rocking from side to side. No one needed to interpret his movements for us. He was a man-bird. But what does a man-bird mean to them? Well, there we would have liked an explanation, but none was offered. His face was transformed by a smug expression and popping eyes. If I hadn't been sure that kava was unknown there, I would have thought Ilabnambenpen had drunk a good share.

Sinmormara, the star of the rite, appeared in front of the Banana Curtain. He was dressed like the others, but with enormous white circles painted around his eyes as well. In one arm he held several stalks of sugar cane, pressed against his shoulder. He danced outside the men's circle for several minutes, following the bird-man. Then he retired back behind the wall of banana trees.

When he left, both music and dancing ceased. All the men froze. The ceremony had already lasted about two hours, but we couldn't believe it was over. Though nothing was going on, everyone seemed to be waiting.

Sinmormara made his second entrance, this time in all his splendor. His costume was painted on his skin. Red spots from his forehead to his toes and black stripes down his back. An armlet decorated with leaves. Several pigs' teeth. Bells made from dried nutshells hung around his ankles. He headed directly for the front of the ceremonial ground, opposite the Banana Curtain. All the spectators and all the participants had watched him. His countenance was that of a "man not man," a spirit. Did he imagine himself a powerful being in the beyond, profiting from his promotion in the Nimangki? Slowly, he got down on his hands and knees. He entered into the V-shaped enclosure, the nelangalanga, like an animal, perhaps imitating the pigs he had paid for this rite. He crawled under the marimba. He stopped. It was difficult to see him through the leaf walls of the enclosure. And then, all at once, he leaped. He burst out of the nelangalanga, shattering the corner of the enclosure by his violent passage. The tom-toms started up again, with a frenzied rhythm. Sinmormara ran and jumped in the air. He danced frenetically around the drums, making as much noise as possible with his little round bells. Two men skipped toward the enclosure. Sinmormara followed them. They took the marimba, carried it on their backs, and headed for the drums. Sinmormara preceded them now, dancing backwards, his arms extended as if to attract the two men carrying the sacred object. As soon as the ritual bearers got near the tom-toms, they planted the marimba vertically into the ground. And Sinmormara collapsed, his head lowered.

The women retreated to a clearing a few yards from the ceremonial ground. They started to dance in place, many with children tied to their backs. Some of them swayed, leaning on two stalks of sugar cane. The drums kept going. The men started dancing again, too, even more energetically than before. They traced large figure eights all over the ceremonial ground. And then there were relay races, run to the beat of the tom-tom rhythm. The first man held a croton branch over his head; the second man stole it from him, thrusting his body forward.

These dances had already lasted for hours. Though I do not consider the Mbotogote in any way more savage than us, the words *savage* and *primitive* came into my head again and again. They are close to nature and their millennial history has not yet suffered the shocks that ours has. And when I thought, when I realized fully, that we were the first foreigners to see these rites, I felt a more powerful sense of displacement than I had ever felt.

A man disappeared into the bush to bring out a spear which he stabbed into the earth in front of the nelangalanga enclosure. Sinmormara also went away and returned trailing one of his tusked pigs. He stopped beside the drums. A solid liana linked one of the beast's paws to one of his master's wrists. Sinmormara tried to stop the pig from jerking, but the animal was excited. It howled piercingly. It knew, perhaps better than we, what was going to happen. The drummers pounded away on their wooden gongs, harder and faster. One of the dancers grabbed the spear and, never stopping for a moment, planted it in the earth in front of the crazed pig's head. The men continued to dance around the little group comprised of Sinmormara, the pig, and the drums. Another dancer took up the spear and, without a pause, he too, gavotting in front of the animal, thrust it a few inches in front of the beast's snout. Each dancer in turn repeated the same menacing gesture, tomcats playing with a mouse. It lasted a pretty long time, as the men were not at all in a hurry. The pig seemed to be aware of what was going on. Sinmormara tightened the liana around his wrist.

Mbatiklao, to whom this pork was being offered, put an end to the game. The second time he had the spear in his hand, he kicked the animal in passing, without halting his dance steps. The next time he arrived in position, he threw the spear toward the pig's heart. The air was perforated with the beast's unendurable screams. The dancers continued their leaping circle, spurred on by the drums. They were still not in any rush. The animal was shakily still standing up. Ilabnambenpen decided it had gone on long enough. Without leaving the ring of dancers, when he came within reach, he grabbed the spear which was sticking out of the pig's flesh. He forced it in still deeper and twisted it. With a last agonizing cry, which I felt deep in my own bowels, the animal collapsed and died. The dogs rushed out to lick up the blood that dripped from the victim's mouth. Sinmormara detached his wrist from the liana. There was no more danger of the beast running away. The blood and the brutality didn't bother him at all. It didn't seem to bother anyone else, either. It was a sacrifice. Ilab-nambenpen whipped the body with croton branches and shouted loudly in an echoing voice, "Akar Marimba! Akar Marimba!" That was Sinmormara's new ceremonial name. The aim was achieved. He had earned a higher grade in the Nimangki.

Each Mbotogote man is not only an artist but a butcher as well. The pig was carved up right away, on the ceremonial ground. The finest morsels were distributed among the men. The scraps were given to the women. The dogs got the fat, the inedible organs, and all the blood they could lick up from the ground. And there was no lack of blood. It flowed copiously. The fascinated children watched the butchering joyously, as if it were a game or a show. They tried to participate. The boys ran to the middle of the ceremonial ground and helped out by passing the pieces of bloody pork to the adults.

Just one pig! All that flesh and blood for one! On the Big

Ritual slaying of a pig. *Kal Muller*

Nambas plateau, they used to kill a hundred during each ceremony. Even now, according to Willy, they kill twenty-five or thirty. I tried to imagine the howling and the floods of blood multiplied by thirty.

I didn't know it at the time, of course, but that was the most rapid and humane pig killing we were to see. The next time with the Mbotogote, it would be more painful.

The women were very happy that evening to prepare a good laplap with pork leftovers. Jacques and Kal, since they were invited, were at that moment being offered the choicest morsels, the half-raw heart and liver. They explained to me the next day how they had dared to ask that their portions be placed back in the fire for a little while longer. The Mbotogote found that very funny. They concluded that whites just didn't know anything about gastronomy.

I wasn't very hungry, even though we hadn't eaten meat for a long time. It wasn't that I was disgusted by the sacrifice. Of course I didn't enjoy watching it, but I told myself that if that replaced sacrificing men, it was probably for the best. In any case, I had no desire to eat. I went to bed as quickly as possible. The drums still resounded inside my head. Trying to think of nothing, I was dreamy. In the night, three or four men came to see their wives. The transport of the rite, undoubtedly. Lonely, uncomfortable, and troubled, I pretended to sleep.

6

The Reincarnation of a Chief

DURING their first stay with the Mbotogote, Jacques and Kal had photographed Tambwebalimbank, an old chief whom they met the night of the cyclone. Six months later this photograph became a precious document. We wondered where it could be. We hoped it had been properly developed. Kal and Jacques reproached each other for not having had the idea of filming the old chief. But to tell the truth, at that time, there was no reason to film him. He was just an old man, a little senile, always staying seated in his hut. All he did was nibble bits of yams and urinate into a coconut shell.

When we returned to Lendombwey, we again found Tambwebalimbank in his hut. But this time he was stretched out on the ground, wearing a new nambas and covered with red paint. Dead. To his right, a row of squatting men cried, lost in lamentations. To his left was a trench to receive the cadaver's humors so that they wouldn't flow toward the family members who slept around the body for a minimum of five nights. A fire burned day and night to alleviate the smell and chase away flies. The weepers performed out of a sense of duty, but they believed in what they were doing. For hours they would sit on their heels, without ever rising, shading their eyes with one hand, watering the ground liberally with tears and mucus.

We saw this scene with the shock of a sudden understanding. We really hadn't understood anything during our previous stay with the Mbotogote! At least, nothing of the underlying beliefs. Now, the importance of death leaped out at us. Death is not the end of life. It is an integral part of life. Life and death are bound tightly by the intermediary of the spirits. But there was a lot that still escaped us. We realized that the texture of this society is much more complicated than it seems at first.

Ilabnambenpen was pleased to see us again, but uneasy at the same time. Behind his broad welcoming smile, I discerned not the sorrow of a man in mourning, but rather the nervousness of a hunted man. He rolled his eyes, threw furtive glances around him, scrutinized the high branches of the trees that surround the village. What exactly was he afraid of? But this is hard to determine around here. We had realized long before that direct questions led nowhere with the chief. He either didn't answer or said something that would appease us without revealing anything. In Melanesia, as in the Orient, precise information can be obtained only by way of long detours. So we detoured for hours, came to interesting crossroads, and finally arrived at an understanding of Ilabnambenpen's behavior. Here, death transforms a man into a formidable spirit. The community owes him honors, lest he avenge himself against the village. Ilabnambenpen feared Tambwebalimbank's powerful spirit doubly: as a vulnerable mortal and also as the chief responsible for the impeccable execution of the rituals honoring the defunct chief. He would have no real peace of mind until the ceremonies were complete.

By allusion to the sun, we asked how long, how many days, the funeral would last. Ilabnambenpen also answered by allusion. He spoke of the planting of the yams, moons, and the harvest. We deduced that he had an unsettling year ahead of him.

Metak was also particularly nervous, being the closest relative of the deceased. Though Tambwebalimbank had a living son, Kamensump, he was considered dead. He was the young man missing two fingers who, on the coast, had offered to be my porter and who had been banished from the Mbotogote territory for adultery. In place of the rejected son, Metak, Tambwebalimbank's nephew, was obliged to take all familial responsibility for the funereal ceremonies to come. If he did the necessary, he could count on his uncle's spirit from then on, like a guardian angel. If he was negligent or if he made a mistake—since actions count more than intentions—Tambwebalimbank's spirit would make Metak's life miserable. A serious mistake could even provoke his death. Metak walked around with his mouth in the shape of an *n*. As for crying, he set records for the flow of tears and mucus. So far, his uncle's spirit and the other spirits who surveyed the unfolding of events were surely pleased with him.

While we were talking with Ilabnambenpen, several men were constructing a funerary platform beside the ceremonial ground. Ritual work, thus slow work. Two men carried Tambwebalimbank's body, already enveloped in a shroud of leaves, on a bamboo stretcher decorated with wild carnations. Very carefully they laid the cadaver out on the platform. It would lie there, in that sacred place, for a year.

From atop a high pole, the modeled skull of one of Tambwebalimbank's uncles watched these preliminaries. This uncle's spirit, which resides in the skull, would participate in the ceremonies to come. I didn't understand why I hadn't been allowed to see the skulls the day they were taken from the sacred hut to be shown to Jacques and Kal, while now I could look at this one freely. Metak explained, today is a special day. The ancestor was presenting himself to the public.

Kal tried to find out if Tambwebalimbank's spirit was actually present, if he saw what was going on. Metak affirmed, without hesitation, that not only was he present and seeing everything, but that he was very happy. We were struck by the firmness of the Mbotogote beliefs. Not yet having encountered the missionaries, they were not harassed by doubts. Ilabnambenpen, despite his worries and preoccupations, was sustained by an internal tranquillity the like of which Virambat will never feel again.

That night the men anointed their torsos with ash, a sign of mourning and purification. The next day, a holy day, they danced, placed yam offerings in front of the platform, and brought onto the ceremonial ground the most important offering, without which no powerful spirit could ever be satisfied: pigs. Since Tambwebalimbank had attained a very high grade and was

Mourning for the dead chief Tambwebalimbank. *Kal Muller*

indeed a chief, his funeral had to comprise a series of pig sacrifices
befitting his rank.

No, I did not want to shrink away from the pig killings. I kept
telling myself that it is a religious rite and, after all, better pigs
than men. But it was painful to watch, and I'll never get used to
it. The fact of knowing there are people in Europe and the United
States as insensitive to the suffering of animals as are the Mbotogote didn't soothe me one iota. On the contrary.

This time, the pigs were killed with bows and arrows. Two
pigs. The second one, screaming and struggling, watched the execution of the first. He must have sensed that his turn was next.
Each graded man shot an arrow. They didn't rush. They played
with the pig as a matador draws out the task of finishing off a bull.
But here there is not even a pretext of sport: the victim remains attached to the arrow. Three drummers enhanced the mood. At
first the beat was slow, but it built up to a rapid, frenetic rhythm.
Blood spurted everywhere. The air was torn by the cries of the
participants and women who watched from a respectful distance,
by the furious barking of the excited dogs, and most of all by the
ear-splitting screams of the sacrificial beasts. I couldn't help think-

ing of the days, not too long ago, of the *"long-pig"* rites, long-pig being a euphemism for man—that is, the cannibal rites that used to take place here.

The appearance of a few men wearing vividly painted masks, decorated with phalluslike noses, pigs' teeth, and leaves, changed the tone of the spectacle. They represented spirits. They swept the ceremonial ground with branches, thus marking the end of the first part of the funeral ceremonies.

Throughout the entire ceremony, no one had paid attention to the birds that always flew around the village. But then, at the very moment the ground was being swept and thus in the presence of those masked men, a big white bird glided in circles over the ceremonial field, hovered for a moment, and headed back toward the jungle. The men all at once became agitated. Though everyone knew we had no guns or bows and arrows, several people warned us we must never shoot at that bird. Why? It was the temporal incarnation of Ilabnambenpen's father, and all the villagers knew it because the bird had made its nest behind the sacred men's hut. His flight at the end of the ceremony undoubtedly signified the spirit's satisfaction.

This ceremony took place about ten days after Tambwebalimbank's death. Five days later, ten days later, fifteen and twenty days later other pigs would be sacrificed. During this first ceremony, the animals had been offered by the dead chief's brother. The others would be successively offered by a man belonging to the clan of the chief's wife, who had died several years before; by a man married to a woman of the chief's clan; by a man of the chief's mother's clan; and by still others whose relations to the chief we couldn't determine.

We left Lendombwey with an invitation to return a year later for the end of the funeral ceremonies. I would think often of the Mbotogote in the months to come, during our stays with other tribes, on other islands. Of course, they had been distrustful of Jacques and Kal at first. They hadn't known what to expect of the first outsiders who unexpectedly showed up one day and moved in. Did my friends' smiles, gifts, and good manners mask the souls of enemies, warriors, sorcerers? How could they be sure, at first? Unhurriedly, they judged us. Even after my arrival, I felt we were still being judged. Jacques and Kal knew it, too. (Actually,

only they were being weighed and measured by the men, for
whom I hardly counted. The women never judged me. The knew
I presented no danger.) Whatever their criteria were, we passed
the test. They decided to accept us. And from that moment on, a
frank and profound human contact was established between us.
No complications, as there were with the Big Nambas. No questions of money, of who profits from whom, no need for anyone to
assert his authority. Among us, there were nothing but the simplest relationships, man to man, woman to woman. Even with the
language difficulties, we always managed to express ourselves mu-
tually, patiently. I already had the idea that the Western influence
on the Melanesians did more harm than good in human terms,
and this idea would be confirmed a hundred times before our
departure from the islands.

When we came back a year later, as agreed, the people of Lendombwey were waiting impatiently for us. They were sure we
hadn't forgotten the rendezvous, but since the ceremonies were
about to begin, they were afraid we would be late. We appreciated their concern for us.

"We" were four this time. The Mbotogote accepted our guest
easily. A friend of our friends is a friend of ours, and so on. The
aforementioned friend's name was Mike Hallston. He was a
young Australian ethnologist. Tall and thin, stoop-shouldered,
pale. We had retrieved him in Lawa where he was unhappily installed in a small hut, as far out of his element as a water lily in
the sea. In order to get his master's degree at the University of
Canberra, he had had six months to prepare an ethnological
monograph and for his subject he had chosen a Melanesian village
where the European influence was minimal. Of these six months,
barely three were left. He had lost weeks in other islands only to
discover that the traditional Melanesia isn't so easy to find. Fortunately, he had landed in Lawa, where the villagers had let him
know there were bushmen in the mountains, but for a month he
had not succeeded in hiring a guide to take him to the interior.

"They're keeping me dangling! They're doing it on purpose,
the bastards," he told us in his thick Australian accent. "Kailuan
always promises me a guide for next week. Each week, of course,
it's still next week. And in the meantime, they're stealing me

blind. For the price of their yams I could be eating caviar in Australia. And to top it off, I've got to kiss everyboy's ass to stay in their good graces. Ugh! If there had been a boat for Sydney, I would have chucked the whole thing."

Poor guy. They had smelled him a mile off, a tourist for the taking. But given that they aren't used to tourists on the island, Kailuan and his troupe are damn fast-talking hustlers.

Mike was delighted when we invited him to come along with us. The morning we set out for Lendombwey, seeing him, I guessed why the Lawa villagers had taken him for a strange bird—an exotic pigeon, let's say—at least if he had been decked out the same way when he arrived. For the long, exhausting, dirty trek he had put on an electric yellow t-shirt and green and yellow checked bermuda shorts. He had hidden his abundant hair underneath a weird golfing cap, his eyes and part of his cheeks under giant sunglasses. There was nothing particularly effeminate about him. It was just that he looked as though he had stepped out of a sporty boutique and was headed for his country club in a convertible instead of for Lendombwey on foot through the jungle. Kal, Jacques, and I looked like veritable island vagabonds next to him.

After the first hills, at most an hour of walking, Mike had already abandoned his cap and sunglasses. His t-shirt was drenched in sweat and stained with mud, and he looked more and more miserable. When we stopped for a few minutes of rest at the Nawaybuss River, he still had enough energy to go frenetically digging through his knapsack. He took out a little lacquered box which held some yellow pills. He quickly swallowed two with the river water then offered the box to us.

"What are they?" I asked.

"They're . . . I forget the brand. They're amphetamines! You don't need a little shot in the arm? Shit. This little trip is a ball-buster."

Jacques looked at me as if to say, what kind of weird egg is this guy anyway? He advised Mike not to count too much on the pills, otherwise he'd never last through months in the jungle. Mike informed us that his mother had been opposed to this trip, and he was beginning to wonder if she hadn't been right.

By the time we got to Lendombwey, Mike seemed to regret ever having been born. It wasn't until after several "vacation" days which he spent sleeping on the ground in Kal's and Jacques's lean-to that he again found some of the enthusiasm he had brought over with him on the boat from Sydney three months before.

We had arrived on time, just before the beginning of the cere-monial period. But we weren't bowled over by the preparations we saw. We didn't see any.

For two weeks our role as spectators would be very limited. Mine would be diminished to zero. For two weeks I saw abso-lutely nothing of what was going on. Being a stranger in Len-dombwey didn't give us any special privileges, and I was buckled in with the other women inside the hut or in the yard in front of the hut. We were permitted to go to the gardens and the closest stream to get water, but we had to go directly to either of these points by the shortest trails. No deviations. No more strolls. If a woman was missing from the yard or the hut, frequently a man appeared to check, to ask where she was. And the answer had to be a good one. I could no longer go to Jacques's and Kal's lean-to, since the path leads in front of the ceremonial ground and I ran the risk of seeing something forbidden. I didn't feel a single re-sentment against the taboos. Although I spent some pretty boring hours because of them, I didn't mind. These taboos symbolize, in a sense, the society's viability. If I could have done what I wanted, I wouldn't have believed in the sacred character of the events.

Jacques and Kal were more privileged than I. They could see everything that was considered semisecret, "taboo little bit." Mike was more or less included. I don't know precisely why, but he didn't get along with the villagers as well as we did. Thus Kal and Jacques, but not Mike, were present when the funerary platform was taken down, Tambwebalimbank's skeleton retrieved, and the skull detached. They watched while all the bones except the skull were buried beneath the catafalque near the ceremonial ground.

Mike was allowed to observe, with the others, ten nights of sacred dances. From the yard in front of the women's hut, I heard bewitching chants punctuated by terrifying howls and raging drums. I couldn't hear very well. There was something in that bizarre music that attracted and held me. I would have liked to get a little closer in order to be able to hear more easily. I knew I hadn't a single hope of being present at the dances. They were strictly forbidden to women. But if I were to go a little closer to the ceremonial ground without seeing anything? My plan was thwarted before it was even hatched. Ilabnambenpen annouced to us, for my intention, that it was taboo, under penalty of death, for a woman to leave the yard during those ten nights. Despite my respect for the taboos, I wondered what they would really do if I went out anyway. I was convinced that at least they wouldn't execute their threat, to execute me! But it would be finished for us in Lendombwey. We would be chased out of the village. We would never see the rest of the ceremonies. I crushed all my rebellious thoughts.

Jacques confirmed, when I had a chance to see him, that these dances were remarkable. Benevolent or malevolent spirits prowled at treetop level. The dancers were in direct communication with them. Jacques described to what a degree it was a serious and profound experience for these men. All the while they danced, they laughed or cried, their expressions terrorized or ecstatic. They rolled their eyes and constantly looked toward the summits of the trees.

At the same time there were many secret things that even my friends could not see, the things "taboo too mass," forbidden not only to women but to uninitiated men as well.

We knew that the men were in the process of reincarnating Tambwebalimbank in a funerary statue which incorporated his skull. The skull, modeled over in clay, was supposed to resemble the old chief when he was living. Other men were making costumes. The information given to us on these activities was very vague.

During this period, there was a basic taboo. As soon as we heard a certain sound, we had to return as quickly as possible to our huts. The sound was a plaintive cry. At first we thought it was the cry of a bird and then, no, rather a series of notes emanating from some kind of flute. Sharp, strange modulations. We learned later, after all the ceremonies, that it was in effect a kind of flute, made from a human tibia.

I hadn't seen Jacques and Kal for several days when I spotted them on a path between the gardens and the women's hut. We took advantage of the occasion to discuss a little our respective experiences. The flute sounded, from somewhere under the foliage, not far away. We dawdled just a minute, time to finish an anecdote. A minute too long. Ilabnambenpen surged out of the jungle with Metak close behind him. He yelled, flaying his arms menacingly. He chased us toward Jacques's and Kal's lean-to. He and Metak came in behind us, barring the entrance. Ilabnambenpen was trembling with anger, letting loose a flood of words which we of course could not understand. "You have broken the taboo," cried Metak, who was as emotional as Ilabnambenpen.

"But——"

They wouldn't let us say another word. "You are strangers. You will not die. But I and the chief, we are responsible for you!"

We protested that we hadn't seen anything. We promised to pay strict attention from then on. Ilabnambenpen and Metak visibly calmed down. They talked softly between themselves. We hadn't seen anything so it was less serious than they had thought. They didn't hold a grudge against us. However, the intensity of their reaction had struck us. Were they afraid to be condemned to death by the spirits, or by the other men, who would judge that they hadn't done their job in relation to us?

Mike, who hadn't understood anything of this dramatic scene but who had nonetheless witnessed it entirely (having been in the lean-to when we arrived), clumsily chose that moment to continue his ethnological studies. "Metak!" he called.

Metak, barely in control of his emotions now, indicated that he was listening. He expected a remark concerning the only subject which interested everybody at that instant: the taboo. Had it been broken or not? What were the possible consequences?

But Mike's thoughts were elsewhere. "Metak," he began, his eyes glued to his notes, full of diagrams and little circles and little triangles illustrating the kinship systems in Melanesian societies. "Tell me, what do you call the husband of the sister of your father?"

Metak stared at him darkly, his eyes full of contempt. For a few seconds we froze. Was he going to explode? With a brisk movement he turned his back and left the lean-to in a huff.

"What's the matter with Metak?" asked Mike.

Mike didn't have the slightest notion of what had just happened, and he would no doubt be surprised when Metak refused from then on to cooperate with any of his research. Kal, manifestly annoyed, but with the perpetual patience of a professor, was the first to speak.

"Forget your notes a little, Mike. You're not in a laboratory. You're dealing with human beings here, not guinea pigs. Stop piling your science on other people's shoulders, and try to understand a little!"

Jacques and Kal started a discussion where they were on common ground. They could each name at least ten ethnologists they had met in the course of their travels who surely would have liked to be able to regroup all the primitive peoples of the world in glass-domed air-conditioned villages, in Parisian or New York suburbia. That way they could study them without the inconveniences of living with them, and without having to get to know them person to person.

The last days before the ceremony seemed very long to us, even to Jacques and Kal, however many more distractions they had than I. They obtained the right to watch the fabrication of the Temes Nevimbur and were impressed by the artists' skill and the astuteness of their methods. For example, to give a greater plasticity to their clay, they blend liana gratings into it. The entire jungle is the storehouse for the Mbotogote palette. They make their beautiful colors from roots, fruits, and stones. But apart from these privileges (which, moreover, I would have paid dearly to share), Jacques and Kal also spent hours and hours without seeing a thing, without anything to do. Everything that was going on was too taboo even for them. The same days must have seemed short to the Lendombwey men, who were secretly busier than ever. On the ceremonial ground they erected a second banana-leaf wall, some three yards high, behind which they did God knows what. My friends more and more lost their right to circulate—like me. They also lost, at times, their morale.

"I only hope," commented Kal, "that all this waiting is going to lead to something worthwhile!"

During the last two days they prepared the banquet. The men and the women made laplaps, working separately. The men's laplaps are among the masterpieces of Melanesian cooking. Pigeons, chickens, shrimp, flying foxes, and coconut are added to the usual yam paste. The women would not partake of these superior laplaps. They do not have the right to eat anything that is cooked on the men's fire. Similarly, all that comes from the women's fire is equally forbidden to men, but the men don't care since they confiscate all the choice ingredients for themselves. Metak explained that the men's food would be shared with the spirits while the women's food, solely for their use, is naturally much simpler.

On the morning of the big ceremony, everyone gathered on the ceremonial ground to await the arrival of the sun at its zenith, the time of their appointment with the spirits. And it seemed the spirits had taken great pains so that the men could read the celestial clock without difficulty. Not a cloud troubled the sky, which was so intensely blue that in a photograph you would attribute the unbelievable color to the effects of a filter. At nine o'clock the heat was already oppressive.

That day the women did not wait to be summoned at the last minute by the drums. They came at the same time as the men. The long wait at the ceremonial ground was part of the day's solemnity. The women stayed in a group in their usual place, a few yards from the ground. They were dressed in mourning, which is to say their faces and naked chests were smeared with ash. Their only role in the ceremony would be to lament, howl, moan, and cry profusely for the deceased. But for the moment they seemed rather to be on a picnic. They gaily passed the smallest children from hand to hand, breast to breast, because here the mother is not necessarily the nurse. Two or three women had caught colds and didn't stop sneezing, a natural function rendered fairly filthy because of the bones they wear in their noses.

The second banana-leaf wall was taken away, and we saw the result of their hidden work. It was the altar where Tambwebalimbank's funerary statue would be placed. It was constructed in split bamboo and generously decorated with leaves and five or six varieties of flowers. Five Temes Nevimbur had been driven into the earth. Today, the puppets represented the five dead children of the deceased. The modeled skull of another of the chief's children, dead when already an adult and graded in the Nimangki, looked out at the spectators from the altar's summit. The other little heads fashioned in clay, the *nembegi*, also looked out with their snail eyes aimed in all directions.

Tambwebalimbank resurrected: his funerary statue. *Kal Muller*

The men slowly brought their offerings, one by one, as if they wanted their good works to be noticed by the spirits. Yams, taros, and laplaps decorated with fragrant leaves and ginger flowers were heaped up before the altar.

And then, without prior notice, at about eleven-thirty, the reincarnated Tambwebalimbank appeared on the ceremonial ground in Ilabnambenpen's arms. We gawked, our mouths wide open. Kal and Jacques almost dropped their cameras. We were expecting the arrival of the *rhambaramb*, the funerary statue, but we hadn't thought it would be such a striking figure. The rhambaramb was more than six feet tall. The arms projected from the body in an upside-down V. The entire object was painted red, white, and black, full of ritual motifs, circles, stripes, and curves. The bark belt was rendered in paint on the body, but the nambas was real—a new leaf covered a larger-than-life clay penis. The testicles were also in clear view, big round globes, highly decorated.

Small heads, ornamented with pigs' teeth, were sculpted on the arms and behind the shoulders. Tambwebalimbank must have paid dearly for the right to these decorations before his death, just like an American might put aside money toward an expensive rare wood coffin. But the most striking feature was the head. It resembled completely Tambwebalimbank's head when he was alive. The mouth and the nose were his. It was a living face. The expression of the features traced a typical look of the old chief, by the forms and lines sharply painted. Even in the empty eyes of the statue we saw one of Tambwebalimbank's habitual glances. A year after his death, with the aid of neither photographs nor drawings, the Mbotogote had reconstructed their chief.

And it wasn't symbolic. Tambwebalimbank saw and heard everything that was going on. His spirit was there, in the rhambaramb. You could say he was more alive, more lucidly aware, than ever. Ilabnambenpen circled the ceremonial ground three times with the statue in his arms before placing it in its niche in the altar.

Masing, one of the most powerful ancients of the village, appeared with a knife fashioned from a human tibia and decorated with sacred leaves. The bone came from the body of a particularly redoubtable enemy, killed and eaten some fifteen years before. Masing used this implement to cut off the head of each yam and each taro in the pile of offerings in front of the altar. These heads would be replanted and produce an excellent harvest, thanks to the help of Tambwebalimbank's spirit.

The villagers glanced often, but rapidly, toward the sun, as a sustained look would have hurt the eyes. It was almost noon. Metak took Jacques and Kal aside to explain to them, as they told me later, that the ceremony about to start had not been carried out since sometime before the time of airplanes in the sky and boats in the sea, that is, before World War II. It had not taken place for more than thirty years because it is reserved for the most highly graded chiefs. Each generation does not necessarily produce chiefs of a high enough grade. It was a historic event. It was the first time that outsiders, as well as many Mbotogote, would see it. The first and the last time, since surely this rite would never take place again. We were convinced that before the death of the next important chief, the Mbotogote society would be broken by contact with the Europeans.

Noon, at last. The spirits emerged from the jungle. They appeared on the ceremonial ground timidly, in Indian file. They
went away and came back, as if they wanted to make the spectators beg them to stay. Each time they came back, there was one
more at the end of the line. A murmur of surprise swept through
the audience. We marveled at the costumes. For Melanesia, and
for anywhere else for that matter, they were a wonder.

The first men-spirits who emerged from the bush were veritable
dark brown balls with a small black ball on top. From their necks
all the way to their feet they were covered with a mass of smoked
ferns. Their heads were wrapped up in several layers of spider
webs.

The women's wails reached a climax. Limbois, Ilabnambenpen's wife, took my arm and looked at me triumphantly. As if I
hadn't believed the spirits would come!

The last brown ball had replaced spider webs with layers of
moss around his head. After him, all the balls were bright green—
men covered with moss. One of them, instead of wearing a spider
web or moss Balaklava helmet, wore an enormous conical mask
made of fernwood painted red and orange. The colors flamed in
the white midday sun. I was sure that the bodies underneath
those fantastic costumes must have been suffering terribly from
the intense heat.

Probably these spirits represented powerful ancestors who had
come to participate at the last rites of a chief who was about to
become one of theirs. In looking more closely, we noticed that
twigs strung with pieces of coconut were stuck here and there into
the thick, bristly suits. All the men had to eat some of the coconut
in order to communicate with the visitors. In fact, it was a sort of
holy communion.

Then came two spirits from the jungle totally unlike the others.
They wore the traditional penis sheath and bark belt, and their
otherwise bare bodies were painted like harlequins in red and
white. On their heads they wore enormous visors made of nargai
leaves, a kind of dark red banana. These spirits wandered all
around the ceremonial ground with crazed eyes, before noticing
the spectators and heading toward them. With long stalks they
whipped members of the audience. And it was not merely a theatrical gesture. They hit hard. The villagers did not protest. On the

contrary, they offered their backs to the whips. It was explained to us that those beaten in this manner no longer needed to fear the other spirits, who might become aggressive at any moment.

Like a phantom procession, the spirits waddled around in a circle, swaying silently, pivoting from time to time. Lost souls. They accepted the yam offerings and then, as if they could no longer stand the ceremonial ground's bright light, one by one and with exaggerated gestures, they threaded back into the jungle. Tambwebalimbank's spirit was doubled. It remained in the rhambaramb's skull but it also left, with the others, for the Land of the Dead at the bottom of the sea. From then on, since the ceremonies had been well executed, the village could count on its protection.

The departure was—naturally—celebrated by killing a pig. These sacrifices are never identical, except in the slowness of the methods. This time the animals were attacked with bows and arrows but put to death, finally, with spears and daggers.

I got a chance to talk with Jacques, Kal, and Mike a little after the ceremony. We were all excited and intrigued by the day's events. From what, from where, did all of this come—the idea of a rhambaramb, the concept of spirits in such fabulous costumes, the beliefs underlying these extraordinary rites? We'll never know the origins since these people, who certainly have a rich past, have no written language and, unlike the Polynesians, no real tradition of oral history. We could only verify that they are remarkable artists, directors, and actors. Kal, who had hoped that the ceremony would be worthwhile, announced that from then on he would be ready to spend weeks in Lendombwey waiting for whatever. With the Mbotogote, we were never disappointed.

He would have the chance right away to put the sincerity of his declaration to the test. We were told that *"c'losup little bit"* there would be another rite, this time for the women. After numerous questions we concluded that *"c'losup little bit"* meant two or three weeks. But we could have been wrong. Our notions of time did not exactly coincide with the native ones. Maybe it would be sooner. As head of our expedition, Kal proposed that it would be best to stay where we were. We agreed completely. When Ilabnambenpen specified later that the ceremony in question would be a Nimangki, the grade-taking ceremony, and for the women, we knew we had been right to wait. Everywhere else in the archipel-

A man-spirit. *Kal Muller*

ago, the Nimangki society is reserved for men. It is uniquely among the Mbotogote that the women too have a hierarchical society, separate from that of the men but equally serious.

During the following three weeks, we didn't even have the time to get bored. Our own health problems provided quite enough distraction. We all had our first malaria attacks. Me first, then Kal, and finally Jacques. We must have been bitten by the Anopheles mosquitoes at about the same time. We all had the most common form of malaria in the New Hebrides: twenty-four hours of alternating fevers and chills, twenty-four hours of rest, and then twenty-four hours of fevers and chills again. The cycle repeats itself every six weeks.

Even if you take quinine regularly, you can't avoid this disease. The mosquitoes bite you and implant the parasites in your body. The quinine diminishes the fever's intensity, which is already very helpful, but it cannot once and for all eliminate all the malarial parasites that are lodged in the victim's tissue. We had the least serious form. In general, in the islands, the more spaced out the crises, the longer they last and the more severe they are. There are people in Santo who have their attacks regularly every three or every six months. These people are seriously weakened physically after each crisis. If they do not die of malaria, they have so little resistance that they wind up catching other fatal illnesses. The natives, without the benefit of quinine, die fairly frequently of malarial fevers and their resulting complications.

The least severe form does not mean it was nothing at all. Our crises began softly with humming in the ears. Then come the pains in all the bones of the body, in all the joints. The first time this happened to me, in Jacques's and Kal's lean-to, I didn't pay any attention, thinking it was just a slight chill. But a little later I began to shiver, to tremble uncontrollably. Under a bright sun, in the tropical heat, I felt like I was dying of cold. Jacques brought me back to the women's hut and put me to bed with his and Kal's blankets as well as my own. My teeth were chattering. The sympathetic women were grouped around me. They knew what it was.

Then the fever started. I was burning. I threw off the blankets. I wanted to get completely undressed. There were minuscule Mbotogote playing the tom-toms inside my head. I had the impression I was in a hostile world. The women were talking on purpose, just to make my headache worse. The pigs reeked to make me vomit. The children did their best to irritate me. I was drenched in sweat. I didn't even know why, but I couldn't stop myself from crying. All of a sudden I missed my parents terribly and cried all the more for it. Something had happened to my mother during my absence—I knew it. I detested Malekula, the tropics, my life. The malarial fever is an irrational and torturous anguish. I finally sank into a dreamless sleep.

When I woke up Woshuk was beside me. She smiled at me. It was over. I felt weak but in a normal state. I couldn't eat and even a glass of water turned my stomach. The next day the fever took hold again. According to Jacques, I was tormented in my sleep, struggling and murmuring incomprehensible protests. Then it was finished for good, or for six weeks anyway. I felt emptied of all my force. I slept a great deal during the following days. I got back on my feet mostly because Kal and Jacques, one after the other, went through the same crises.

On top of this, we were all plagued by dermatological irritations. Fungi proliferated on our skins as they do in American forests. But on our bodies it's not pretty. The infections were a tenacious drag. I lost my fingernails and toenails, and I had a blotch as big as a silver dollar on my thigh. Kal and Jacques never stopped scratching the folds of their groins and rear ends, and Mike, decidedly born under a bad sign, developed a particularly bad case at the tip of his penis. Very put out, he didn't say anything at first. But Jacques and Kal had seen him wake up, tossing and in a sweat, for fear that it would all turn out badly and he would lose his masculinity. Mike at last confided in them and we gave him all the unguents and antibiotic powers we had. The infection didn't get any better for all that, and Mike began to go crazy. It was because of this that he abandoned his Lendombwey monograph.

It was a good excuse for leaving a place, and maybe a profession, that he didn't really like. Metak found a guide to take him back to the coast, where he hoped to get the first boat headed for Santo or Vila, anywhere, as long as it was more civilized. He would get back to Sydney as fast as possible. For the walk back to Lawa he put his yellow t-shirt and his yellow and green bermuda shorts back on. He had washed them in the stream but been unable to get out the mud stains. He cut a sad figure.

At the end, prey to last-minute compunctions, he wasn't too sure whether he actually preferred to throw in the whole thing or stick it out with us after all. But he couldn't help confiding that from the start he would rather have pursued urban studies than ethnology. Okay, we answered, a bit taken aback, you're good and far from cities around here. Maybe it would be best for you to go back to Australia. Since he chose to interpret that as our way of kicking him out kindly, he left with a clear conscience. We never saw Mike Hallston after that day. Did he become an urbanist? I hope so for him, because his heart is in the right place and I would be pleased to know he's happy. Maybe, after all, he went into business with his father, who directs an important insurance company in Sydney.

We succeeded in pumping a little information out of Metak

about the coming rite. It was indeed a Nimangki for women! So, the Mbotogote women also have their Nimangki society, in which grade-taking has the same significance as for the men: prestige and power, in life and in the afterlife. We tried to get some particulars about the ceremony itself, but for the moment Metak wasn't talking. He informed us, with a strange smile, that we would find out soon enough.

A few days later we understood what he had been getting at. I was in Jacques's and Kal's lean-to. Jacques, the last of the three of us to suffer a malarial crisis, was just beginning to recover. Kal and I were boosting his morale a little, as he had done for us. We were fairly surprised to see Metak, Ilabnambenpen, and his wife, Limbois, arrive. It is rare to see a woman in men's company. We quickly understood, moreover, that Limbois was the head of this delegation. And for once, it was me instead of Jacques and Kal they were looking for. Limbois, as chief of the women, or the most highly graded woman in the community, spoke. She invited me to participate in their Nimangki, to take a grade and consequently become an honorary member of the society. This was a present that hadn't even been offered to my friends during the men's Nimangki we had witnessed. I was flattered.

"What do I have to do?"

"First, you pay a pig to the chief," translated Metak, half in pidgin, half in Mbotogote, which we were beginning to understand. At the same time, he assured us that we could get a pig for several knives, axes, and cigarette packs.

"And then? What do I do during the ceremony?"

"You dance with the other women. Then you bring out your pig. You stun it with a club and then you kill it with a spear. You butcher it and distribute the meat. And then you have one of your front teeth knocked out."

That's all! A moment of silent stupefaction. Kal encouraged me to say yes, saying that it would make an astounding film sequence and that I could always get a beautiful artificial tooth in the States. Jacques, on the other hand, was negative. He was thinking of me rather than spectacular sequences. For me there was no problem. I wouldn't do it. I wasn't particularly anxious to slaughter a pig, and the tooth bit was really too much. I told Kal rapidly in English that he could take me for a chicken if he liked, but I had the right to dispose of my body as I chose. And I say no!

I was a bit more tactful in explaining to the Mbotogote my refusal of the honor they were offering me. I explained that in their community a gap in a woman's mouth is a symbol of prestige, but where we come from, in my country, at the least it would be viewed with prejudice. They understood very well, and they were not offended.

Since I was not participating in the ceremony, I didn't have the right to see the preparations. Jacques and Kal were always with the men, as usual, but I could no longer stay with the women. I spent my days alone. I explored the surrounding jungle. I bathed in the closest stream. I returned to the hut to read. In fact, I regretted not having brought an entire library, even though it would have meant another porter. I went through Melville's *Typee* for the third time. The women going and coming didn't know what a book was. They saw me bent over a tiny insignificant object for hours, and they thought I was most bizarre.

During one of my solitary jungle walks. I came upon an old woman painting some objects. She perceived me and started howling. Paralyzed with panic, I didn't know what to do, run away or explain myself. Limbois arrived, running. When she saw me, she was furious. The old woman was painting ceremonial headdresses, and I shouldn't have seen them. Limbois yelled. She was very upset. She made me understand that not only had I broken a taboo but she had broken one, too, because of me. She should never have let me go out without surveillance. Henceforth, I would not have the right to stray from the women's hut until after the ceremony.

On the day of this ceremony, as on the Ceremony of the Spirits day, we waited for the sun to reach its zenith. Since there is no exception to the rule that the ceremonial ground is taboo to women, the rite had to be accomplished in a clearing outside the village. In the middle of this land, there was a funerary structure whose four legs were connected by a thatched trellis. I wasn't even surprised to see this symbol of death manifestly imposed on the decor for a joyous rite. I had understood that the Mbotogote live in the shadow of death and that the ceremonies around which their lives are organized are—first and foremost—preparations for each person's departure into the beyond. The structure before us was a model of that which will receive the bodies of the two women and two girls who were rising in grade that day if, of course, they don't obtain even higher grades before dying.

As everywhere else in the archipelago, the women in Lendombwey occupy a position in life clearly inferior to the men's, but the Mbotogote women have hope. After death, their spirits can be as powerful as those of their husbands or fathers.

A little girl about nine years old carried a skull, modeled in clay and painted, on the end of a stick. It was the skull of her mother's elder sister, a woman who had been very highly graded in the society. She attached it to the trellis of the funerary structure so that her aunt's spirit could enjoy the ceremony and also so that she could bless the proceedings.

The male orchestra took its place at the edge of the clearing. The men began to sing, beat the drums, and strike the ground with bamboos in cadence. Limbois was the first to emerge from the jungle. She entered the scene like an old and venerable actress. The other women and girls trooped behind her in Indian file. Their faces were painted in bands of red and green, red and black, or red, green, and black, according to their grades. All but the youngest girls wore bones in their noses. We had finally learned the significance of these bones. At all costs, one's nostrils must be blocked so that an evil spirit could not introduce his penis into the opening during the night. Since a nose is sexless, it is obligatory for men as well as women to wear a bone, particularly during the sacred rites. The women and girls wore on their heads the magnificent taboo headdresses that I had glimpsed illegally in the jungle. They were like upside-down raffia baskets, embellished with horns and painted in red, white, and black. The women had to buy these headdresses for pigs and chickens.

They started dancing. First in place, then around the funerary structure, following the rhythm of the men's music. There was very little movement, just a tiny step, always the same, a simple swaying from one foot to the other. They continued this way until sunset, which must have been tiring all the same. Then on a sign from Limbois, they stopped. The people began to disperse. The rite seemed to be over.

"And what about the rest?" I asked. "The teeth? The pigs?"
"Tomorrow. Day after tomorrow. The day after the day after
tomorrow. Everything in its time."

The women's Nimangki lasted six days. Dancing all day and
night. Ceremonial exchanges of yams, coconuts, and bananas. On
the fourth day there was a strange rite, a kind of Melanesian baptism. In the nearest stream the men had constructed a dam covered with a dome of ferns. The women who were taking a new
grade waded into the dammed-up water, which formed a pool.
The men beat the dome with sticks, then went inside to hit the
two women and girls, who screamed at the top of their voices.
They weren't really being hurt. They were acting. The watching
spirits had to be persuaded that the women were suffering. The
rite ended by the men's sprinkling them with water and finally
submerging them completely.

The real drama occurred on the sixth day with the pig killing,
which was much more lively than any of the dances. The drum
rhythm excited the spectators as much as the participants. The
women began by tapping the pigs on the head with branches
decorated with sacred leaves. This wasn't really meant to stun the
animals, as the branches were much too light. It was simply the
inauguration of the sacrifice. The definitive work was executed
with a spear, stab by stab, by each woman and girl in turn. The
two girls, who were about nine and twelve years old, were not
particularly strong. Their spears hurt the pigs but didn't finish
them off very quickly. In any event, that was all right, since the
beasts must not die fast. Each strike affirms the existence of the
woman or girl and the importance of her new grade in regard to
the spirits.

The tooth extractions were even more painful to watch. The
first participant was one of the women. The other woman and the
two children who were waiting their turns watched the spectacle,
staring tensely, perspiring profusely. To be precise, the teeth are
not extracted. They are loosened by repeated blows until they can
be simply plucked out like chicken feathers. The woman sat and
two men held her in place, by the head and the shoulders. With
her molars she bit a piece of wood. The end of a stick is placed
against the tooth to be taken out, and the other end is struck with
a rock. It is not a rapid method. The women's groaning and the

Ritual tooth removal. *Kal Muller*

girls' yelling attest to the pain. One of the girls struggled so much against these brutal dentists that they had to lay her on the ground and pin down her arms and legs. Her mother came to caress her, to comfort her, from time to time. She had solid and healthy gums, and it took two hours of hitting to get the resistant tooth out. At the end her furious screams had dwindled to pathetic moans. She was half-conscious.

I suddenly had a crazy idea, but maybe not so crazy. The pigs have their upper canines taken out so that the lower canines will grow into curved tusks. This is the same operation! Do they hope, or did they hope at the time this practice originated, that the women's teeth would grow in ivory circles as do the pigs' teeth? It's unthinkable, but, after all, women are actually worth less than pigs. You can buy a wife for pigs, but you can't exchange an entire harem for a single tusked oinker. My head swam with these disquieting reflections.

The flood of blood from the victims' mouths was stopped with plant stalks warmed on hot rocks. For at least two days, the two women and two girls walked around with a hand glued to their lips because of the persistent pain. It was only later that we saw the big smiles—toothless and proud. The women and girls had paid the price to raise their grades. They had earned prestige. And they had the satisfaction of knowing that after death their spirits would be more powerful.

During our last evening with the Mbotogote, we did some trading. In the women's hut, Mdrouk, one of the youngest women, brought me a raffia miniskirt in the Lendombwey style. It wasn't exactly a gift. I had to offer her something, too. And I saw right away what she wanted. I had an old green woolen cardigan which I wore when it was cold during the night. Mdrouk pointed out to me that with this sweater she wouldn't need to sleep close to the fire anymore, and she wouldn't need to risk burning herself. Of course, I gave it to her.

Jacques and Kal received real presents, each one a Temes Nevimbur puppet. They were even allowed to choose the ones they liked best. Even though Ilabnambenpen and Metak didn't ask for anything in return, my friends offered them all the provisions we had left: knives, flashlights, cigarettes, everything but the film and photographic equipment. And then—truly unexpectedly—the chief offered Kal and Jacques other art objects, other Temes Nevimbur, sculpted heads, clay flying foxes and pigeons, and more, but not for them. Kal had explained one day the principle of museums in our countries, and Ilabnambenpen wanted Mbotogote sculptures to be admired by everybody. Nothing in the whole lot was really sacred, but it was all beautiful. Jacques and Kal were moved, because Ilabnambenpen was putting his faith in them and because normally these objects are destined to rot in the jungle. Once they have served in a ceremony, they have outlived their use. They must be newly fabricated for each rite.

These objects ended up in the Musée de l'Homme in Paris and in the Brooklyn Museum in New York—but not without difficulty.

When we got back to Santo via the *Windua* there was a local European VIP waiting to meet us, partly to greet us, but mostly to see if we had brought back native art objects. Our sculptures were covered only with leaves, and he spotted them right away amid the pile of baggage. He suggested that he could easily make trouble for us if we wanted to take them out of the country—black-mail. We protested that we were perfectly within our rights. According to the law, you can export all objects that are not more than twenty years old, and that was the case for everything the Mbotogote had given us. Yes, said the gentleman, this model citizen so well considered by all the "right people," but you cannot prove that these are not ancient objects and I am in a better position than you to insist before the customs officials that all these sculptures are at least fifty years old. What did he want as payment for his kind cooperation? That was simple. He wanted nothing more than the best of the objects for his own personal art collection. Jacques and Kal were furious. They sent him packing. They visibly contained their profound desire to hasten his departure with a few well-aimed kicks. This pillar of colonial society, fat, red-faced, raised his fist as he was leaving. "I'll make trouble for you," he promised.

And so he did. That bastard, in his starched white shorts, made trouble for us. Because of him and his lies, Kal was almost expulsed from the archipelago, accused of illegal trade in native art objects. At the last moment we succeeded in establishing the truth before the authorities, but the true swindler in that affair will never be punished. He no doubt continues, even today, to add to his treasury of Melanesian art by threatening every easily intimidated traveler.

7

The Red and the Black

Cook was the last great explorer of the archipelago, but in the years to come the natives here and there were to see in the distance the white sails of other navigators. It is believed that La-Pérouse passed through the north of the archipelago in 1788. Since all his expedition was lost—drowned? attacked and eaten?—we'll never know exactly how it ended or what his precise route had been. His disappearance without a trace, no shipwrecked sailors or floating boards, remained a mystery for almost forty years. D'Entrecasteaux crossed the New Hebrides in 1793 looking for La Pérouse, but he found nothing.

It was an Irishman who discovered on Vanikoro in the Solomons traces of that unfortunate expedition. His discovery won him membership in the French Legion of Honor if no material compensations. But Peter Dillon was a merchant and preferred discoveries with a return. He was most interested in sandalwood, that rare substance so valuable because of its scent, which was avidly sought in China. For centuries it was thought that the tree grew only in India. Toward the end of the eighteenth century it was found and exploited in Polynesia and Fiji, but these resources were exhausted in a few years. Peter Dillon discovered it in 1825 in vast quantities on the southern New Hebrides islands. He didn't even profit from his discovery, however, because he didn't have the heart to confront the hostile natives. He was a romantic and wanted the islanders to be his friends. Perhaps because he had no intention of exploiting this wealth himself, he announced in the *Sydney Gazette* on March 3, 1825, the news of his discovery. All available Pacific adventurers flocked to the New Hebrides. Because of Dillon, a new epoch began for the island natives.

The explorers had wanted nothing of the natives but a little fresh water and just enough tropical fruits to avoid scurvy. Queiros, or his crew members, had stolen pigs when they could, but this was much less catastrophic for the New Hebrideans than the large-scale robberies to come. The explorers were most interested in discovering the islands, making maps, studying the flora, and doing a little astronomy. They were scientific expeditions, at least from the time of Bougainville on. But the Europeans who would come during the nineteenth century all wanted something from the natives. The sandalwooders came for their trees. The "blackbirders" wanted their bodies. The missionaries wanted their souls. The colonists wanted their lands. It was a bloody century, without a government to protect either the Melanesians or the minority of "white" Europeans, turned pale by the misdeeds of the majority of their compatriots.

There were honest sandalwooders like Dillon, but the business seemed to attract mostly lawless and faithless rogues who, as a contemporary sailor said, "will treat the proprietors of the land like the trees they exploit, knocking down everything they come across." In 1849 the English admiral John Erskine, commander of the *Havannah*, went to the New Hebrides to investigate the abuses perpetrated by the Europeans. He declared, "Commerce in these islands is conducted in a manner which discredits the white traders, who often show themselves to be more advanced in cruelty and treachery than the natives, and with the exception of cannibalism, in the practice of all vices which we attribute to savages."

Erskine was sent primarily to look into an affair concerning the *Sophie*, a British sandalwood vessel. The *Sophie*'s Captain Henry had augmented his crew with Tonga Islanders. On Erromango a crew member didn't hesitate to kill a native for stealing an ax. On Efate, the Tongan crew members, undoubtedly carried away by the novel feelings of power due to their firearms, indulged in an orgy of massacres. After having stolen taboo coconuts, those reserved for religious rites, and insulted the proprietors, they shot their rifles in every direction and killed some sixty natives. The terrorized survivors took refuge in a cave. The Tongans blocked the entrance with branches and pandanus thatching torn from hut roofs and set it on fire. We don't know how many Efate Islanders perished in that cave, but we do know they were mostly women and children. The crew continued its work by burning the villages and gardens. The boat stayed several more days in mooring and was loaded with sandalwood.

Later, the captain and the other whites swore that they hadn't known about the massacre. But there was one white on board, the second mate, who did have a conscience and who gave honest testimony. The captain and officers had known very well what was going on. They pretended not to notice the flames that were devouring an entire section of the island. Nonetheless, no one was punished. The murderous crew members received one hundred pounds in wages, good money at the time, as the work was classified "perilous."

From then on, the Efate people were prepared. They awaited their chance for revenge, and the next two boats to arrive, the *Cape Packet* and the *British Sovereign*, provided the opportunity. The natives massacred the crews of both boats by treachery, since they still didn't have firearms.

These first traders depleted the abundant New Hebridean supply of sandalwood very quickly, in a matter of a few years. The traders who succeeded them were after ebony, figuratively speaking. The French used that term in general, but the men engaged in the trade found another euphemism, in the realm of ornithology: blackbird. The blackbirders were officially called manpower recruiters. From time to time they were also called, frankly, slave traders.

The first person who had the idea of employing South Seas Kanakas was an Australian, Benjamin Boyd. In 1847 he caught sixty-five New Hebrideans and took them straight from the tropical jungle to the New South Wales plains, where he raised sheep. Because of the change in climate and food, as well as their homesickness, his sixty-five shepherd-prisoners didn't take very long to die, down to the very last man.

But the worst was to come. The cotton plantations and particularly the sugar cane plantations in Queensland and in the Fiji Islands had an insatiable need of cheap labor, capable of working long hours under the tropical sun. And the Melanesians were "capable" of this, according to the bosses' definition of the word, anyway. Under those circumstances, Kanakas die slower than Europeans. In any case, the Europeans didn't want to undertake such labor and you can't force *them*. Besides, the death of a white provokes all kinds of problems, while the death of a native meant only one less beast of burden. The blackbirders were well paid, about twenty-five pounds, or sixty-five dollars, per head. Thus, it was in their interest to return from the islands with a maximum of human cargo. The problem was that there weren't enough native volunteers. But as the blackbirders were not scrupulous men, they didn't hesitate to use force and treachery to fill their ships' holds. Two methods of kidnapping seemed to be the most popular: attracting the natives on board by offering them presents and then keeping them prisoner; and simply overpowering a canoe and grabbing the men in it. Anyone who tried to escape was to be recaptured if possible, if not, to be killed.

Dr. Murray was the owner and commander of the *Carl*. He used the method of pirating canoes. He threw iron weights into the canoes, stunned the natives so he could hoist them on board with no resistance, and closed them into the hold. One particular voyage started well. His hunting technique had brought him ninety slaves, which was a lot for his boat's tiny hold. During the day, the men, who were suffocating, began to struggle madly. A guard shot his pistol into the air a few times to calm them, but it didn't work. The crazed natives began to riot. They used the wood from the bunks like battering rams to break through the hatchway. Then the crewmen, under the doctor's orders, started shooting their rifles into the hold. Once it was begun the firing didn't stop. The frantic tumult in the hold gave way little by little to plaintive howls of pain. And then, nothing. Silence, broken only by moans. However, the sailors continued to shoot. All night long.

In the morning, the hatchway was opened. Five uninjured natives came out, helping nine others who were only slightly wounded. Sixteen others had serious wounds. Sixty were dead. In

order to pull them out of the hold, the crew members floundered
in blood up to their ankles. The sixty dead were thrown overboard right away. The sixteen badly wounded, too. Their hands
and feet were tied to make absolutely certain that they never
reached land to tell their tales.

Murray gave the order to clean the hold, and none too soon.
The H.M.S. *Rosario*, which was navigating those waters precisely
to survey the actions of people like Murray, boarded the *Carl*.
The British officer who came on board to make the inspection
found everything in order. The few recruits he saw seemed to be
there voluntarily. He noticed the freshly whitewashed hold and
appreciated its cleanliness, but he didn't notice that it was riddled
with bullet holes.

The bloody history of the *Carl* became known anyway, and the
two crew members who had done most of the shooting faced trial
in Sydney. At that time in Australia, the courts almost never accepted a native's testimony. The pretext was that the natives, not
being Christians for the most part, were not bound by the oaths
inherent in Anglo-Saxon justice. The two accused from the *Carl*
were acquitted.

The *Hopeful* had been a suspect boat for quite a while when, finally, it was investigated upon arriving in Australia, after a typical
voyage, with 103 recruits, not one of whom had been engaged voluntarily. An episode among many others: off an island, canoes full
of men bringing fruits to offer to the whites in exchange for a few
scraps of cloth advanced to meet the boat. The launches were put
into the water, and the crew armed with rifles set to hunting
blackbirds. One canoe tried to get back to land. The native helmsman was shot and killed instantly, as well as the man next to him.
The other islanders jumped into the water and were scooped up
by the crew, as was the helmsman's corpse. They decapitated and
mutilated the latter, "as a lesson for the others." In another canoe,
there were six men and a little boy. As the child was too small to
be of any value, they attached two coconuts under his arms and
threw him back into the sea. A few minutes later, in plain view to
everybody, including the little boy's father, the coconuts came undone and the child drowned. According to the witnesses, many
men were killed in the course of this single trip.

Two of the *Hopeful*'s crew members went on trial in Sydney.

New Hebrides recruits—"blackbird-ing" days. *Mitchell Library Archives, Sydney*

They were condemned to death and pardoned. The defense attorney's speech that saved their lives was striking as a legal argument. The atrocities of which he admitted his clients guilty were the widespread practices of this trade so it would be unjust to punish these two men for the crimes perpetrated by hundreds of others as well!

These "manpower recruiters" didn't count on force alone. The astuteness they employed to achieve their ends was infinite. They would take a hostage from one tribe and offer him, all tied up and ready for the slaughterhouse and stone oven, to an enemy chief in exchange for a specific number of "volunteers." Since the chiefs were all-powerful, they could command young men of the tribe to go with the whites and thus profit from the situation. For a rifle, a chief often gave three or four men. The traders even had the idea of arming one tribe against its neighbors, so that these latter would try to escape from the island before being exterminated.

Carl Satini, called "Satanic" by some, generally nicknamed

Captain One Eye, displayed a certain black humor in the use of his glass eye. Instead of giving presents to the chiefs, he threatened them, promising that if he didn't have so many recruits by the next morning, he would take one eye from each man in the village. And then, to prove that his personal sorcery included such powers, he took out his glass eye in front of all the terrified natives. One Eye rarely had to use rifles to fill his hold.

There *were* men who signed up voluntarily—that is, who scribbled crosses on the whites' contracts without being forced in one way or another to do so—and for various reasons: disputes or dissatisfaction at home, a recent defeat as a warrior, a desire for adventure, and so on. The great majority of these men were cruelly deceived. The recruiters never explained to these illiterate men the real conditions blatantly written into the contract. The "volunteers" therefore had no idea that they would be going so far away and that they wouldn't see their native islands for at least three years, if they were lucky enough to live that long. Many of them didn't even realize that the labor contract specified bondage on a distant plantation. Indeed, a fair number didn't even know what a plantation was. Because of the recruiters' lies and insinuations, the majority of the men believed that they were bound for a quick sail over the Big Water and would soon return home, laden with precious gifts.

Technically, the victims of this black trading were not slaves since they did earn wages. In this, the whites were fairly reliable. They did pay what they had promised. True, the expenses did not exactly deplete their bank accounts. One worker, who labored ten to fifteen hours a day and was fed on yams and rice, cost a grand total of a rifle, an ax, a few strips of calico, and a little tobacco after three years of labor. Very frequently the repatriated worker didn't even profit from the fruits of his labor. The profits were confiscated by the chief or elders of the tribe. But that certainly was no concern of the whites. The whites were guilty only of sometimes confusing the islands and repatriating a man in enemy territory instead of his own village. If he were killed and eaten as a result of these geographical errors, the blackbirders didn't want to know anything about that, either. It was none of their business.

The rifles were a poisoned present. Using bows and arrows,

clubs and spears, for centuries, the various tribes had maintained an equilibrium among themselves. Now, with the superior force of guns, a tribe didn't hesitate to wipe out its neighbors. The face of war changed: two tribes armed with spears irritated each other; two tribes armed with rifles massacred each other.

But the deadliest poison introduced by the recruiters, as well as by the planters and even the missionaries, was microbes. Epidemics ravaged all the islands. The New Hebrideans were fairly well immunized against malaria, but they had no resistance to European illnesses. On Aneityum Island, cholera killed one-third of the population. Thousands of natives on Tanna succumbed to smallpox. Measles took two-thirds of the Erromango Islanders. With influenza, chicken pox, whooping cough, and dysentery, the archipelago's population was decimated. And, inconceivable but true, the most sadistic black traders took advantage of the islanders' vulnerability. To get revenge against a tribe who had killed one of their men, or quite simply who wouldn't furnish any "volunteers" for recruitment, they didn't hesitate to land a diseased man on the island. Knowing that a single person was enough to provoke an epidemic, they rubbed their hands gleefully and had happy dreams of moribund black enemies. The natives defended themselves against all these atrocities as best they could by killing and eating whites, any whites, whenever the opportunity presented itself.

On this sinister canvas the portraits of the first missionaries were painted. These honest men came to the fore as champions of the "poor savages," doing everything they could to protect the islanders from the abuses of the less scrupulous whites. But at the same time, with only the best intentions, they attacked (in their own way) the very people they sought to protect. In the name of Christianity, they destroyed as much as they could of the Melanesian culture. The Presbyterians, who landed first in the archipelago, were the severest. They outlawed in a single blow the chants, dances, ceremonies, traditional costumes, polygamy, sacrifices, and much more, too—everything that was at the heart of the native civilization.

The emotional reaction of the Melanesians was predictable. Why don't these whites have rifles? Perhaps the natives asked themselves the question, without finding the answer. For them, "European" was synonymous with killer, thief, liar, incendiary. So who are these people who talk about the *"big fella on top papa b'long you-me"* and want so badly to cover the breasts of all the island women? First and foremost, the Melanesians were on guard, as with all the whites, even if these whites had sweeter methods.

The Presbyterian John Williams, representing the London Missionary Society, sighted the New Hebrides on November 16, 1839, from on board the *Camden.* He was the archipelago's first missionary, and his career would not be a long one. On that day he wrote in his journal, "I consider the coming week as the most important of my life." And that it was. Four days later, before he was even able to start his work, he and his assistant, James Harris, were killed by club blows on Erromango Island before the horrified eyes of their ship's crew. Williams had ignorantly insisted on trekking directly toward an area where a taboo native ceremony was being prepared. Later, it was learned that there was a second reason for his murder. A few weeks before Williams's arrival, the sandalwood traders had landed on Erromango and had killed a chief's son.

The day before his death, Williams had dropped off three "teachers," evangelists or subpastors, on Tanna Island. They were Samoans. Other Samoans and Rarotongans were landed on other islands. It is true that the first missionaries were courageous, but because there were too few white volunteers for this dangerous work, they weren't to be exposed to needless risks. For years, the courage of Christian missionaries would depend on Polynesian teachers—Christians themselves for only a short while, not knowing their adopted religion too well, but martyrs of their calling nonetheless. They preceded the white missionaries in most of the islands. If the teachers were not killed, then the whites could land without too much danger. This was a fairly successful method of evangelism. The royal trail of Christ was blazed with a few crosses representing a few dauntless Europeans whose memory is still honored, and with numerous anonymous crosses in vague memory of forgotten Polynesians.

The Presbyterians concentrated their efforts in the southern part of the archipelago because of the sandalwood commerce.

Turner and Nesbit arrived on Tanna in 1843 and soon after were forced to flee in the night in a dinghy. The resistance and ferocity of the Tanna Islanders discouraged the whites from trying again for years. When they finally would come back, they would be even harsher than their predecessors. In the meantime, they continued to land Polynesian teachers. In 1845 the *John Williams* left a party of zealous Samoans and Rarotongans. Two were martyred quickly, but others would replace them.

John Geddie, a Presbyterian missionary from Nova Scotia, was the first to succeed. He arrived on Aneityum Island in 1848 with his wife, the second white woman in the archipelago (the first being, of course, Jeanne Baret, disguised as a boy on Bougainville's *Boudeuse*). He would succeed not only in doing his work, but also in staying alive on that savage island for twenty-four years. He had chosen his island well. He was poorly received by the natives, but they were less inclined to violence than the other New Hebrideans, and to stop this tenacious pastor, they would have had to kill him.

The second advantage of Aneityum was that the natives spoke a single language, while elsewhere languages differed from tribe to tribe. For the Presbyterians, the question of language was fundamental since their evangelism was based on the diffusion of the Bible. Geddie learned the native language and set to translating the Bible. He had a press shipped to the island and printed the texts himself. Since the islanders had to be taught how to read in order to read religious literature, the minister founded island schools with the aid of teachers and a second European missionary.

Geddie's strength was his intransigence. This quality—or fault, as you wish—allowed him to crush all resistance. His house was set on fire while he and his wife were sleeping within. This was discouraging, but not enough to make Geddie quit or even falter. He saw the universe in black and white: everything that was Presbyterian was good; everything else was bad. He didn't even have much sympathy for Christians of other confessions, particularly not for the Catholics. When he saw Marist missionaries landing on Aneityum, he declared: "A new enemy has entered the field . . . dressed in long priestly robes. In this we recognize at once the mark of the beast. The battle is no longer to be fought with Paganism alone, but with Paganism and Popery combined." The Marists did not stay very long, so Geddie quickly got back to hammering away at paganism alone.

Everything that was native was particularly black. Black is the devil's color. Geddie did not even try to learn about a few local customs which could have been valuable to him. A native who sang anything but the Presbyterian hymns was a criminal. And drinking kava, smoking wild tobacco, dancing—for him, these were sins no less serious than the Melanesian practices of strangling widows and prostituting girls. In a few years, Aneityum's traditional society was completely broken. The joy of living was buried as a shameful memory. But on Aneityum, the natives were good children. On Tanna, where the people are tougher, the crop of the first missionaries' intolerance is being harvested even today.

The island of martyrs was Erromango. Island of sandalwood also. Six Presbyterian missionaries left their skins there. John Williams and James Harris died violent deaths a few hours after their arrival on Erromango in 1839. George and Eleanor Gordon, a young, handsome, and enthusiastic couple, came to Erromango in 1859. They managed to last through two difficult years on the island, two years of thankless work, of vexations and privations, before they were killed. Ironically, their deaths were caused by their own countrymen. In 1861 the *Bluebell*, a sandalwood trading boat, left a few Tanna men who had measles on Erromango. A sadistic joke. A vengeance. A few months later, one-third of the island's population succumbed to this imported disease. The sandalwood traders then suggested to the natives that this plague was caused by the missionaries, that by their prayers they had incited their God to punish all nonbelievers. It took no more. The Melanesians were convinced of the power of spirits, native or foreign. The choice seemed simple: accept Christianity or die en masse. But the Erromango Islanders were crafty. They rapidly saw a third possibility: kill the representatives of this malevolent god in order to stop the prayers. A party of nine warriors ambushed Gordon and, thanks to the Europeans, accorded him a quick death. They broke his spine with an ax obtained from the sandalwood traders. Mrs. Gordon came running when she heard her husband's cry, and another ax took care of her at once. Then the two were killed again, symbolically, their wedding portrait being hung in a tree and shot full of arrows.

James McNair came to the island in 1870 and was killed before the end of the year. George Gordon's brother, James Gordon, took up the cross in 1871. Meaning to be helpful, he gave medication to two sick children who died all the same. For the parents it was white sorcery that had killed them. Without delay they took their revenge—more mortal ax blows.

Today we can hardly help criticizing the aims of these first missionaries, but we must admit that as individuals, they were not lacking in courage. Their courage was composed of fanaticism, cynicism, masochism, recklessness, and sincere beliefs, along with hidden motives Jesus surely would not have appreciated. It is undeniable that these ardent Presbyterians deliberately destroyed as much as possible of the native cultures, but they must be compared with the other whites in those parts who destroyed not only the cultures, but the Melanesians themselves. We can understand why the islanders, after their initial distrust, asked for missionaries. And the men of religion were proud to be requested, declaring that Christ's light, through them, had inspired the pagans. In reality, the missionaries were the Melanesians' only protection against the evil doings of the sandalwood traders, the blackbirders, and the first plantation owners.

John G. Paton, the first missionary to stay on Tanna, an island particularly dangerous for outsiders, explains in his autobiography, *Thirty Years with South Sea Cannibals,* how he brushed with death time and again. In general, each time the savages advanced toward him with clubs, knives, rocks, and rifles, it was Jehovah's hand that stopped them. All of Great Britain and Australia wept over Paton's story and contributed tens of thousands of pounds for his undertakings. At the time, a gentleman aboard a warship sent to discharge its cannons against the natives who mistreated the whites was less convinced than Paton of Jehovah's direct intervention in these cases.

Paton didn't hesitate to call his technical superiority a manifestation of God's power. According to him, he had "broken the backbone of paganism" on Aniwa Island by digging a well. The "pagans" were dazzled. Their own gods could send fresh water from the sky, but they were incapable of making it surge out of the earth! In Paton's 317-page book, we see the unconverted natives as beings totally preoccupied with murders, treasons, robberies, wars, and other diverse atrocities. Only once does he let us glimpse any other aspect of the "savages' " life. He describes very briefly a ceremony: dances with men in the middle and women all around, accompanied by chants and hand clapping. However, he concludes, "I was never able to associate dancing with things lovely and of good report."

Paton was to be one of the most influential founders of the Condominium.

An anecdote from the *New Hebrides Magazine,* October 1900. One Sunday morning, the catechist, who was teaching the youngest children, explained the story of John the Baptist. "And when the girl had placed the head of John on a plate, what did she do with it?" he asked. A small boy answered without hesitation: "She ate it!"

The Anglicans (the Melanesian Mission), the second missionary group in the archipelago, had another style and another idea. Contrary to the Presbyterians, they saw the world in shades, not in black and white. They did not speak of poor pagans and degraded savages. Of course, they too wanted to convert the Melanesians, but it was strictly a religious question. They made a distinction between what was and was not religious. For them, singing and dancing was not at all an insult to God. Thus they tolerated practices that the Presbyterians rejected as the devil's work. The Melanesian Mission was fortunate also in being directed, three times running, by erudite humanists.

George Augustus Selwyn, a New Zealand bishop, was the first Anglican in the New Hebrides. If he hadn't been a missionary, he would have been a professor or man of letters rather than a businessman or politician like Paton. A fellow of Cambridge, his powers as an organizer were strong and most useful in the Pacific. His lack of contempt for the members of other societies made him a precursor, advanced far beyond the thinking of his time. Selwyn treated the New Hebrideans as equals. His style of evangelism was to offer the islanders a general education, to train native pastors exactly as European pastors are trained. His ideas were far from those of the Presbyterians and their teachers or subpastors.

Selwyn's successor was George Coleridge Patteson, who had been a brilliant student at Eton and Oxford where he had particularly excelled in languages. He spent years perfecting his knowledge of Latin, German, Hebrew, and Arabic. During his life he learned to speak fluently twenty-three languages. In the New Hebrides he followed Selwyn's example. He took Melanesian children to New Zealand to study for six or eight months a year and repatriated them afterwards. He respected the Melanesians and treated his students "as if he were dealing with Eton scholars."

Patteson fought against the recruiters' methods and, because of them, he died at the age of forty-four. He landed on Nukapu in the Santa Cruz Islands just north of the New Hebrides. And as was his usual practice, he went ashore unarmed. He ignored a recent incident in which a blackbirder, disguised as a bishop, had attracted natives on board his ship in order to kidnap them. Their relatives had sworn to avenge themselves on the next white who arrived. It was Patteson. He was killed on the beach. At least his death caused some healthy reactions. A decree called the Kidnapping Act was promulgated at the next session of the English Parliament to regulate recruitment by British subjects in the Pacific. Unfortunately, this law was not very effective since without adequate surveillance it was impossible to ensure its application in the distant islands.

Patteson was followed by Dr. R. H. Codrington as the head of the Melanesian Mission. He is remembered as an ethnologist and linguist rather than as a missionary. He was sincerely curious about and respectful toward the beliefs and mythology of these peoples. His work involved a constant exchange. He taught the island children and, at the same time, was instructed by the islanders. In 1891 Codrington published his remarkable *The Melanesians: Studies in Their Anthropology and Folklore,* which is reedited regularly and is still the authoritative work on this subject.

Why did these Anglicans fail? The results of their efforts did not last. The native elite they began to create no longer exists. And the elite that is painfully beginning to take shape now in the New Hebrides does not come from the Banks Islands, the Mission's territory. The Banks people are still Anglicans in name, but they give the impression, if we can say it, of having lost their souls. I don't think Selwyn, Patteson, or Codrington would rejoice in seeing them as they actually are. Perhaps the fact that missionaries of these three pioneers' caliber are rather rare, and that their successors were not up to par, might explain somewhat the sad state of Banks society today.

The Marist missionaries settled into the archipelago in 1887. If the Anglicans had their Codrington, the Catholics were all more or less amateur ethnologists. Throughout the islands I found old notebooks written by these Marists, full of details about the traditional societies. I was impressed. Here it is at last, I thought, a group of missionaries who were sincerely interested in the customs and beliefs of others, who looked to understand and not to destroy. I saw all of them, naïvely, as brave humanists disguised in cassocks.

Then, one day, I found the diary of Father Salomon, the first missionary in north Malekula, who came to his post in 1899. The journal was very moving on first view, with its delicate and careful calligraphy half faded by the tropical rains, half eaten by rats. These notebooks were more frank than most and certainly not written to be read by *me*. Father Salomon quickly set my ideas straight about the Marists: "The knowledge of a country and its men can serve evangelism marvelously. . . . This study of native customs and superstitions is most useful to the missionary. Knowing the superstitions in detail, he can attack them successfully if he takes them one by one. Attacking them as a whole through logic, or trying to crush them all at once through ridicule, is not generally a good means to success. One is taken for an outsider, an impious person, and one is not listened to. . . . Moreover, the knowledge of native superstitions and customs can serve, as comparison, in the explanation of the truths of our holy faith."

Well, that's it for the relativism of the Catholic missionaries. At least they did not forbid all the traditional customs as the Presbyterians did. Like the Anglicans, the Catholics attempted to "find out what was good and bad in the beliefs and practices [of the Melanesians] so that each might be officially tolerated or eliminated." The Anglicans and Catholics were capable not only of judging the customs of others but also of transforming their judgments into laws.

Despite his intentions and his commentaries, Father Salomon presented a real treasury of knowledge about the region's peoples. He studied in depth the *demets*, the spirits, and he even translated and wrote down a few of the prayers these people addressed to them: "Little ancients, push the water, stay on that wave that it become calm sea, nalol, sea without ripples like a bay. . . . Ancients, come out of the bush today. Bite this yam that all the yams may grow tall and that our garden be plentiful." For Father Salomon each prayer was a challenge. "See," he said to an almost converted pagan, "it is not the demets who bite your yam in the night. Look at the teeth marks, you can see clearly that it was rats." The polite native replied, "Yes, Father, it was rats . . . demets in the form of rats!" The Malekula men were still not ready to accept the logic of the Europeans.

In these societies, where a woman is considered impure by nature and at the bottom of society's ladder, where everything that is sacred is automatically taboo to her, I would have liked to hear the first minister who spoke to the people about the Virgin Mary. What dialogues must have taken place! All the missionaries' notebooks are silent on this subject. One day I listened to a sermon delivered by an Italian missionary in which he did his best to move the natives with stories of the Madonna. They were completely impervious to these tales.

All the missionaries had as enemies not only paganism but the other Christian denominations and their representatives as well. The number of Protestant sects multiplied with the arrival of the Church of Christ Mission, the Seventh-Day Adventists, the Apostolic Mission, and even a few Jehovah's Witnesses and Ba'hai'. But the bitterest hatred followed a line of fire between the "papists" and the "heretics." The New Hebrides had become a microcosm of this traditional European rivalry. The French and English newspapers, magazines, and books perpetuated the antagonism. Paton (trying to be witty? I doubt it, as it would have been the very first time in his sober life) wrote: "There is a sort of freemasonry in heathen religions; they have mysterious customs and symbols, which none understand except the priests and sacred men. It pays these men to keep their devotees in the dark—and how much more to deceive a passing inquirer! Nor need we hold up our hands in surprise at this. Nearer home, it pays also to pretend and to perpetuate a mystery about beads and crucifixes, holy water and relics—a state of mind not so very far removed from that of the South Sea islander, not disproving but rather strongly proving that, whether savage or civilized, man must either know the true God, or he must find an idol to put in His place."

In the other camp, Monsignor Fraysse declared: "We must hasten to arrive in the field of the Father of our family before the enemy has planted there the darnel of error. There is no time to lose." As the Catholics arrived in the islands much later than the "enemy," Monsignor Douceré, chief ethnologist of the Marists, noted sadly, "The passage of the infidel to Protestant heresy is one of the hardest obstacles to conversion."

This polemic, founded on the differences in beliefs, became more and more political. It was a struggle to conquer territory and spread the spheres of influence. It was Protestant England against Catholic France. The Melanesians, pawns in the game, understood very little of it and still don't understand very much. Today, there are natives who change religion about as frequently as they change shirts. Numerous families send one child to a Catholic school and one child to a Protestant school. Hearing the first speak of the Trinity and sing the "Marseillaise" while the second pores over the Bible and hums "God Save the Queen," the parents attribute it all to the same thing: white men's mysterious customs.

A conversation at Goddyn's in Santo concerning the differences between Catholic and Protestant missionaries. A planter who found my questions on this subject too complicated bluntly explained to me, amid laughs and snickers, "the only difference that counts."

"The ministers fuck but they don't drink. The priests don't fuck but they get smashed. That's it! All any of them do is deprive themselves of one vice to indulge all the more in the other!"

Albert Goddyn, preparing another round at the bar, two bottles in his hand, raised an eyebrow and pulled himself up straight with a swagger. *"The-o-retically!"* he barked, directing a significant and cagey glance toward one member of the uproarious bunch.

Albert's target did not lower his eyes but couldn't help blushing. It was Father Sicot, Marist missionary, Santo's priest. The planters got into the game and egged him on.

"Isn't it true," roared one of them, "that you like the ladies as much as you like your whiskey?"

Goddyn, the old rascal, put on a serious face and leaned over on one elbow toward Father Sicot. "Now listen, no kidding," he began, "the Catholic missionaries always borrow other men's wives. Don't you think that priests should be allowed to marry after all?"

"Not in these parts, in any case," replied Father Sicot. "A priest cannot permit himself to be ridiculed. A cuckold is always ridiculed. And in this blasted country, every married man is a cuckold. Thus, I am formally against the marriage of priests."

In the midst of the general clamor which followed, some talking still about priests, others about a certain Protestant missionary who never drinks in public but who has a wine cellar any Frenchman would be proud of, Father Sicot raised his hand. "You will excuse me," he said, "I have to go say mass. Shall I reserve seats for all of you in the first rows?"

In the course of our peregrinations in the archipelago, we often had to deal with the missionaries, since the missions are located at strategic points along the coasts, in the places where we landed in order to proceed toward the inland villages. The clergy's reactions to us varied from excessive amiability to aggressive hostility. But it seemed to me that almost all came from the same source: basic distrust. Their attitude toward us was: they are potentially dangerous so we must either coddle them or be harsh with them. What danger did we represent? First, since we were interested in traditional Melanesian customs, we could encourage the pagans in their resistance against the missionaries' efforts. Second, we could look too closely at the activities of the missions and, being journalists, photographers, and film makers by profession, we could create undesirable publicity. Because it was not in the missions' interests to have the activities of certain missionaries examined too closely, even in speaking with us, most of them were visibly on guard.

On Aoba we knew a young minister of the Apostolic Mission,

John MacKenzie, who encouraged his students to write essays and make drawings with traditional legends as subject matter. Unfortunately, he was judged "progressive" by his mission, which for his superiors was a reproach, and was recalled.

On Malekula we had known Father Faure, who had taken an unhappy Big Nambas boy under his wing. Gerard, as the priest had baptized him, was unhappy not only because he had lost his mother, but also because he was born with defective eyes. Little by little, the child was going blind. As the Big Nambas are not very tender with their handicapped, Gerard would have probably led a short and miserable life on the plateau of his ancestors. Gerard's father had voluntarily given the boy to Father Faure, who, more personally Christian than many missionaries, had cared for him tenderly for years. Gerard's vision was too poor for him to go to school. The missionary gave him private daily lessons and recopied the texts in large letters for him. At his own expense, and not without difficulty, he sent him to Paris for surgery. The operation did not succeed. In such congenital cases, there isn't much hope and Gerard was destined to become blind. This was not enough for Father Faure to abandon his efforts with the child. To the contrary.

The only time he cried, "All this work for nothing!" it was not because of Gerard but because of the mission. And it wasn't because of the followers, but because of his colleagues. For twelve years Father Faure had worked to develop a large, dynamic mission. Then he was sent off to a small outpost where, before his arrival, a lay sister had done alone the little work there was to be done. What had happened? We don't know. Knowing Father Faure's frank character, he must have had some differences with his superiors. But for an active and ambitious Marist like him, that was not an acceptable punishment. So, he turned in his collar.

The last time we saw him was in Tahiti. I shouted, "Hello, Father." I was jabbed with an elbow and told I had put my foot in my mouth. I should have said "hello" quite simply. Ex-Father Faure had become a teacher, married a lay sister, and legally adopted the ex–Big Nambas Gerard (who wore the thickest glasses I've ever seen and seemed to be a very happy boy). I would have liked to talk with Mr. Faure, to learn the details of his story, but I sensed that those experiences were far too profound to be confided easily.

On Malekula we had also known Father Soucy, an American Marist, who is still working there. He has created a mission that operates like a modern business in which all the workers are shareholders. He believes that economic development must precede religious and philosophical questions. "Later, they'll understand better what I have to say, and they'll be able to judge for themselves." Economically, the people under this mission's influence seem prosperous in relation to the other New Hebrideans. We went to a church fair organized by Father Soucy. Among other things, he directed a booth where the clients came to be photographed with a Polaroid for ten francs. "One photo, one pound," just like on the Big Nambas plateau, but this time it was not the photographer who paid. Father Soucy made many people happy with his little business! He even had the idea of borrowing a large motorcycle on which the delighted natives posed. I was surprised to see the same clients come back four, five, and six times. New Hebrideans in other regions would never have had so much money to spend.

Jacques and I got a good general view of the Marist mission (and the others are not very different) in the New Hebrides during a cruise on the *St.-Joseph*, the mission boat. We boarded at Santo to go down to Ambrym to meet with Tofor, chief of the northern region of the island. We were to stay for two or three days, waiting for the arrival of the *Konanda*, on which we intended to return to Santo. Planes cannot land on Ambrym and boats pass very irregularly, but that time the *St.-Joseph* and the *Konanda* were both certain to call at the northern end of this isolated dot of land. Of course, it didn't go as planned. In the New Hebrides, you can never count on announced schedules.

The ambience on board the *St.-Joseph* was friendly from the start, thanks to Captain Pascal, a Malekula native, who knew the sea well and was hospitable by nature. We ate on the bridge with him and one or two crew members. They offered us fresh fish and we had thought to bring canned food and soda for everybody.

The first port of call was Craig Cove in the west of Ambrym, a volcanic island dominated by two active volcanoes, Mount Marum and Mount Benbow. Craig Cove is a small bight bordered by black sand and defined by a precipitous cliff on one side and cascades of consolidated lava on the other. All around is a delirious growth of vegetation. In the middle of the bay is the small mission headed by Father Gomez, a Spanish Marist. I found the site somber and menacing, but undeniably beautiful. I said this to Father Gomez. He looked at me oddly, incredulously.

"Beautiful?" he repeated. "You find this *beautiful?*" He sincerely could not imagine the association between that adjective and the place where he lived.

Father Gomez is about sixty years old. He seems to have stepped right out of *Don Quixote*. A classical Castilian peasant. A broad beret. Old baggy pants ornamented with a new patch over the backside. He is small, bent over, dry like a Sierra olive tree, with a round, flabby belly and a hard and linear will. He has the calling, if not of a martyr, at least of an ascetic. I had the impression he was as hard with the natives as he was with himself. And hard means hard in every sense. He has been in the New Hebrides for over thirty-five years.

The priest kindly invited us into his house, which was very old and made of wood in the country's colonial style. It must have been very pretty some fifty or sixty years ago, but now, half eaten by termites, it is a warehouse for broken and forgotten objects. A collection of old storm lamps, a massive bronze chandelier in a dark corner, big empty quinine cans full of nails and unsharpened pencils, books more or less nibbled by the rats, things and pieces of things impossible to identify—all modestly covered with a shroud of volcanic dust more than an inch thick.

Father Gomez could get everything he needs to repair the house. He could hire a woman to clean the house. He could order a minimum of supplies via the *St.-Joseph* instead of eating only yams. But he couldn't care less about all these petty material concerns. His only interest is in leading souls down the straight and narrow path toward spiritual perfection. We talked a little. He is absent-minded. For him Europe is a distant memory, a mythic land. A few men of the mission came to ask him something. They displayed respect mingled with fear and spoke as they might if they were in the ward of incurables in some hospital. For the Melanesians this is not natural behavior.

We went down the coast as far as Sesevi, a small mission outpost dependent on Father Gomez. A pale young man, wearing rimless glasses, with shy eyes advertising poetry, intellectualism, and anemia, came to greet us. He was surrounded by about twenty inhabitants of the village. Brother Antoine was a Trappist monk. We couldn't get over it. What was a Trappist monk doing in a mission? It's hardly the place for the contemplative life.

"In these underpopulated islands," the brother told us, "I thought I could get far away from everything. But you can't survive alone in the jungle around here. So, I came down to help Father Gomez." The two of them surely got along well.

The Trappist's experience did not last very long. We learned a few weeks later that Brother Antoine had been seriously weakened by his first malaria attack and had to be repatriated to Noumea.

We crossed the strait which separates Ambrym from Malekula to see Father Mutter, another but no more typical style of missionary. Mutter, an Alsatian, is as tough as Father Gomez, but you would take him for a general or a gym teacher rather than a saint or a mystic. He bursts with energy. He jumped from his jeep before it had even stopped. He didn't walk, he bounded. He had manifest difficulties in standing still.

A surprise was waiting for Captain Pascal and us at Father Mutter's. He introduced us to Mr. Grasset, a representative of the French Catholic Aid Society on an official tour of the islands. From then on, the *St.-Joseph* was at his disposal, by order of the Port-Vila bishopric. He was accompanied by Mr. Biron, the Vila scoutmaster. Here was an unexpected title. So there are boy scouts in the New Hebrides?

Father Mutter, playing master of ceremonies, organized us. A chair for everyone, and he took the drink orders. Then he took care of Jacques and me.

"May I invite you to share our little meal?" he began in a voice hard but sugary at the same time. "But you will remember me when you make your films and books, won't you?"

His "little meal" came on like a regular feast. The mission boys must have spent hours gathering the oysters and catching the crayfish! And the excellent chilled Alsatian wines in the heart of Melanesia were unbelievable! But the atmosphere at the table was not worthy of the victuals, and I had the regrettable impression that it was our fault, Jacques's and mine. Our presence seemed to bother Mr. Grasset, Mr. Biron, and Father Mutter. They weighed their words, glancing at us from time to time to be quite sure that we had no microphones hidden under our napkins. After the meal, we left these gentlemen to their business and strolled around the mission grounds.

A girl about fourteen years old ran to catch up with us. She introduced herself in good French, which is rare for a young New Hebridean. Her name was Martine. She came from Pentecost where her father, Matthew, was the chief of a Presbyterian village.

"I've been watching you for a little while," she said with a nervous little laugh, "but I couldn't bother you, because you were with the Father."

I saw right away she had something to ask us, but in the Melanesian manner she took her time. Little by little, it came out. She had been at school in Santo. She had enjoyed it and spoke of the experience with a child's pride. "The teachers liked me a lot because I always did my homework and I had good grades." (Later, in Santo, a woman teacher told us that certain male teachers didn't just like her a lot, but liked her too much. In the tropics, a fourteen-year-old girl is already a woman.) Martine wanted to continue her studies, and she could without any great difficulties since there is a high school in Port-Vila. But her father wanted her to return to the village. We understood immediately. Her father didn't see the use of schooling once you had learned to read and write. Secondly, he must have already been thinking of marrying her off. She would certainly bring a good price. A chief's daughter. Pretty. And it's always handy to have a wife who can read. Martine was staying at Father Mutter's mission while waiting for the next boat that would pass by her village. She was unhappy.

"What am I going to do there? I won't be able to read any more. There's nothing to read except the Bible. And my father wouldn't even like me to read that. He'd think I was wasting my time. He'll send me off to work in the gardens all day long. And I'm afraid I'll forget my French. In my village, we talk native language or pidgin, but neither English nor French."

"Have you spoken about this with Father Mutter?"

"No . . ."

"Why not?"

"I don't dare."

So, Jacques and I promised we would present her case to Father Mutter. There are few young New Hebrideans who express a desire to study. The priest would undoubtedly agree with us that everyone who does should be encouraged, all the more since he directs a large school, financed in part by the French government, at the mission. And who could explain the situation better to Martine's father than a missionary?

We spoke too soon. When we told Father Mutter the story, his attitude was totally negative. And his reasoning was based on a general viewpoint which he was careful not to explain directly. The missionary thought Martine should go home because when "they" are too educated: (1) "they" cannot readapt anymore to village life (we interpreted: "they" don't know their place); (2) "they" become antiwhite (he meant "antimissionary" certainly); and (3) "they" become Marxists.

The man said "Marxists." The New Hebrideans are still far from having such ideas. And if a few have the vague beginnings of such thoughts, it is a spontaneous and natural reaction to their circumstances. You can count on the fingers of one hand the New Hebrideans who know someone called Marx ever even existed. But the farsighted Father already fears the possible consequences of "too much education." And this missionary does direct a school. He is responsible for the education of hundreds of New Hebridean youths.

On board the *St.-Joseph* between Malekula and Ambrym, I talked a little with Mr. Grasset. He didn't want to talk to me, but he wanted even less for me to write later, in a book, that he had refused to talk with me. He is a big wheel in Catholic Aid, traveling constantly, visiting missions in all the countries under French influence. He knows all the French-speaking African chiefs of state. And as he travels to find beneficiaries worthy of his organization's gifts, you can imagine that he is in general very well received.

"Do you already know the New Hebrides?"

"No, this is the first time I've come here."

"And what is the purpose of your trip?"

He mentally drafted his text before replying. "To meet the priests, to help them discover methods by which they can morally and economically ameliorate their missionary efforts. And to see how Catholic Aid could render charitable services, according to the Christian ideal of charity."

A pretty answer and a fairly ambitious project for someone who doesn't know the country and who plans to stay for only about a week, of which at least three days would be spent peacefully in the small capital's bishopric. It was very instructive for us to see how Mr. Grasset would conduct his brief study of the islands. We were to see this at close range because, instead of getting off at the next port of call in northern Ambrym as expected, we stayed on board during the entire tour.

When we arrived off the Ambrym coast, the captain had barely had time to drop the anchor when a hardy human form charged into the waves, waving his arms in a warm gesture of welcome. No, we were not foolish enough to feel flattered by the enthusiastic reception. We guessed right away that the honor was reserved for the pocketbook of Catholic Aid. Father Vanderborg helped Mr. Grasset climb out of the launch, without even glancing at us. On the beach, face to face, he was obliged to acknowledge us, but he didn't offer his hand. He informed us coldly that the *Konanda* would not be coming to Ambrym to pick us up as planned. Since the boat had taken on a full load, it had already returned to Santo, according to the radio. Nice guy, I thought. After all, he could have let us get off and get stranded, without informing us of anything. The next boat was due in a month or two, maybe.

"That's a shame!" replied Jacques. "Oh well, we don't have any choice. We'll go see Tofor and his men right away so we can be ready to leave with you on the *St.-Joseph*."

"You know," Father Vanderborg said to Jacques, "we'll already be four on board: Mr. Grasset, Mr. Biron, myself, and my aide, Gilbert. I don't believe the *St.-Joseph* can take six passengers."

"I believe, sir," Jacques said to the missionary, "that I do not need your permission to stay on board. We have our places with the bishopric's agreement. And if changes must be made, I believe that any such decision is up to the captain. But don't you worry about it, Father, I'll go ask the captain myself if he has any objection to our remaining on the boat."

Vanderborg's red face turned a little redder. Grasset coughed. Scoutmaster Biron lowered his eyes.

They climbed the hill toward the mission house and the good meal that awaited them. We took the path toward Fona, the village where Chief Tofor was waiting for us. On a grassy slope in front of the village's cooperative store we had our own little feast: canned corned beef, cold yams brought by Tofor, warm beers and sodas. Captain Pascal had come with us. He hadn't been invited to the mission table.

Departure the next morning. Mr. Grasset came from the mission laden with presents from Father Vanderborg. Mr. Grasset was very proud of his booty. They were Ambrym "art objects," which is to say, imitation traditional objects, made to be sold in Santo and Vila to tourists: miniature statues and drums, mass-produced masks.

Tofor wanted to come on board with us to meet the "Capman"—a pidgin word which means "important white man," generally a government official, in this case Mr. Grasset. All Tofor knew about him was that he was a Capman who gave money to the missions. On the bridge of the *St.-Joseph*, with the proud bearing worthy of an important chief, he offered his hand to Mr. Grasset, saying, *"Thank you too mass b'long all something, b'long money, b'long school, b'long medicine."* Mr. Biron, who spoke pidgin, began to translate. "He's thanking you for——" But Mr. Grasset cut him off and pretended not to notice Tofor's outstretched hand.

"I know, I know. That's an old refrain, and I've heard it hundreds of times," he sighed. And he sent Tofor packing with a gesture that needed no translation.

He didn't understand that Tofor was reciting his monologue, above all else, to affirm himself as *chief* in front of the Capman. When anyone takes an interest in northern Ambrym, he ought to address himself to the chief. If matters concerning the island are decided between the Capman and the missionary, Tofor feels unjustly bypassed, even dishonored. You don't have to know a people that well to understand certain universal reactions, and we were fairly shocked by Mr. Grasset's total lack of comprehension. We told Tofor we would come back soon. He paddled back to shore in his canoe, and the *St.-Joseph* took to the open waters.

A hierarchy was quickly established on board. The single small cabin contained the helm and three bunks, the captain's and two others. But the captain's was no longer the captain's, as Mr. Grasset figured he had the right to borrow it. The other two bunks were taken ex officio by Mr. Biron and Father Vanderborg.

We were on the bridge with Gilbert. No. Not with Gilbert, next to Gilbert, since he was following the missionary's example, pretending not to see us. He was a skinny, frail, young seminarian with thick glasses and a thin beard. About as friendly as a prison door. The sky clouded over, the sea rose, and the boat began to dance on the waves. Jacques said to him, "Not very nice out, huh?" He didn't answer. His face turned a sickly green. He went and knocked on the cabin door. He was admitted. He sat down on the floor, the only place left for a seasick clerical aide.

Father Vanderborg emerged furtively from the cabin to relieve himself over the rails on the boat's stern.

They all came out on the bridge before we got to the next port of call, Father Gomez's mission. Since this priest had been a New Hebridean missionary for so many years, Mr. Grasset had to see him. Vanderborg was already making excuses: "You know, it won't be very . . . comfortable. Still, we ought to stay for lunch. But don't worry, we'll eat much better afterwards."

I would have been surprised to see Father Gomez charge into the water, like Vanderborg, and bend over backwards to court Mr. Grasset. I was right. He didn't.

On the beach, Gomez told Jacques and me, "I would like to invite you to lunch with us, but Father Vanderborg tells me we have to talk about mission matters, privately. . . ."

Crossing the Selwyn Straits between Ambrym and Pentecost the sea was rough, as usual. The water builds up force coming from the Fiji Islands some six hundred miles to the east. The waves broke over the bridge. Moreover, it had begun to rain. Soaked and shivering, I became indignant about our fine traveling companions under their peaceful shelter.

"Talk about Christian charity!" I yelled. "How would it hurt them if they let us into the cabin? Are they afraid we'll steal their bunks? I've had it up to here. I'm going in there, invited or not. I defy them to throw me out!"

Jacques didn't want to come with me. He preferred a wet bridge to hostile company. I knocked on the door and asked the captain if I could enter. But he was no more privileged than we. If we were treated like criminal suspects, he was treated like a servant. Captain Pascal, with whom we got along well, shot a worried glance at the others. Gallantly, Mr. Grasset invited me to come in. Under the circumstances, it would have been difficult to do otherwise. Grasset, Biron, and Vanderborg were stretched out on their bunks. Gilbert huddled in a corner. Vanderborg got up, dropping his book, not because of my presence, I saw that right away, but because of the seasickness he hadn't yet been able to master. His face gray, and with a mean look toward me, he rushed out of the cabin onto the bridge in the pouring rain, to avoid vomiting inside, in front of everybody. Mr. Grasset invited me to sit on Vanderborg's bunk. Even if he distrusted us and would mainifestly have preferred to be without us, Mr. Grasset was always civil. And I wondered, once again, sitting on his bunk, what Father Vanderborg could have against us. We hadn't done anything to him or to anyone he knew!

Since Vanderborg didn't come back, out of boredom I picked up the book he had dropped: *OSS 117 and the Black Forces*. It was one of a series of the very worst spy books in modern French. In the first paragraph there were violent winds, doors cracking like pistol shots, and Nadia, the beautiful secret agent, who drew away from the window with a sensual shiver. I couldn't help laughing.

The radio was transmitting at that hour. Without asking permission, without saying please or thank you, Gilbert turned on the receiver in the captain's stead. Pascal was annoyed—he let it show—but he was used to such annoyances. I went on the bridge. All things considered, I preferred to be with Jacques, out in the rain.

The next stopover was at Father Karana's station on Pentecost Island. He is one of the rare native priests, and our aristocrats on board left him on the sidelines to talk with the European nuns.

Anyway, it wasn't the kind of mission that interested them very much and we didn't stay long.

Father Karana was not to last very long in the mission. One of the good sisters surprised him in a compromising position with an island woman one day. He was expedited to New Caledonia and locked up in a monastic prison.

At the next mission Father Vanderborg found a colleague to his liking, Father LeBeru, who came out into the water up to his waist to greet Catholic Aid. If Father Vanderborg had been disagreeable with us from the beginning, he was a choirboy next to this priest. LeBeru eyed us as a tough judge might stare at two young hoodlums accused of mugging an old lady. He is a young man, cut out of the hardest wood, with hard crystal eyes. He seemed to be quick and clever. I mistrusted him instinctively. With a sweet smile he invited the others, clearly the others, for a drink in the mission house before dinner. They left, leaving us on the beach. A nun popped out from behind a tree and waved. She invited Jacques and me to tea. Two minutes later we found ourselves in the simplest house of that wealthy mission, around the kitchen table with five French and Italian sisters.

Since our fellow voyagers never seemed to be in a rush to leave the prosperous missions, we had lots of time to walk around. An island man, about twenty-five years old, intercepted us. He asked us to follow him a little farther, behind one of the buildings. I assumed he didn't want to be seen talking to us.

"*Name b'long me, Cyril. You-fella you savvy Mastah Pierre Theuil, long Malekula?*" he asked.

"Yes."

"*Mastah Theuil him tellem long me, suppose you wannem school long mechanic, you come work long place b'long me. Me givem long you plenty shillings! One year, two year, you mechanic numbah one! My word, me wannem go long Mastah Theuil!*"

"Well, why don't you go?"

"*Father he sing out no! He cross too mass! He strong too mass!*"

After numerous questions we learned that Father LeBeru had taught Cyril how to paint the mission buildings. Cyril didn't particularly want to be a painter, but the priest needed one and Cyril was capable. Now the missionary was saying, basically: I taught you the work; it's this work that you'll do; and you'll do it for me and no one else. Cyril wanted us to talk to Father LeBeru about this. This time we refused, explaining that the missionary would undoubtedly not listen to us. But we told him that the priest clearly did not have the right to keep him. If Cyril wanted to leave, if he really wanted to learn to be a mechanic, all he had to do was get on the next boat and go! He was free! LeBeru couldn't do anything. There was nothing for Cyril to be afraid of.

The young man nodded his head sadly, slowly. *"You no savvy,"* he whispered. *"Father he strong too mass!"*

Jacques was disgusted.

The next time we would see Father LeBeru was a ceremonial day. All the local villages had gathered for a traditional dance in front of the mission. We were there, along with Kal, to film and photograph the event. After hours of work under the burning sun, Kal asked the priest if he might have a glass of water.

"No!" answered the missionary. "There isn't any! There's barely enough for us!"

After LeBeru had stormed off, a native from a nearby village brought Kal a quart of water and offered to get more if he wanted it.

There is no lack of water on Pentecost Island.

The rest of the voyage on the *St.-Joseph* continued in pretty much the same way. Vanderborg didn't talk to us, not even to say hello. But he developed the habit of talking with Grasset in front of us, as if we did not exist. Their conversations most frequently revolved around meals. They judged the last one, planned the next. They were rushing toward an Italian priest's mission, Vanderborg swearing that even in these islands he found the means to make delectable spaghetti Bolognese. Moreover, he had an excellent wine cellar. They decided not to stop at a native priest's mission, even though it was the outpost of the first native priest in the archipelago, since it was too late. That meant it was too close to lunchtime. Vanderborg had discreetly slipped into the conversation the fact that Father Sola had retained many of his Melanesian customs: he ate nothing but yams and taros and drank nothing but water.

I noticed that Grasset displayed a remarkable lack of curiosity throughout the trip. He didn't even ask the names of the islands we saw. He never spoke to a native, which seemed rather odd since the New Hebrideans, in theory anyway, were the future beneficiaries of Mr. Grasset's "Christian charity." His only questions came up when we passed by a cluster of houses on the coast of this or that island: "Is that a mission? Which denomination?"

Back in Santo, we went to see Father Sicot, one of the nicest missionaries, who took life as it came and to whom we could talk frankly. We reported, without enhancement and with precise details, Father Vanderborg's behavior. Father Sicot was not surprised. He laughed his giant elephant laugh.

"What do you think," asked Jacques, "he has against us? Is it just that he doesn't like our looks, or what?"

Father Sicot's reactions were clearly readable. We saw that he vacillated between a tendency to defend his colleagues in general and an undeniable lack of sympathy for this particular colleague. The reason was clear, but we hadn't thought of it. Father Vanderborg bragged many times to Mr. Grasset (and undoubtedly to others before) of the veritable miracles he had accomplished in his mission, which had been catastrophic before his arrival. To hear him, you'd think the buildings had been falling in ruin, the coconuts rotting at the foot of the palms, the people not working, not going to mass, not having the slightest idea of discipline, and so on. Implicitly, it was a severe criticism of his predecessor. And his predecessor was Father Sicot.

We never learned what the results of Mr. Grasset's study trip were. We never saw Mr. Biron again. He must still be Port-Vila's scoutmaster. In fact we never got to see a New Hebridean boy scout, but I'm willing to believe they exist.

Father Vanderborg continued his pious work in the islands. And we noticed in his mission, a few months later, a brand-new luxurious Land Rover. A mission servant was busy polishing it. Gilbert, his assistant, the seminarian, had renounced his ecclesiastical career. Like Father Karana, he had been surprised in a shocking position with a native woman. Since Gilbert was not yet a priest, he wasn't sent to a monastic prison. Instead, he was forced to marry the woman.

8

Entente Cordiale at the Antipodes

Jонн G. Paton, that dynamic and harsh Presbyterian missionary, wrote to Sir Henry Parkes, Prime Minister of New South Wales, on March 28, 1887. In this long, handsomely written letter, which resembles a petition more than a letter, Paton presented his opinion in an organized fashion: "I. Why Great Britain and Australia have the right to annex the New Hebrides." Fourteen numbered reasons followed. "II. We protest against France's annexation because . . ." A list of nine developments then followed. There were economic arguments: "The rich volcanic earth . . . will make these beautiful islands, if they are in British hands, tropical gardens of an inestimable commercial richness for Australia. . . ." Political arguments: "The spacious and deep New Hebridean ports will constitute a danger for Australia in times of war if they are under French control." And above all else, there were the moral arguments. What morality? A year before, the Melbourne newspaper *Argus* had called France "the most immoral nation on the earth." Paton, somewhat more diplomatically, seemed to share this opinion. He railed against the ill-fated influence of the "papist priests," against the French sale of alcohol and arms to the natives, against the New Caledonian ex-convicts who would settle in the New Hebrides if the archipelago were French. Paton already foresaw the arrival of a hundred thousand jailbirds in his beloved islands. He was a man who had come to think only in big numbers.

The Marists had similar reactions. The missionaries were not only God's agents, but the state's agents as well.

If English or English-speaking missionaries cried out for annexation by Great Britain, a certain number of British planters preferred to live under the French tricolor. Great Britain had very little desire to get involved with the New Hebrides.

As much as possible, England discouraged her subjects from colonization and handicapped them relative to the French colonists. The British government's principle was not to tolerate what could not be controlled. Thus, the English and Australian planters did not have the right to recruit labor in the islands, to legally register their property titles, to sell alcohol and arms to the natives. In London and Sydney, these restrictions were considered to be moral laws destined to protect the Melanesians. But since the traders from France and other countries were not subject to the same laws, the result was chaotic. The English planters broke every rule. They did what they wanted in hiding; or they operated through the French, who were acting legally; or else, weary of being forced into outlawry, they asked for French citizenship. Their government was not pleased; the Protestant missionaries, even less.

An Englishman with Irish origins, brought up in Australia, a naturalized Frenchman, basically an Anglophobe, did much to change the equilibrium in the New Hebrides. John Higginson is an important figure in the history of the Pacific. He was the principal owner and director of the nickel mines in New Caledonia. He wanted France to annex the New Hebrides, for reasons of general Francophilia and particular personal interests, since he needed a large, cheap supply of labor for his mines. Well placed to make waves, he led a propaganda campaign which reached the ministerial level in Paris. Nonetheless, in 1878 France and Great Britain signed an accord guaranteeing the independence of the New Hebrides. This did nothing to stop the political activities concerning the archipelago, which had no real value to London or Paris.

Higginson was not a quitter and he had a good idea. If the land belonged to the French, France would have a good excuse for annexing the islands. In 1882, already in possession of some 250,000 acres himself, he formed in Noumea the Caledonian Company of the New Hebrides, which bought up another 250,000 acres with dizzying speed. The natives would have sold almost anything to obtain a share of the treasure carried by the *Ne Oblie*, Higginson's boat—bottles of gin, carbines, beads, calico scraps, axes, and knives. In some cases they voluntarily sold their well-placed lands. In other cases, it is not at all certain that they knew they were giving up their real estate in exchange for tempting gifts. At least, let's say that there were "misunderstandings." When many of the titles were examined fifty years later, the distances were found to have been measured in estimated walking hours (since the company's officials had no desire to leave the boat to verify the boundaries on foot); that the limits were "a certain tree here, a certain rock there," often impossible to distinguish; that in at least one case, the village name given as a boundary meant "mountain" in the native language—and as there were many mountains on the island in question and no village called Mountain, this particular title gave the right to anything and everything. But Higginson was a businessman and not a moralist. His aim, in his own words, was "to be able, by any means, to buy as many lands as possible. . . ." He was more chauvinistic than any born Frenchman. When an important Port-Vila chief ceded to him "a fairly considerable territory of excellent land" and agreed to recognize a French protectorate, Higginson wrote, "For me this was one of the most beautiful days of my life . . . among enthusiastic cries of *Vive la France! Vive la République!*"

Neither were there any difficulties in buying land from English planters, since many of them were on the verge of bankruptcy. But the Protestant missionaries, particularly the Presbyterians, and some of the planters were as tenacious as Higginson. In 1883 a petition "signed" by the Tanna natives asked the *"big-fella Queen"* to send a *"big-fella boat"* to protect them against the *"wee-wees"* ("oui oui," or Frenchmen).

Thanks largely to Higginson, France now had something to defend in the New Hebrides. In 1886 the New Caledonian governor sent two naval infantry companies to the islands. Their presence enraged the Presbyterian missionaries. Great Britain still did nothing toward annexation, but it was clear she would not permit the French to annex the archipelago either. The New Hebrideans scarcely suspected that their islands were such a thorn in the side for two important world powers.

Things were really getting out of hand. In this archipelago British missionaries and planters, French missionaries and planters, and the Melanesians all rubbed shoulders, and most problems were settled with gunfire. There was no government at all to protect any of them.

In 1887 France and Great Britain took their first step together. A joint naval commission was established in order to "maintain order and protect the persons and properties of French citizens and British subjects in the New Hebrides." It was an ineffective compromise. The warships tried to defend the Europeans against the Melanesians by means of punitive expeditions after each aggression by the natives. But no one, at least officially, defended the Melanesians against the Europeans, or the French against the English, or the English against the French. Most disputes arose over land. And though the commission was supposed to protect the properties of all nationals from both countries, it had no authority whatsoever to determine the ownership or extent of the properties to be protected. If an Englishman, a Frenchman, and a Melanesian each claimed to be the proprietor of a certain beach or a certain tree, it was still the boldest or the best-armed man who won.

In 1906 the New Hebrides was declared a "communal zone of influence." The Franco-British or Anglo-French Condominium (depending on the speaker's nationality), a government unique in the world, was born. It was reinforced by the Protocol of 1914. At the time no one believed a colonial marriage between the French and the British could last. Surprisingly, however, not only did it last; it has remained practically unchanged since 1914.

I went down to Port-Vila to see how the Condominium could have shown itself in the tiny capital. The Union Jack and the tricolor were waving side by side, at the same height. But I understood the country's style all at once when I saw the French residence at the summit of a hill which dominates Vila Bay—and in the very middle of this bay, on an islet, the British residence. A veritable microcosm of Europe. With opera glasses, each resident commissioner could even keep an eye on his fellow commissioner's living room.

I was given the honor of hearing the following story within twenty-four hours after my arrival (and many times since). It was introduced as the clearest and most concise possible explanation of the Condominium and its workings. One Sunday morning, a French planter decides to drive into town. At the same time, an English functionary sets out for a tour of the island. Since both of them have the tendency to conserve their national habits, the Frenchman drives on the right and the Englishman on the left. The inevitable result occurs around a sharp curve: two cars are transformed into accordions, resulting in one terrible argument. The Queen, the Republic, and the good Lord are invoked in two different languages. But since disputes between the French and the English are never too serious in the New Hebrides, our two heroes end their adventure peacefully in a café, one seated behind his anisette, the other behind a gin and tonic. The Entente Cordiale is cordial once more.

Whether a Frenchman or an Englishman, the teller of this story will inevitably add at the end, with a wink, this little tip. In a Vila bistro you can always tell the French from the English by the color of the liquid in front of them. If it's clear and looks like water, it's gin. If it's milky white or yellow, it's some kind of Gallic anisette brew—a picturesque if invalid way of identifying people, since many Europeans in this country have a penchant for whiskey and beer. As for the New Hebrideans, the only alcoholic beverages they are permitted, by law, are beer and wine. I have seen some of them drinking a mixture of the two and others drinking cologne!

It's interesting to note that in this country equally governed by the English and the French, cars do drive to the right all the same. Why? Any European on the street (the New Hebrideans couldn't care less) will tell you that the first person to bring a car to the New Hebrides was a Frenchman—and he made the law! It's possible.

Vila is a model of the smart little tropical capital. Enlivened by the sailboats, trading skiffs, and from time to time even a big freighter or cargo-passenger ship, the town embraces the deep bay, vibrant with intense colors; the bluish green Melanesian vegetation, the turquoise Pacific irradiated by coral, and the reef's white phosphorescence.

Main Street winds along the bay. Behind the waterfront, small streets bordered by Vietnamese and Chinese shops and wooden houses, decorated by bougainvilleas and frangipani, climb steeply. They cross a sinuous avenue and disappear into a jumble of tropical gardens. Dreadful concrete buildings, called "modern" by their proud inhabitants, dot the little city without managing to spoil its overall appearance.

I arrived by taxi from the airport. In the center of town, two officers, one in an English uniform topped off by a Scottish pompon, the other in a French uniform with a colonial garrison cap, blocked all access to the principal street. The Condominium's advisory council was meeting that day, presided over by the two President Commissioners representing the Queen and the Republic. And they could not tolerate the noise of cars.

This council is the only "representative" assembly at the Condominium level, even though the majority of its members are not elected. It has no legislative function. Its members advise, no more. The governed thus have the impression of participating in the government. Nothing very important comes out of this assembly. It's hardly taken seriously. As with all aspects of the Condominium, appearance is the key. The major decisions come from Paris and London in any case.

To govern only about eighty thousand people, three administrations—the French, the British, and the Condominium—each follow their own laws.

The two Condominium powers conserve their authority over their own citizens by means of the two national administrations. Moreover, each foreigner who visits this country must choose to submit to either the French or the British administration. Thus the visitor becomes, for the duration of his stay, or for his lifetime if he resides in the New Hebrides, subject to one or the other, an honorary Frenchman or Englishman.

What becomes of the New Hebridean natives in all this? They do not have the right to choose either French or British nationality. They are New Hebrideans, of course, but this nationality does not exist. They are citizens of no country. At home, they manage mostly by playing the English off against the French. The

The native English police force. *Kal Muller*

Condominium is pandemonium. The joint administration of the Condominium includes the services of the public works, customs, agriculture, post office, and telecommunications, everything that concerns the archipelago in general and does not concern, at least in principle, the politics of the two countries. But even there, at the heart of this cooperative system, the English and the French find the means to neutralize themselves. Shall we construct a landing strip on a given island? Oui, because there is a French school. No, because there is a French school and no English interests. When I was in Santo, the discussion centered around the necessity for public toilets at the port. I couldn't see how the national interests were involved. But in any case, for months the English and the French couldn't come to an agreement. Should people be allowed to relieve themselves under proper conditions on the quay, or no? Would it be worth the cost? When people land, can't they wait to get home or to a hotel or a bistro? Can't the dock

The native French police force. *Kal Muller*

workers just as easily find a quiet corner in nature? All decisions of this kind require agreement between the French and the English. And since about all they agree on is the principle of change without risk or disruption, the status quo reigns. (Public toilets finally were installed, undoubtedly because some French or English dignitary was too uncomfortable while waiting to get to a suitable location.)

Services as important as education are left for the two national administrations working in isolation. The New Hebrideans have the right to send their children to the English or the French schools. And then there are the mission institutions, that is, the various Protestant and Marist schools. A complicated rivalry has resulted, which is not necessarily in the New Hebrideans' best interest. Often in one part of an island, you'll find two schools trying to attract the same native students, while on the other end of the island, there will be no school at all.

And justice—sweet justice!—is more complicated than everything else. One court is reserved for French subjects, another for the British. A third exists for native matters. In the islands the lower courts are presided over by a French or English Delegate. But the key to the system is the Joint Court in Port-Vila, conceived in the Condominium's spirit of international cooperation. It rules in all cases between New Hebrideans (and also serves as the court of appeals in native affairs) and between New Hebrideans and Europeans. There is one French judge, one English judge, and the president who, in principle, must be of a neutral nationality. At first, the King of Spain nominated the court's president, and for years the post was occupied by Tomas Alonso y Zabala, Count of Buena Esperanza. As a neutral president, he was the ideal choice. The Count spoke very little English or French. He didn't understand a word of any of the native tongues. Moreover, he was deaf as a post. For years now the English and the French have been fulfilling the role of president together.

In matters between natives and Europeans, or between English and French, the machine grinds away with difficulty and sometimes breaks down. So poorly does it work that we saw a Frenchman accused of murdering an Australian (and with witnesses!) who was released on his island with a provisional liberty—which seemed to become liberty, plain and simple—as gradually the whole business was forgotten.

And this wasn't the only unpunished murder. I concluded that in the New Hebrides, it is better to kill someone than, say, to insult a judge. During our stay, for example, a woman who runs a bistro was brought before the tribunal for not having respected closing time. She dared to call the magistrate every name under the sun. She was thrown into jail for one month. But Monsieur Bob, with his pistols and his brutality, has certainly never served a stretch in the New Hebrides.

To praise somewhat the Condominium's inventiveness, take the case of the archipelago's currency: the Australian dollar and the New Hebridean franc (not the same as the Pacific Colonial franc used in Polynesia and New Caledonia). The value of the latter has been based on the value of the first since World War II. One hundred New Hebridean francs equal one Australian dollar. This would seem to simplify things—but try to mail a letter. The post office depends on the Condominium, and since the English and the French have never agreed on the franc or the dollar for the sale of these pretty New Hebridean stamps, they are sold for "gold cents" or "centimes-or," coins that don't really exist. For the price in gold cents you still pay in Australian dollars or New Hebridean francs, and the postal workers do some fancy arithmetic acrobatics trying to figure out what you owe. To send a letter, as with so many other things in the New Hebrides, you cannot be in a hurry.

The French and the English understand each other best when it comes to national holidays. The rule of thumb is that there must be an equal number of English and French holidays. It's something like a parlor game. I'll give you Ascension Day for Prince Charles's birthday and so on. The New Hebrideans do not take any umbrage. They have nothing against days off.

November 11 is a holiday shared by the English and the French, and the ceremony they sponsor in Port-Vila is worth seeing: real hand-in-hand solidarity, with the native police forces lined up opposite each other in parade dress.

No one has yet suggested that Queiros's discovery of the archipelago or Cook's baptism be added to the long list of national holidays. Perhaps it will come.

The Melanesians don't have any luck. Having no traditional written language, they cannot give the exact dates of their history as pretexts for days off. One of these days, though probably not too soon, maybe they'll have the anniversary of their independence to celebrate.

If the Europeans have a tendency to make fun of such a government, they nonetheless remain fundamentally in favor of it for one precise reason. The French and the English could never agree on the principle of taxes. Thus, though the customs bureau functions outrageously well, there is still no income tax in this country. For numerous people, for no other reason than this, it's a dreamland.

For us, Vila represented a few days' worth of the good bourgeois life every once in a while. As a number of publicity folders boast, Vila does have its charms. It is truly a pretty little city. The climate is better than in the northern islands. All the hotels are adequate and there is even one international-class hotel. There is a small cultural center which interested us. Sunk into the ground in front of the center is La Pérouse's massive anchor, salvaged from Vanikoro, an impressive symbol of the lost expedition. There are also some amusing stores where you can buy all sorts of overpriced New Hebridean souvenirs, from false native sculptures to real, if often inferior, pigs' teeth. A warning to tourists who hope to uncover a beautiful art object (the real thing, not the Melanesian equivalent of the small bronze Statue of Liberty): for a long time now, in Vila, they haven't existed. And if the owner of a junk shop who pretends to be an explorer takes you into a corner to swear to you that he brought this statue from the depths of Malekula where it was used in pagan rites, or that it was adored for generations by the savage tribes, well, don't believe a word of it!

European art in Port-Vila is a different story. Tahiti had missed out on Gauguin. No one knew, before his death, that he was an important painter. The Tahitians made fun of him and refused to pay a cent for his canvases. In Vila the same mistake will not be made! On the contrary. Each dabbler in art is treated like a potential Gauguin. You never know. The local painters have even developed a very effective gimmick as a result of this attitude. They do not like to talk about it, for fear of breaking the charm, but I'm going to tell all anyway. The principle is this: get one of your paintings sold to a high functionary in the country. Give it to him if necessary, but only on the condition that he promise to give the impression he has paid dearly for his work of art. Numerous other functionaries and a good portion of the good bourgeoisie will compete, in New Hebridean francs and Australian dollars, to be the first on their blocks to have one of your works. They'll even commission paintings and pay in advance. It's a simple system, but it works. Oddly enough, there is a real painter in this tiny archipelago. Tatin d'Avenières believes in his art, and over the years his reputation has grown steadily throughout the South Pacific.

Despite all the amenities, our stays in the capital became more and more tiresome—we had not come so far for that—and we avoided going there as much as possible. We preferred the less pretty, more rude and empty Santo. At least Santo had maintained its blunt Far Westness, while Vila had become pretentious, like a lovely island girl who makes the mistake of wearing makeup and going to the hairdresser. Vila "society" takes itself seriously. Too many beautiful people and beautiful manners for a small capital lost in a far corner of the Pacific. Between the French and English functionaries, between the Europeans and the New Hebrideans, an ambience of distant politeness reigns.

We were invited for a drink at the home of one of the most beautiful people, an important, now old, planter, who lives like an old aristocrat. I have never been so ill at ease in anyone's house. His living room is furnished with four deep easy chairs, one in each corner of the room. Right in the middle is a small, low table, which serves as a bar. It is impossible to converse normally across yards of emptiness. I had the impression that the effect was intentional. The master of the house could control the situation better if his guests were uncomfortable. The whiskey was served, not by one of his servants, but by one of the guests, another pillar of Vila society, who effaced himself voluntarily before a larger bank account. In direct proportion as our aristocrat lowered the level of his high-quality bottle of Scotch (surely not the first he had opened since that morning) he became loquacious. Knowing that I was a journalist, he wanted (with the manner of one accustomed to being obeyed) me to help him write his memoirs. There are misunderstandings in my life, he said, and I want to explain myself. If I hadn't said I would return to interview him, he would surely keep me prisoner in his domain. So, I said it, but I didn't go back. I knew what it was all about. High Society does not talk about it, but among ordinary Vila people this gentleman has a dirty reputation. His name evokes stories of illegal recruitments for his plantation, of poor treatment of his laborers, of dubious trafficking. Moreover, what is unpardonable for the large majority of New Hebridean French people, he spoke out a bit too much against the English and against the Franco-British alliance at the beginning of World War II. At that time, political dissension was no joking matter. Our planter was expelled from the country, and it took him years to be allowed to come back to his properties.

For Port-Vila 1940 was a momentous year. After the capitulation of France in June, Henri Sautot, the resident commissioner of the New Hebrides, declared his personal intention to continue the struggle. He assembled all the French in town and invited them to join him. If they said no, he would leave his job to go offer his services to the English. More than six hundred men and two hundred women, coming from throughout the archipelago, were present for Sautot's second important meeting in Vila. They all backed him solidly except for three men and one woman, who were asked to leave the room. Thus, with a telegram to De Gaulle to announce the quasi-unanimous decision, the New Hebrides became the first overseas territory to rally officially behind Free France.

The Americans landed in 1942. Vila, with the entire island of Vate, took the code name Rose. Santo was called Banyan. Guadalcanal, that dangerous neighbor just to the north of the archipelago, teeming with Japanese, was Cactus.

During our last visit to Port-Vila we stayed at Henri Joly's house. We had met this entrepreneur and his charming English wife on Malekula. The Jolys have a lovely house and large garden in the center of town.

We arrived early in the evening. We were tired and went to sleep early. Henri settled into an armchair to read. It was very hot and I could only doze. As if in a bad dream, I heard very disturbing sounds—scratchy chants, furious yelling, and cymbal claps. I woke up with a start. Was it a demonstration, a revolution, or what? I left my room and found Henri, still reading peacefully.

"It's nothing," he assured me. "It's the madmen."

For, as we would see the following morning, the Jolys live just across the street from the native lunatic asylum, a large cement building with barred slits seven or eight feet off the ground which serve as windows. Through them you see the unhappy heads of the "patients." They hoist themselves up by the bars to get a view of the outside world. The children in the street throw stones at them.

"If you're not crazy when they lock you in there," said Mr. Joly, "you are after two or three months. I know just how it happens, and how long it takes. Whether I like it or not, I have the sight before my eyes, every day."

According to the Jolys, the French have wanted to move the asylum outside the city for a long time, but the English have not agreed to the necessary funds.

That night, the noise was even louder. It grew intolerable. Even Mr. Joly, who is used to it, lost his patience. He called the head doctor.

"This is inhuman!" he shouted. "Come do something for those poor people. They're in a harrowing state!"

"Don't get so upset," replied the doctor, yawning. "I'll send over a nurse right away to give them some shots to calm them down. In just a little while, you'll be able to sleep undisturbed."

Bravo, Condominium.

9

Slit-Gongs, Black-Palms, and Bank Accounts

H I M , *little chief*," said Tofor, pointing a finger at one of his brothers. "*Him, big chief little bit*," he continued, indicating a second brother. "*And ME*," awarding himself a big punch on the stomach, "*ME, MUCH CHIEF PLENTY BIG!*" His words were laced with French. Normally, he spoke to us in pidgin, but for such declarations, he liked to show off his linguistic versatility.

Tofor is north Ambrym's important customary chief. His authority extends over all the non-Christianized population of the region, and even the Christian natives treat him as an important chief. Tainmal, his father, was an extremely powerful chief, an implacable traditionalist who led an extremely harsh resistance against the influence of the Europeans, particularly the missionaries. Now an old man, he had already passed on his chiefly offices to Tofor when we met him in his village, Fanla. It is not a hereditary chieftainship as on the Big Nambas plateau, but as is often the case, the chief's oldest son was the most highly graded man in the society after his father. Tainmal impressed us. It is true that old age had stolen his ardor. In his heyday, we would have been poorly received. However, he has lost none of his dignity. He's a handsome old man, with fine features accentuated by a white beard which tapers down to two points.

Tofor is also a handsome man. He's about forty-five years old, but you'd say he was younger. Not the typical Melanesian pretty boy. He's got character. He's alive, intelligent, crafty, shrewd, and his expressions display these qualities. Tofor perpetuates, more or less, his father's principles. He prevents the missionaries from setting foot in Fanla and in the other traditional villages. Moreover, he is not afraid of them. He feels superior to them. Who needs Christians, he asked us one day, to tell you there's a God? We've always known there's a God, but—here's where the others are wrong—he's not called God. He's called Barkulkul! Tofor is diplomatic enough to maintain good relations with the missionaries. However, he would never compromise with them. The reason for this intransigency has less to do with theological questions than with questions of customs. The missionaries insist on monogamy. And that is an idea that Tofor finds, quite frankly, stupid.

Like Tainmal, he is in favor of custom. He keeps up the traditional life to a large extent in Fanla. But we quickly understood that he knows European civilization well—very well, in fact—and that he doesn't disdain all its elements. He particularly likes money and alcohol.

A Chinese skiff, the *Ling Sing*, dropped Jacques and me on the coast of Ambrym after a horrendous night at sea. (Kal would arrive by another boat a few days later.) What a rotten tub! Leaving Santo the night before, the smiling and friendly captain, Raymond Chan, had told us to go sleep in the hold, since we were in for some bad weather. Anyway, there was not enough room to stretch out on the bridge, overloaded as it was with cans of gasoline. There wasn't much space in the hold, either. We were forced to settle down right next to the motor, which made a deafening noise, released sickening odors, and smoked so much that one crew member's only work was to stay beside the cursed machine and pour water into it every five minutes. I seriously wondered what the risks of an explosion were. All the same, we were finally falling asleep when the rain began, and the hold was closed so the cargo wouldn't get wet. After a few minutes it was unbearable.

I was the first to give up. It was stifling. The boat rocked to such a degree that I had trouble climbing the narrow ladder which led to the small steerage. I went out to breathe, but I couldn't stay outside. The waves crashed over the slippery bridge, and the *Ling Sing*'s rails were no more than two feet high. It was impossible to wedge into a corner because of the cans of gas. My chances of falling overboard were excellent.

I returned to the minuscule steerage. The captain was kind, but there really just wasn't enough space. In the bulkhead, though, there's a niche referred to as the boat's "store," containing the breads, rice sacks, rolls of calico, and other odds and ends that are sold in the islands. I sat, as best I could, at the edge of this recess. Jacques, half asphyxiated too, soon came up to join me. The steerage, like the hold, was completely closed because of the torrential rains. The little air there was, was impregnated with smells of gasoline, copra, and mustiness.

How could the captain take it? How could he breathe normally? Undoubtedly he was used to it, like people who live across from a celluloid factory get accustomed to that, because he seemed completely at ease. Jacques and I both had an urgent need to go out, to not be sick inside the steerage. The captain asked us to stay put. It was too dangerous to move around. Evidently, if we had an accident, he'd have a lot of explaining to do.

"If you are ill," he recommended delicately, "relieve yourselves in a corner of the niche. Don't worry about the stock!"

We tried to squeeze the merchandise together a little, in order not to ruin everything. It was impossible. The little space was ready to burst. The inevitable moment came when we could no longer hold back. We spent the rest of the night vomiting on the breads. The captain watched us, amused.

"Don't worry about it," he clucked, "it's not serious. I'll still sell them to the natives!"

Filthy rotten boat! When I learned a few months later that it had given up its soul by sinking all at once, for no apparent reason, I was neither surprised nor saddened.

To say we were not fresh when we landed at Fona, a Presbyterian village on the northern coast of Ambrym, would not be an exaggeration. Tofor was on the beach to greet us. He had told us not to bring any presents, that he would choose them himself in the Fona cooperative. He had come down from Fanla to make his choice without delay. We went to the store together. He chose for us at the same time. *"Two cases beer b'long me, two cases beer b'long you. Man b'long me savvy carryem cases long Fanla. Hey-hey! Allez! Quick-time!"*

Tofor is always exuberant. We were very happy to buy him a stock of beer. Ambrym is not Malekula. A good part of the man-bush population, like the man-salt-water, consume a considerable amount of alcohol. But since we were still sick from our little jaunt on the *Ling Sing*, we were not too keen on buying beers for ourselves. Tofor explained that it was necessary. We had to have them to be able to offer them to him and to others in the village. We gave in. He was the boss, and we were the guests.

We all went to Fanla together. For once, it wasn't a difficult walk. True, we climbed continually, but next to the Mbotogote trek it was a stroll in the park. Tofor set us up immediately in his guest hut, constructed with plaited walls in the Ambrym style, but topped with a corrugated metal roof of which he was very proud.

Tofor was a personage and we knew it right away. If you saw a photo of him dressed, as he was, in the customary nambas and bark belt with a red hibiscus tucked behind an ear, you'd say he was a real traditional Melanesian, under no European influence, like Ilabnambenpen. Not true. He parked us in our hut, asked us to wait a few minutes for him, and then, to our stupefaction, returned with a bottle of Beaujolais and a bottle of Côtes-du-Rhône which he had dug up from the earth floor of his own hut! We had to drink to our arrival. There was no corkscrew and Tofor asked Jacques to get the bottles opened with a nail. That done, we were ready to enjoy ourselves. But Tofor warned us immediately that if anyone should come, it was *our* wine and we were drinking alone. In Fanla there is a taboo against wine and beer.

"Time me drink, head b'long me no good," explained the chief. He showed us a little wound on his leg. The last time he drank too much, he fell somewhere in the jungle. He added, however, that we could offer beers to his brothers if they came. We didn't understand the situation. There was a taboo against alcohol. Tofor had made us buy beer. Certain people could drink alcoholic beverages openly in the middle of the day, and others drink them in hiding. What's the story?

Finally, we got to the truth. There was a taboo, but a special one, which Tainmal had decreed though he was no longer chief at the time. Tainmal was still the most highly graded man, and he was Tofor's father. This was an important fact, for the taboo concerned only Tofor. In other words, Tainmal had forbidden his oldest son to drink. And Tofor, being the good Melanesian he is, called that a taboo. We were intrigued. We asked the chief why his father had set the personal taboo. No more dissimulating. Now Tofor spoke frankly, though his terms were a bit euphemistic. The last time he was drunk, he had *"talk-talked long belly"* of a married woman, his cousin Luan's wife. Tofor had had to pay a penalty of one pig and a few Australian dollars. In Ambrym you don't play with a woman's honor under any circumstances. Since Tainmal had judged that the evil came from the beers which Tofor had consumed during the day, he had also punished his son with this taboo outside the normal ones. Tofor didn't take it all too seriously. He had every intention of continuing to drink. Only he didn't want his father to know. For an important chief over forty years old, this was something.

Tainmal, who felt his age, spent his days sitting on the ground, watching people pass before him, sighing toward the treetops. Occasionally during the day he shifted position, following the sun. In this country, where everyone is used to excessive heat, old bones require a maximum. Tainmal was uncomfortable in the shade. In a society where the aged are usually honored, no one seemed to pay attention to him. We often spoke to him. He hardly knew pidgin, but we got along well with this ancient chief who had hated whites in the old days. He must feel that the world is changing very fast. During our stay, we bought him a gift at the coastal plantation store: a pneumatic mattress to cushion his aching joints. His daughter Massi appropriated it at once. "Old men don't need modern things like this. Young women do."

Without meaning to, we brought some entertainment into Tofor's life. The day after our arrival, we had to spend the afternoon writing certain brief letters so we would be able to send them on the boat that would be bringing Kal. We hadn't had the time to write these letters before leaving Santo on the *Ling Sing*, which had hoisted anchor a few hours earlier than expected because of the weather. Tofor set us up in a small kiosk, open on all sides, filled by a rudely cut table and two benches. The chief was proud of it. It was his "dining room."

The important little missives in question were invitations to our wedding. Because, yes, at last, it was set. Jacques and I were to be married. Without waiting to return to France or the States. We had both written letters to our parents which began with the words: "Sit down. I have some news for you. . . ." Okay, we're "hip" and a marriage was not going to upset the world. But you don't have to be Melanesian to have your traditional side. It was a very serious matter for us. The very modern Tofor, on the other hand, thought it was a scream. *"Hey-hey! Zak! Woman b'long you! You payem how many pigs long papa b'long Sarrlin?"* What a wonderful thought. I could just imagine my father summoned to O'Hare Airport to pick up the squealing bride-price.

Tofor had two wives at the time. His first wife had died, apparently of old age. His current wife-number-one was no spring chicken herself. Her age was perhaps fifty-five, but since New Hebridean women age so quickly, you could easily believe at first glance that she was seventy. Tofor explained to us that he liked to have a wife older than himself as number one because *"old-fella woman him savvy work good too mass."* And besides, Tofor added with a wink, she permitted her husband to "walk about," that is, to play around. His second wife was about thirty years old and rather pretty.

Tofor had had, very briefly, a third wife who was very young. He had paid 11 pigs and 140 Australian dollars (about 165 U.S. dollars) for her. Only his two first wives did not want to accept the third. They threatened to kill her if Tofor did not return her. He consulted a Condominium Delegate and concluded that if there were a murder, he would have had *"plenty too mass trouble."* So he returned the young woman against his own wishes and was reimbursed.

Tofor has never been satisfied with this solution. In the good old days, he swore, it never would have happened that way. In the name of Barkulkul, I never would have let my wives push me around like that! But Tofor told us he still had every intention of getting a third wife one of these days. And if his other wives give him any trouble next time, well, he'll just get rid of them! The third, he explained, would have to know how to read and write.

That would be very useful. And then, he added, wryly giving me the once-over, if she were a European, that wouldn't bother him at all!

As for children, Tofor has a daughter in her twenties by his deceased wife. She is now married and lives in Santo. There are three other children by his present second wife. One of them, Bongalibu, about ten years old, clever and full of humor, became our good friend right away.

We invited Tofor to our marriage. He knows Santo. He would not have felt lost in town. We offered to pay for the round trip. No chance. There would be quite a number of Europeans at the ceremony. And Tofor likes very much to welcome Europeans in Fanla, but he does not like to expose himself alone in the world of whites. I understood. In shorts and a shirt he is just some New Hebridean, automatically placed in an inferior position to the Europeans of the archipelago. In nambas on Ambrym, he is the big chief. Why, then, doesn't he go to town in nambas? Because, in town, a New Hebridean in traditional costume, even a chief, is too much of a spectacle. A circus sideshow attraction. A "real live native chief," not a man. On Ambrym, explained Tofor so that we would understand perfectly, a man who wears a nambas is a *man!* No, I saw there was no way. Tofor could not celebrate our marriage with us comfortably. The realities of this situation distressed us.

If the chief was already amused by the writing of our invitations, he was even more so to learn that it was my birthday. *"Fete b'long Sarrlin! Hey-hey!"* he screamed, thrusting his arms toward the sky.

In Fanla, any excuse is good for making a night of it. We tried to calm Tofor down, feeling that things could easily get out of hand. Nothing doing. A party is a party. At three o'clock in the afternoon, about twenty villagers came to give me a little concert. Traditional music is reserved for traditional ceremonies, but in Fanla everybody also knows "plantation songs," typical South Seas tunes. Tofor's young sister Massi, who is about seventeen years old, played the guitar. Someone had a ukelele. Twenty strong voices sang in pidgin with spirit. The words pleased me and I recopied them later with Massi's help. Among others:

Tchou tchou tchou tchou
Papa push mama
Tchou tchou tchou tchou
Papa push mama
Me askem you-ou!
Long plantation!
Me jealous long you
'cause me wannem one thing
Me jealous long you
'cause me wannem one thing
Me askem you-ou
Long plantation!

And also:

Long Aori one place b'long me go round,
Me no findem one place allsame Aori,
Early morning sun he rise up,
Me look so very nice,
Buttercup allsame bow-lily,
I'm crazy in my heart.

And just one more:

Long Santo long half past ten
Me shakem hand long sweetheart b'long me
Me think-think me sorry too mass
He good you-me turnem round.
My darling I'm still remember you,
Ta-ta! C'losup me drown.
Lucky makem plenty work long ship,
C'losup me losem home.

They had a considerable repertory, and with the guitar and the ukelele it was captivating. At about five o'clock Tofor, acting as master of ceremonies, announced that it was over. He sent the musicians away so that they could prepare dinner.

"You see?" I said to Jacques. "You thought it was going to degenerate, but it was a wonderful little party!"

Tofor overheard me and, understanding French fairly well, answered by laughing out loud at me. This wasn't the party, he proclaimed. That's to come. First, everyone had to build up his strength by eating some yams. And after, since it's your party, you buy the drinks, hey-hey! Oh no, I protested, but Tofor cut me off. Yes! He's the chief and he made the rules.

We ate. Since the sun sets at six o'clock, it was already night. Afterwards, Tofor ordered us to bring out the two cases of beer which we had in our hut thanks to him. But not both cases! Yes! Hop to it! He's the chief, and he gives the orders. You'll buy more tomorrow morning. Tonight we drink everything!

In a small clearing more than fifty men, women, and children were gathered. Only the most highly graded men, Tofor's brothers and cousins, had the right to drink the beer. Tainmal, leaning on a branch to support his weak legs, was served first. In honor of the occasion he lifted the taboo against his son for the evening. So Tofor had the pleasure of downing the Australian beers in front of everybody. What joy! He wanted us to dance. First, traditional dances. He yanked Jacques off to dance next to him. He put me in between his two wives. Then he wanted to show that he knew European dances, too. He led Massi in an unrestrained number that should have been accompanied by a rock group instead of the Fanla chorus. We were all brothers and sisters! Tainmal watched us, bent over his cane, laughing softly. I had the impression they had drunk more than our beers. Tofor set to pulling his aged father, the one-time big chief, by his pointed beard to get him to dance. Poor old Tainmal, he had a hard time just standing up. Enough. Jacques and I suggested strongly that "*you-me go sleep now.*" Tofor was undoubtedly waiting for that, because without hesitation he sent everyone away except his father and brothers, the elite. He whispered to us with imperative motions, "*You wait small!*" When the people had left, he brought us to the little kiosk and had us sit on the benches around the table. He brought out, from I don't know where, a bottle of whiskey. He took a good hit and then passed it on. "Okay, okay," he sputtered. "*Now here you-me talk-talk long something taboo!*"

Two weeks later there would be a grade-taking ceremony, a Nimangki, in Fanla. In a month we would see their Rom Dance. Because, in Fanla, even if the people are considered to be "*false-man-bush,*" tradition holds strong at the center of their lives.

In Fanla each Nimangki grade is associated with a sculpture. For each of the thirteen grades that exist in northern Ambrym, there is a different statue. We were going to see the ceremony for the sixth grade, *Sagaran*. The ceremonial period began with the

An Ambrym man at work on a black-palm-trunk statue. *Kal Muller*

fabrication of the statue *maguene sagaran* cut from the trunk of a
"black-palm," as the islanders call them, that is, from a tree-fern.

Several men went into the jungle to find a tree of the appropriate size. They brought it back, singing all the while, dragging it
with lianas to the middle of the ceremonial ground. Their arrival

was celebrated by a drum concert. Baskets of yams were brought as an offering. A pig was sacrificed. The meal was prepared and eaten in front of the black-palm trunk, in honor of the statue that would exist very soon.

Tofor and his brother Itoul had the privilege of starting the work and executing much of it. Itoul traced designs with a leaf which left stains on the trunk. Tofor began to follow the greenish lines, gouging them out. But on Ambrym all the men are artists, and many participated in the making of the statue, cutting a bit here or painting a stroke there. Little by little the forms emerged. At the top of the trunk there was a human face about a yard long. Below, a lizard almost as long climbed toward the mask. It was intriguing. I asked what the drawings meant. No one could explain them to me. It was something *"b'long custom,"* that's all. The completed statue was put in place under a sacred platform at the edge of the ceremonial ground. Tofor began the painting. The surface was prepared with a mixture of volcanic ash and coconut milk. There were four colors: black made with ash, white from crushed coral, green from a hard clay, red from dried fruit. The methods were masterful and the result was beautiful. Four pigs were sacrificed to celebrate the handsome colors and the end of the ritual work. But the sculpture is not made to last. Each ceremony demands the same work. A statue that has already been used is left to rot somewhere in the forest.

The extraordinary Ambrym drums, on the other hand, last for generations. They are wooden slit-gongs, shaped from the trunk of a breadfruit tree. The tallest one I saw was over six yards high. A human head with saucer eyes was sculpted above the slit. Sometimes two or even three heads are sculpted, one on top of the other. These drums are unique in all of Melanesia. I was very curious to know how this form had evolved on Ambrym and nowhere else. But even the islanders don't know how, or when, except that the drums are old-old-old. Kal, Jacques, and I were fascinated by the artistic sense of these men and by the important role art plays in their lives.

How do they learn it all? As the statue was being set in place, a boy about fourteen years old casually picked up the base of a coconut frond used for beating the biggest drums and played at playing. Honghong, Tofor's cousin, noticed him, encouraged him to try, tapped out an accompanying rhythm on a small drum. Afterwards the boy was too shy to meet the eyes of the others, who were smiling kindly, but too proud of himself not to smile, too.

Just before Kal got to Fanla two other Europeans came up to the village. Tofor looked for us at our hut. *"You come, you come, quick-quick,"* he called. *"Father he stop!"*

"What Father?" asked Jacques distrustfully.

"Father Vanderborg more Father LeBeru."

Those two! Forget it! After their attitude toward us during the trip on the *St.-Joseph*, we didn't have the slightest desire to see them again. We didn't explain our point of view to Tofor. He was already against the missionaries and we didn't care to influence him any more. So, we used our work as a pretext. Jacques rushed toward a camera and began taking it apart. I plunged into one of my notebooks. We couldn't go out because we had too much to do. But Tofor wasn't born yesterday. He thought our reaction was funny.

"My word!" he said comically, pretending to be shocked. *"You-fella no likem Fathers?"*

We replied vaguely and he saw we weren't going to give him

The Ambrym drums: wooden slit-gongs over six yards high. *Kal Muller*

any tasty tidbits to gossip about later. Playing his role of dignified chief to the hilt, he strutted off alone to receive his visitors.

The next day, Jacques and I decided that enough was enough concerning the missionaries. We still wondered what they could have had against us, particularly Vanderborg, during the little cruise that circumstances had forced us to take together. We decided to go ask him frankly why he disliked us so without even knowing us. With that kind of confrontation, we knew that either we would work out whatever problem existed, or simply aggravate the hostility. When we got to the mission, LeBeru had already left. We found Vanderborg, who watched us approach as if we were evil spirits. Jacques opened the conversation bluntly.

"If you don't want to see us, Father," he said firmly, "just say so right away. But if you wish, and that's why we came, we can have it out, and maybe come to an understanding."

After a moment's hesitation, Vanderborg invited us onto the porch that surrounds his large colonial house. He looked sheepish. He must not like confrontations. He had chilled drinks served and chatted about the weather. Jacques grew impatient. Okay, okay, let's get to the facts. Just why had he treated us so badly on board the boat? Answer: because he had been told earlier that we were working "against the mission's interests." How so, against your interests? It appeared that we had told the natives that the missionaries wanted to do them wrong, that all missionaries were nefarious individuals. But who told you that? Vanderborg was undone now. Finally he put the blame on the shoulders of the easiest scapegoat around, Father Karana. We can't accept that. We get along very well with Father Karana. He would never have spoken of us that way. So who? Well, actually, said Vanderborg, it was perhaps Father LeBeru. And where did he get his information? I don't know, but he has sources. So you never even thought of asking us our own point of view, of letting the accused defend themselves before being condemned? Vanderborg reddened and finally exploded.

"What do you want of me?" he shouted. "I accepted Father LeBeru's word. He's a missionary! A priest! He wouldn't lie!"

The discussion was so ridiculous that it was better ended. If not, we would have been taken for secret agents, sent by the Russians or the devil, to make trouble for these men of God. As if we didn't have anything else to do! So that he wouldn't be forced to admit that his colleague LeBeru had erred, we concluded gaily that the whole thing was caused by a regrettable misunderstanding. After that we were all buddy-buddy! Vanderborg even invited us to dine with him some evening.

On the way back to Fanla, Jacques and I couldn't help laughing. It was unthinkable! We laughed less, however, when we thought of Father LeBeru. We understood. He knew that we were interested in the traditional life of the New Hebrideans. Now, for him, the single fact of being polygamous, let alone not being baptized, was equivalent to a one-way ticket to hell. With him we could never get along.

During the week before the Nimangki, Tofor left us to circulate among the other villages. We asked him what he was doing. *"Business b'long custom,"* he replied laconically, with the air, despite his nambas, of a corporation president. Massi laughed, saying he was taking us for a ride, that he was going to drink with his friends *"no more."* In fact, both of them were telling the truth. Tofor came back to Fanla pretty well looped in the evening, but he had negotiated lots of details concerning the ceremony. People from several villages participate in each of these rites, even the Christians, since on Ambrym they have kept some bonds with the pagans regarding the carrying out of ancient traditions.

The morning of the Nimangki, people arrived from all the villages in the vicinity. Six Fanla men were going to rise in grade. Sagaran is only the sixth grade, but the men were all young, between twenty and thirty years old. It was an important event. The rite was fairly simple. It was, however, carefully and artistically executed, as is everything the Ambrym Islanders do. The participants arrived in single file at the ceremonial ground, tapping on coconuts and dancing around the two large slit-gongs standing vertically in the center of the ground. The drums were played at the same time. One by one, the men who were taking a new grade climbed onto the platform, about twelve feet high, and danced above the statue. Climbing onto the platform symbolizes rising in the society. But so that the newly graded are not too proud of themselves, the dancers below throw stones at them in passing.

All alone, Tofor turned around the other dancers. He was completely carried away by the music, yelling, "Ou-ah! Ou-ah!" while bending his back and throwing his arms above his head. He made no compromises with custom, but I noticed all the same that he often danced in place, right in front of Jacques's camera, which was fixed on a tripod on the edge of the ceremonial ground.

Then, of course, came the pig killings. After each whack of the club, each man who was taking a grade shouted, as loudly as possible, his new ceremonial name. "Sagaran betneim!" "Sagaran mili!" "Sagaran lonu!" and so on. The club struck many times, and there were many shouts. Then the bill was paid ritually. Each of the six men gave Tofor between three and five pigs, according to the beasts' values, and some money, too. I don't know how much they paid (Tofor didn't want to tell me when I asked later), but I saw fat wads of bills swallowed by the chief's hand and slipped into his bark belt. The payments used to be made uniquely with pigs. A man paid as many as twenty pigs for one rite. But now, as the handsome pigs with well-advanced teeth are more rare and the ordinary pigs are worth less, the difference is made up in Australian dollars.

The ceremony ended as all the ceremonies we had seen at Fanla, with a general drunk. The "beverage" shelves at the Fona co-op had surely been emptied of their entire stock for the occasion.

After the Nimangki and before the preparations for the Rom, nothing extraordinary happened, and I had time to take in the details of these people's life-style. Life in Fanla is agreeable. There is less segregation between the sexes than on Malekula. Only the most highly graded men may have "taboo-huts," huts for one person where a woman must never enter. And only Tainmal and Tofor have high enough grades to merit them. But there aren't any nakamals, those sacred men's huts, exclusive male clubs. In general, the people live in familial huts. In fact, in Fanla, the segregation that does exist is rather among grades. Tainmal, Tofor, and Itoul each have a "taboo-fire." They must make their own food and eat alone. This taboo undoubtedly comes from the traditional poisonings. This subject interested me, and I talked to Tofor about it. He assured me it was serious. The custom is more important than friendship, he said. If he had only one yam and

Tofor's brothers playing their bamboo flutes. *Kal Muller*

we had nothing to eat, he couldn't offer us any of his. And conversely, even if he were dying of hunger, he could not eat any of ours. Tofor was very anxious to find a chance to travel. I asked him, if ever you came to see us in France or the United States, how will you be able to keep up the "taboo-fire" and eat alone?

"*Suppose me come,*" he assured me, "*me kaï-kaï long witem you-fella. Time me come back long Ambrym, me killem one pig.*"

This is the normal fine for breaking a taboo that concerns food. However, Tofor added quickly, the taboo does not apply to drinks, and he asked if there weren't a little old can of beer around that he could share, in most sincere friendship, with us.

The Fanla people never lack for ideas when it comes to enjoying themselves, and they love music. From different spots in the village we regularly heard bits of songs. One day Tofor was bored and he had a sudden, luminous idea. He sent for his brothers, and they all came out with their flutes. On Ambrym, bamboo flutes are played as well as the ceremonial drums.

An open-air Melanesian chamber orchestra! We listened, dumbfounded. These Ambrym people had a real talent for pulling surprises. After the concert came story time. Tofor enjoyed telling us that once upon a time on Ambrym a man called Dangdang lived in a bamboo trunk. Dangdang found that in blowing he could produce an enchanting sound with which he could seduce any woman. Thus he attracted two sisters whom he had ogled for a long time. They wanted to marry him and brought him to see their father. Papa couldn't have cared less about the pretty melodies; he noticed only that Dangdang didn't have any pigs, so he was opposed to the marriage. Dangdang went away into the jungle with his flute. He played his magical music. Pigs fell from the trees. Since then, there have been wild pigs in the region. I asked Tofor if Dangdang had been granted the young women after this remarkable exploit, but Tofor was not sure.

Tofor is a modern man-bush. However he believes in the legends as much as he believes in the taboos, spirits, and Barkulkul. We heard him one evening, when he was returning a little late from a drinking bout at Fona. He was far away in the jungle. He was singing as loud as he could. I pointed out to Massi, who never liked her older brother's excesses, that he must have been going pretty strong to howl like that. No, she told me, or anyway, that has nothing to do with what you hear. He's singing loud to protect himself during the night in the forest. It was a chant to frighten off the "wild-man," the evil spirits that roam in nature.

Nevertheless, for a traditionalist, Tofor is one of the most up-to-date and in-the-swing New Hebridean Melanesians. In business he manages better than many of the archipelago's Europeans. He likes to say that he doesn't *need* money. His nambas, yams, taros, and leaf hut cost him nothing. But money has changed *"business b'long custom."* Everything that used to be bought solely with pigs—wives, superior grades, and so on—is now bought with pigs and dollars, too. Tofor insisted that that's not very important, as the idea remains the same, and in traditional life the role of the pigs is still primordial. More important, he said (since in at least one sense he looks beyond Fanla and Ambrym), is that the Europeans control everything and they do this with their money. It was difficult for the chief to express these opinions in pidgin, a language not made for abstractions, but he got along very well all the same. It was the Europeans who established the rules by which he, the customary chief, is quite willing to play.

The rules must be respected in order to win the game; and that is just what he intends to do, sooner or later.

A large part of his revenue comes from "custom." The pig commerce alone is profitable. As a highly graded man, he also receives a good bit of money from ceremonies such as the Nimangki. He has discovered, moreover, that he has a product to sell to the Europeans: art objects. That's a subject he loves to talk about. Gone are the days, he declared, when you could buy a statue from him for a bottle of rum and a scrap of calico! Now he knows what things are worth. Operating like a professional, he even offered a large drum as a present to the Queen of England and to General De Gaulle, and ever since, he's been able to sell his drums at unthinkable prices to international art collectors. He controls a veritable assembly line of trinkets to sell to tourists. He knows very well that these objects have no value, but he also knows that they bring in the bacon. In this domain, he has no scruples. The true custom is not compromised if imitation ritual objects are fabricated and palmed off on unsuspecting foreigners.

Tofor is possibly the only man-bush in the archipelago who knows how to swim in the waters of European capitalism. He bought a Port-Vila taxi and pays a man from Paama Island to drive it. He owns a half interest in a trading boat. He is sorry not to be able to read and write, but he is instinctively strong in arithmetic. He does not bury his profits, like his bottles of Beaujolais, in his hut. He has a bank account in Vila.

From time to time, however, he demonstrates that he hasn't yet mastered all the ins and outs of *"custom b'long you-fella."* In some cases it's comical, like his "New South Wales State Lottery" affair. One evening, Tofor and Itoul showed us the fistsful of tickets they possessed, at fifty cents each. Either they were victims of some chicanery in the selling, or they simply misunderstood. They believed that every ticket was a winner and were waiting for the money to come rolling in. I tried to explain, but they were slightly drunk and couldn't discuss anything rationally. I could see, though, that the matter did puzzle them a bit. Why, for a half-dollar ticket, should they automatically collect a hundred dollars or more? But, no worry. If it's a curious white man's practice, at least it's a pleasant one.

The question of the road led us to a political discussion with

Tofor. In northern Ambrym there was no trail practicable even for a jeep between the principal villages. The Condominium wanted to create one. Tofor also wanted a road, but he always tries to remain as independent of the government as of the missions. He believed that if the Condominium did the work, the road would essentially be government property from then on. And who knows? Those Vila people could claim even more rights afterwards. The chief wanted the road to belong entirely to the islanders. So, during our stay, with remarkable energy, he organized the affair. He asked for manpower and contributions toward the costs in all the villages. The Presbyterians and Seventh-Day Adventists cooperated. Only the people of the Catholic mission refused. According to spokesmen for this group, they didn't want to be directed by a pagan. We watched them working with shovels and picks. Clearly, in this rugged terrain, it wasn't easy. Tofor would have been very pleased to have a bulldozer, but he preferred to do without it rather than accept help from the Condominium.

During this time, the Na-Griamel, the New Hebridean movement directed by Jimmy Stephens, was seriously trying to root itself on Ambrym. Tofor was cynical about this, too, but he accepted the movement as a counterweight to the European influence. He set up a confrontation between them, to see which side defended itself best. The day the French Delegate was due to come meet with the regional inhabitants, Tofor promised to have a representative of the Na-Griamel on hand. For the chief, the main matter at hand was still the problem of getting a road built. The Delegate explained that since the official establishment exists, it should be exploited. The Condominum funds belong to all the New Hebrideans, and if the Ambrym people don't want their share, well that's fine, others will get more, but how silly that would be! The native audience more or less believed the Delegate's reasoning.

The Na-Griamel representative started forcefully, talking of the New Hebrideans, *their* country, *their* lands, and the like. But anything would have been better than talking about his movement's financial strength. At that time, the Na-Griamel bragged that it had twenty thousand members. Now, to be a member, the annual dues came to nearly $2.50 for a man, $1.20 for a woman, and 50 cents for a child, even an infant. If the Na-Griamel really had twenty thousand members, it also had quite a stash of Australian dollar bills. What were the heads of the movement doing with all that money? It was the same question Kal and I had asked Jimmy Stephens when we first arrived in the archipelago, but he laid on the slickest nonsense imaginable disguised as an answer. The Delegate couldn't have been happier. The Na-Griamel's accounts aren't about to be made public any time soon.

For an ungraded man to see the fabrication of the Rom masks, he must pay a pig (or its dollar equivalent) to the chief and then submit to a physical trial. We paid the price Tofor asked and literally laid the physical trial on Kal's back while Jacques filmed it. The villagers constructed a low bamboo tunnel, several yards long. On the inside hung branches of *nangalat*, a wild nettle which hurts like the devil. Kal, with no shirt on, had to stoop deeply to get through the tunnel. To make sure that the leaves had stung enough, two men whipped him with other branches when he emerged. Then, his back was rubbed with a leaf-antidote to calm the burning somewhat, but his skin would be on fire anyway for several days. He didn't complain. On the contrary, I think he enjoyed the possibility of testing his physical endurance. Later on, he would have a superb chance to do so, on Pentecost.

While all the other traditional dances of the archipelago have a metaphysical aspect, the Rom dance is performed mostly for enjoyment. It is also a good excuse for an exchange of pigs and yams between villages. And perhaps it used to be a means of firming alliances between villages. Only the men participate in the dance. Tofor explained why. Very, very long ago, a girl fell in love with a man who wasn't at all interested in her. To attract his attention, the clever woman made a beautiful mask and banana-leaf robe with which she disguised herself. The man believed he was seeing an apparition. She signaled him to follow her. When they were deep in the forest, she undressed. The man couldn't have been more surprised. He thought he was dealing with a spirit! He begged her to tell him how she had made her fantastic costume. Thinking this was how she would win his love, she explained everything, whereupon he coldly killed her. Thus, only he knew the secret of the Rom masks and robes. So he astutely combined his contempt for women with his knack for commerce and sold his secret very expensively only to the men of his village.

It is a dance full of momentum and rhythm accentuated by the wicker cones full of nuts which the dancers shake on beat. Like everything fabricated on Ambrym, the costumes are magnificent. The thick coat of leaves which covers each man's entire body transforms him into a marvelous bird. The meticulously crafted triangular masks painted in gay colors and ornamented with banana-fiber beards and long hair are taboo masks. The secret of their fabrication is jealously guarded by the artists, who sell their works at a very high price. Kal had earned the right to see how they were made, but he wasn't shown everything. Museums would pay dearly for a few of these splendid objects. However, after the dance, the masks are burned, in part because the artists do not want their methods studied too closely, but mostly because some of the spirit of the man who wore the mask could remain in the mask. The eventuality of such a doubling of the personality is profoundly feared: a man would no longer be his own master.

The Rom dance. *Kal Muller*

One evening, a barefoot young man with curly chestnut brown hair appeared in the Fanla clearing. He spoke French and English, but he was Spanish. Juan Villar had come to get a look at the island's interior and was leaving for Santo in his sailboat, which was moored in Fona. I decided to go with him. Before my wedding, I wanted to spend a few days in more civilized territory. A shower, a bed with sheets, and so on. By that time I had adapted well to jungle life, but my wedding was my wedding, and I wanted to be in good shape. Five or six days later, the *Red Shark* was to pick us up, but I wanted to have a little jump on my future husband. So, I left with Juan. Seeing his sailboat, I was full of admiration for this young man. It was very small—a nutshell a few yards long. To think it had crossed oceans! We got to Santo with no problems. The weather was beautiful. The sea was calm. When we arrived in port, Juan had to stay on the boat for a little while, waiting for the harbor master to assign him a mooring. I dashed to Chez Goddyn.

Our Santo headquarters was now the establishment of that old pirate Albert and his wife, Anna. Their two darling daughters, Yvonna and Astrid, jumped up to my neck to hug me. It had been a while since we had stopped staying with the Ravons. I had brushed aside the events on the night of the cyclone, but because of another incident later on I would never have anything to do with them again, at least not with Elsa. One fine day when we were out, Elsa unashamedly stole my notebooks and read them. Naturally, she particularly looked for the pages where I talked about her and her husband. She was furious. I was philosophical. I said to myself, if she dared to read someone else's private papers she deserved to know exactly what was written there. That's what I told her, too.

We had asked Albert to organize a little dinner party for our wedding, for us and our friends. "We're not rich," I said to him. "What can you serve that won't be too extravagant?" He stared down at me mockingly. "Hamburgers and Coca-Cola!" he roared. "That's what Americans eat, right?"

He refused to speak about it any more. Albert would be Jacques's witness. Ernst Lamberty was supposed to be mine, but the *Konanda* would still be out in the islands. So, I chose Pépé

Procureur, the one-time cowboy who now spent his time putting his cattle into cans.

I spent my days admiring the Mexican wedding dress, ideal for hot climates, which my mother had had the good idea of sending me, and taking warm showers at Marjorie Harley's house. Marjorie, Santo's English schoolmistress, pampered me like a big sister. Life, in short, was beautiful! My happiness had no bounds, until the day the *Red Shark* arrived in port without Jacques and Kal on board. The captain had been forced to skip the stop on Ambrym. The weather was too bad and the sea too rough. He wouldn't have been able to approach the coast safely, he explained by way of apology. My happiness was drowned all at once in a wave of panic. How would Jacques get to Santo? The marriage was four days later. Not a single boat would be passing by Ambrym in the meantime, and the weather forecast was hardly encouraging. It was no longer cyclone season, but the barometer continued to drop abnormally fast.

Jacques called me over the mission radio. "You hear me? Send me a boat! Hire anything! Don't worry, *cherie*, you'll find something. You've got to! You hear me? We're prisoners on this goddamn island!"

My heart pounding, I ran like crazy to see all the captains and all the owners of anything that floated. No success. The boats were on other islands, already chartered or incapable of confronting the bad weather. No one could or would rent me a thing. I noticed with anxiety that even on the Segond Channel, which is sheltered, the waves were getting higher and higher.

Juan Villar kindly offered to save us, and he didn't even want to be paid. But his sailboat is minuscule, and I couldn't see how he could transport two persons and all the film equipment without winding up at the bottom of the sea.

It was thirty-six hours before the big event, and it takes at least eighteen hours to make the round trip. I made the round of the captains one more time. I begged them. I pleaded with them. I finally found one who would hire out his boat for twice the normal price. I grabbed the chance.

Jacques got to Santo at the eleventh hour. He looked like a shipwrecked man barely rescued, but he never stopped smiling. He was here!

When we had time to exchange experiences, he told me of his encounter with George Staempfli, a New York art collector, and his young wife, Barbara. Jacques, having told me over the radio to send him a boat, was more or less camping on the beach, waiting for it. He knew I'd do my best, but he was worried that the circumstances might be just too stacked against me. He cheered aloud when he saw a majestic sailboat approach. Not only did she do it, he thought, but she was lucky as well; he was figuring I had found and chartered one of the infrequent private boats passing through Santo. Their meeting, on that deserted Ambrym shore, must have been something to see: the Staempflis, all decked out in the finest Abercrombie & Fitch–style explorers' gear, and Jacques, haggard and ragged, permeated with volcanic ash after a couple of months of jungle life on one of the only islands in the group that doesn't even possess a fresh-water source.

"Hi!" screamed Jacques, shaking their hands with his very heart in his own. "I'm all ready! I'll just go get Kal, and our things. And thank you, thank you so much!"

The dignified Mr. Staempfli was decidedly nonplussed.

"Who *are* you?" he inquired. "And just what are you talking about?"

When Jacques learned that I had not sent this boat, that the Staempflis were there on their own, his first reaction was to say he would give them anything, anything, if only they would take him up to Santo. But Mr. Staempfli had come for business reasons. He wanted to meet Tofor and buy some drums and statues for his gallery.

"I know the chief well," pleaded Jacques. "I'll take you to Fanla, and even intercede for you personally, if only you'll get me back on time!"

The Staempflis found this proposition reasonable, and off they all went, on the Tofor trail. Halfway up, completely out of breath and drenched, George regretted his whole adventure.

"I'll go to your wedding if I can," he puffed, "but you may have to come to my funeral first."

He made it up to the village and he got his art objects. When they returned to the coast, Jacques found the boat I had sent awaiting him. Mr. and Mrs. Staempfli, with good winds behind them, arrived in Santo just in time for our wedding, anyway.

It was the most romantic wedding I could have hoped for. The young French Assistant Delegate, who had never married anyone before, was as excited as we were. The Santo missionary wasn't exactly used to marrying people either, as most folks in these parts dispense with such formalities. He was flushed with excitement. We went to Albert's only to find the most magnificent feast possible in the islands. A mountain of crayfish. Two suckling pigs staring out at us from the middle of the table. A royal cake. Champagne for everybody! I couldn't get over it.

"How did you do all this, Albert?" I asked, beaming. "I've never seen anything like it!"

"I just didn't have any more hamburgers!" he replied proudly.

With the fifty or so Santo people we liked best—representing Melanesian, French, English, Australian, New Zealand, Belgian, Chinese, Vietnamese, Javanese, and Tahitian origins—we did honor to the chef.

We danced until dawn on the *Polynésie,* a handsome Pacific-based cargo-passenger ship. She was passing through on her way to Sydney. The party continued all the next day on an islet inhabited by a French Robinson Crusoe, Jacques Binet. On his dream island you don't even have to bring provisions. All you have to do is wander among the mangroves or among the rocks, with a screwdriver and a hammer in your pocket, and choose among the thousands of peacefully living oysters.

But it all happened too fast. Only two days after the marriage, we had to leave each other. Jacques and Kal went to Mbotogote territory. I went to the Big Nambas plateau. Separated already, and by more than thirty miles of virgin forest!

10

The Master of the *Konanda*

W<small>E</small> were back with the Big Nambas, for the fifth or sixth time. Because, finally, we were going to see a ceremony in Amok. It would be a Nimangki in honor of Nisaï, Virambat's eldest son, the future Meleun.

The last time we arrived in Amok, we fell out of the sky, in the belly of a large mechanical bird. At least, that's how the Big Nambas saw it. More simply, we arrived in a helicopter. The Amok men had never seen anything better or worse. At first they thought it was an evil spirit. When they approached and timidly touched the Plexiglas, they saw that it did not bite or burn, that it seemed in effect to be harmless. Our friendship with Nisaï was secured when we invited him to take a little trip in the air. Was he proud! But at first he was petrified. So that he wouldn't fall out the window, he wrapped an arm around the pilot's leg, as if it were a lifebuoy. After the first tumultuous moments, however, he didn't want to land. But we'll run out of gas! He didn't understand. We'll be mangled in the trees! That, he understood perfectly. He got out of the helicopter with the air of a dignified warrior before the awestricken population.

Now we were going to see Nisaï become important in the society. The men had already been rehearsing the dances for two months. If a woman accidentally saw these rehearsals, her husband or her father had to pay the Meleun a tusked pig.

Nimangki is a pidgin word. In Amok it is called *erpnavet*. By any name, the Big Nambas ceremony we saw was particularly impressive.

The men smeared their bodies with coconut oil. Then they covered their faces and torsos with black paint made from a mixture of burned coconut and coconut milk. Blacks who want to be as black as possible. The men of the chief's family wore drawings in red paint on their faces and backs. Everyone wore brand-new nambas, *bancoul* nut bells around their ankles, and "*grass b'long fowl*," or feathers, in their hair.

The dance took away my breath. I have never seen such a Melanesian ballet anywhere else. The choreography was perfectly timed and intricate. Men on their knees, men huddled close, splitting apart, coming back. Lines of dancers wound in and out of each other, tracing 8s, Zs, and Os on the ceremonial ground. The bells and drums produced a bewitching rhythm. One dancer detached himself from the others. He had a bow and arrow decorated with white feathers. He pretended to shoot at the men. He represented the chief's power over the members of the tribe. At the same time everyone sang, and the song was full of praise for the chief. The water is good; we have many pigs, many yams; we have made peace with our enemies—thank you, Meleun!

Going back to the hut to get more tapes for the tape recorder, I saw the beginning of a parade that was coming along a small trail. I shouldn't have seen it. It was taboo for women. It wasn't my fault, I didn't know. Twenty-nine giant pigs were being pulled by liana leashes onto the ceremonial ground. In Amok all the pigs are sizable because they are castrated at the age of four or five months. The superior canines are taken out at four years.

All twenty-nine had to be sacrificed. But since the Big Nambas are clever, and since they don't have refrigerators, they have developed a singular manner of killing pigs. Some are hit lightly on the head, killed symbolically. They are the lucky ones. Others are clubbed with extraordinary skill, so that they will die in two, three, four days, up to a week later. I wondered how the men could calculate the impact of their club strokes so precisely. But they never made a mistake. Several pigs are killed straightaway

A dance from the Big Nambas Nimangki ceremony. *Kal Muller*

for immediate consumption. Nisaï himself killed six; his younger brother Rabi killed two others. Eight pigs would be enough for the evening's banquet.

Just after the rite, I got sick. I had a fever, and it wasn't a malaria attack. I vomited my guts out. My teeth chattered almost hard enough to break. One of these filthy tropical diseases, I thought. But Willy and Virambat had another diagnosis. It was because of Tama. And who is Tama? He is the spirit who follows the Meleun day and night and tells the chief of chiefs what he must do. If the Meleun doesn't obey, one of his children will die. And Tama was after me because I had seen the arrival of the pigs onto the ceremonial ground. If I had been a Big Nambas woman,

I would have been dead already. Since I was an outsider, Tama had punished me by making me sick *"no more."* Moreover, Willy announced, I didn't have the right to eat any pig that evening. That didn't bother me too much, since I didn't want to eat anything at all. After a Nimangki, the women are not allowed to partake of the sacrificial meat until the next day.

As young as Nisaï is, he had become a highly graded man. He immediately was allowed to take two wives, the first as a servant, the second to bear him a child.

This time we left Amok rapidly to cross the island as far as Norsup. The Figas greeted us with Peter Wright, then the assistant manager and later the manager of the plantation. With this high liver whose origins are Fijian and Tongan, and with our friends, we spent a day seeing how a coconut plantation works. But we didn't have much time to lose. We had to rush back to Santo, to leave with Captain Lamberty for Pentecost.

The *Konanda* is a ship, a real ship, in a country of rotting Lilliputian skiffs. More than four hundred tons. Over fifty yards long. The smokestack is painted in Burns-Philp's black and white checkerboard pattern. The *Konanda* sails under the British flag. She was docked at the Burns-Philp wharf, left over from the American World War II base. Above the hangars, the Burns-Philp flag waved softly in the wind. Ernst Lamberty brought Jacques, Kal, and me down in his car to load our baggage. Kal and Jacques had some work to do before leaving Santo. So, Ernst addressed himself only to me. Besides, he prefers the company of women.

"Listen, darling, I've got to go see Burton, the director of B.P. Come back into town with me if you want to. We'll have one for the road at the Corsica and Chez Mao. What do you say, darling? One for the road?" Even today, when I hear that expression I can't help thinking of Captain Lamberty.

There's nothing of the jealous husband in Jacques, and he sent us off cheerfully. Ernie expedited his business at Burns-Philp. Across from the store is Mao's Tahitian bar, and we lost no time getting there. Ernie is a solid drinker. In his life he has downed gallons upon gallons of beer, wine, aperitifs, drinks of every color. He is a real Dutch seawolf. However, I have never seen him drunk. Given his size and natural force, that's not too surprising.

On land, he starts his bistro rounds in his red Toyota early. He gets out of the car, his Tahitian shirt flapping in the breeze, without ever closing the door, which yawns the entire time he is in the café. Pernod, whiskey, gin and tonic, beer, mixing drinks doesn't scare the captain, who likes to converse with the proprietors and the other customers, and any liquid that lubricates the throat is fine. Doing the bar circuit with Ernst is a memorable experience. We left Mao's bar to stop in at the Ravons'. Since they were staging a flying saucer session, as the captain called it, we left the Marine quickly for the Corsica.

The Corsica is Santo's most "respectable" hotel. At the bar, Frenchmen and Englishmen gather in a rollicking ambience, and the rounds unwind to the sounds of old country and western. I often accompanied Ernie during our visits to Santo. I knew what to expect. With him, I always had three full glasses or bottles of beer in front of me. The captain always fills up before taking off, since on board he drinks nothing but water. "One for the road, darling," he said to me again, and that one was really the last, since it was almost time for our departure.

Two minutes later, we had driven to the pier. Ernst left me for a few minutes. He went to the hangar to find his supercargo, lost among copra sacks, girders, sheet metal, boards, and sundry mysterious cases. I had a few moments to study the *Konanda*, bound tightly to the wharf with heavy hawsers. The small cargo ship is no longer young, but she symbolizes all the romanticism of the South Seas. On the gangway, you are as high as the fourth floor of a building. The *Konanda* is first and foremost an enormous copra hold, above which the landing masts stretch their arms amid a complicated system of cables and pulleys. Aft, behind the gangway, the large smokestack spits out soot and crude oil vapors. Ladders everywhere, longboats, two levels of portholes. A sailor on the pier pointed out the captain's cabin, where I was to be installed, on the principal bridge, just under the gangway. The storeroom was on the quarter-deck. Natives bustled all over the ship while the pulley-blocks hauled oil barrels on board. The machines humming, the draw works straining, the sailors shouting, metallic equipment clashing—the soundtrack that lightheartedly carried along the film of the departure, and I wanted to remember as many of its Santo sunlit sequences as possible.

"We're off," called the captain, bounding across the plank that linked the quay covered with copra debris to the principal bridge. I followed Ernst hesitantly over the long narrow board. Despite myself, I was afraid of falling into the water, or worse, onto the cement pier. I wasn't really afraid of killing myself, just of looking ridiculous in front of everybody. Lack of confidence. But no problem. Of course I got onto the boat, and I went up the gangway. I lit a Rothman's happily. Leaning on the gunwale, I watched the natives taking their posts. I saw Jacques and Kal come on board. I waved to them, but they didn't see me.

Now, everything happened very fast. The captain was at the transmitter, which rang like a telephone amid the machinery roars and grunts. Ernie yelled orders through the open bay window that looks out on the bridge, where Jimmy, the first mate, supervised the crew and looked extremely busy. The machinery puffed away. The hawsers aft were released, and the *Konanda*'s stern came unglued from the quay. Ta-ta, Santo! The native dockhands shouted good-bye, ta-ta, and howled with laughter at the jokes tossed from above the railing by the men on board. The *Konanda* was now withdrawing perpendicularly from the quay, foaming up the sea. Ernie gave orders to the helmsman to correct the effects of the current. We left the pier very quickly and straightened out. The wheel rolled this way and that. Ernie activated the transmitter, pointing the needle to "full speed ahead." Santo was some two hundred yards away. The sea in the channel was pure blue, like the sky. It was hot. The work was done. For the moment, the rest was routine. Ernie summoned us to the cosy little dining room for a bit of kaï-kaï.

The captain told me to wander wherever I wanted on board. "The boat's yours, darling!" What chivalry! So I did some exploring. I went as high as I could to change my perspective. On either side of the enormous smokestack and windsails, I noticed two small buckets full of water. This intrigued me. I went down to ask Ernie what they were for.

"In case of fire," replied the captain.

"But there are fire extinguishers and hatches everywhere!"

"I know that very well, but the English are sticklers for the rules, and that's the rule, even if it isn't very logical."

Two preposterous pails of water in the middle of the ocean!

Anyway, the *Konanda* is a sturdy boat and you feel at ease aboard. And safe.

Ernie had some work to do in his cabin. He told me to come down and join him whenever I wanted. I walked around a little more on the bridge. I relished the sea view and the whiffs of salty wind. Finally, I went down the alleyway which gives onto the main deck to find the captain's cabin. I guessed right, right away. I saw a pareu rippling in the wind, covering an open doorway, and I was sure the captain was behind it. I pounded on the metallic wall, loud enough to be heard over the machinery that throbbed below. "Come in!" The captain was sitting at his desk, his legs spread around the safe nestled under it. He was examining the manifest. Just a large captain in a small cabin, but it felt like all the Pacific was in that little room.

"Sit down!" he said amicably. "I'll only be a minute getting through these papers."

Yes, all of the Pacific as I would have imagined it was there in Ernst's cabin. Two berths covered with vivid red and turquoise pareus. Books in a small windowed cupboard, since the captain is a man of letters. Jars full of shells, native statues, Tuamotou fans, Tahitian necklaces. All these objects stood out strikingly against the cabin's dark wooden paneling. Two little ventilators at the bulkhead hummed. Fresh air entered by the three round copper portholes, through which I could see the vegetation and beaches of Aori Island. I looked at the photographs pinned above the captain's berth. A picture of his pretty Polynesian wife. A picture of his fifteen-year-old daughter with a Tahitian face, blond hair, and blue eyes, a lovely antipodal Dutch girl. Next to her, there was a picture of his pretty New Hebridean wife.

"You're not bored, are you?" asked the captain.

"Oh no, Ernie, not at all!" And it was true. I was completely taken by the atmosphere, full of feelings of well-being.

"Look, for a little distraction while I finish my work, glance through this."

He handed me a manila folder full of old newspaper articles in several languages, with photographs. I looked at Ernst as a young man, a handsome young Dutchman, slender, blond, and suntanned, standing on his sailboat *Kroja*. One photo that reappeared frequently was Ernst with his young Marquesan wife, a strikingly beautiful island girl. Both of them, dressed in pareus, looked at each other romantically on a beach bordered by coconut palms. There it was—the South Seas paradise. When I started to read the texts I was even more impressed. The captain's life was not a common one!

"Ernie!" I cried. "You should write a book!"

"It's done," he answered laughing. "I've even written two. But you can't read them, no one here can read them. They're written in Dutch and have never been translated!"

I wanted to ask some questions, since the articles I could read revealed only certain details, but the captain had to go up to the gangway. He invited me to follow him, which I did gladly. It was raining now. Warning. The sea was strong. The wind had fallen. The sound of the waves knocking against the tarred hull covered the noise of the panting engines. We wound toward Malekula in the scrambled liquid weighted here and there by low, gray cotton clouds. On the gangway, the captain listened to the weather over the Fiji radio.

"The barometer is dropping," announced Ernie. "We'll see what's going on; we may have to shelter the ship in Port-Sandwich."

"Funny," I remarked, "the way it can be so cold in the tropics."

"Darling, if you want to warm up, we're going back down. We'll drink some tea in my cabin. You, *keepem ship long 170!*" he commanded to the native helmsman.

The rain lashed us as we went back down the ladder. In the alleyway, the English supercargo, John Woodrow, was filling his pipe with fragrant tobacco from a round can. "Nice weather for whales," he said to me. Indeed.

"Hey, John," joked the captain, "despite the bad weather, you want to leave the Pacific and return to England?"

The supercargo smiled, steadying himself on the bulkhead. "No, Ernie. Going as far as Australia is like going to the end of the world for me now. You know that. I'm not complaining." John is one of the few Englishmen married to a New Hebridean. His heart is totally in the islands.

Passing through, we greeted Jacques and Kal, who were set up at the small dining room table with papers spread out everywhere. Film talk—what's already shot, what they need, the condition of the cameras, some of which were beginning to show the effects of the humidity, and so on. Ernie offered them tea, too, which they gladly accepted, and we left them to their work. I followed the captain and we settled down comfortably in his cabin. In response to my questions, Ernst began to tell me of the events in his life. After several such discussions, I would end up with a fairly detailed portrait of the captain.

Ernst-Wilhelm Lamberty was born in Nimeguen, in the Netherlands. The sea had always attracted him. When he was fifteen he attended a school that prepared merchant marine officers, but he didn't like institutional life. At seventeen he ran away on a German yacht that was going around the world. They were shipwrecked off the coast of Brittany. Ernst then enlisted in the Dutch Navy. It too was much too constricting for an independent man's taste. He applied for a discharge before the end of his engagement. Request refused. So he left without permission. Once again he tried nautical school, but he was just not made to be directed by a group of conservative professors. At twenty he ran away to join the French Foreign Legion. He remembers it well. His new name was "Number 61842." This is also the title of one of his books. He served in Algeria and Morocco. But the Legion also deprived him of too much of his liberty. He tried to desert. He was caught and spent fourteen months in the Legion disciplinary sections in Colomb-Béchar in the Sahara. Forced labor, constructing roads in the desert. His punishment had been only twelve months, but in the meantime he tried to escape again, which cost him the two additional months of prison. Afterwards he returned to service in Morocco.

When World War II broke out, volunteers who knew how to ski were sought among the legionnaires, to go to Finland. Ernst was the first to raise his hand. He had never skied in his life but had had enough of Morocco. In France, on the way to Finland, while his feet were being measured for skis he didn't know how to put on, he got word of the armistice—Finland had laid down its arms. Ernst went to fight in Norway. He participated in the Narvik battle and earned the prestigious French war cross with two citations. He returned to France just before the Pétain armistice. On a small coal ship he fled to England, where all legionnaires were suspect, half of them being German or Italian. He was imprisoned at Trentham Park. He was freed because of De Gaulle. He battled in Gabon and the Cameroons.

When the Dutch returned to combat, Ernst naturally requested permission to go rejoin them. But permission was denied. Since he couldn't have cared less about such formalities, he again took French leave and landed in an internment camp in Durban, South Africa. The Dutch consul got him out so he could rejoin their Marine Corps. But once more he was arrested in England, this time by the Secret Service, who thought he was a spy. He finally managed to reenlist in the Dutch Navy. Ceylon. Madagascar. He joined the American fleet in Australia. He fought against the Japanese at Sumatra. Years in Indonesia. When he returned home to the Netherlands after all his experiences, he tried to make a little money smuggling tulip bulbs into England.

Ernst earned enough to buy a sailboat, the *Kroja*, and he set off for the Pacific alone, with two cats to keep him company on board. He stopped at the Marquesas Islands, where he met an important Marquesan chief's daughter, a true Polynesian princess. The French authorities didn't want him to stay at first. The Marquesas are protected. But for a young man Ernst had so much military service to his credit that the government left him alone. A few months later, while he was courting his beautiful Rebecca, sheltered from a raging storm, an island native came looking for him on the run. "Captain, captain, your boat!" The wind had thrown the *Kroja* against a reef. What was left of the boat wasn't worth saving. Ernst promised his pretty princess he would return to marry her. She said something in her Marquesan language to the effect of "whites are all liars." But she agreed to wait. In any case, if he hurried.

Ernst got himself hired on a Tahitian schooner. At Papeete he was picked up by a Belgian yacht headed for Honolulu. He spent Christmas on Christmas Island. He crossed the States as cheaply as possible, by bus, as far as Chicago. He locked himself in a cheap hotel room to write a book so he could earn enough money to continue. The book allowed him to return to Holland, to buy another sailboat, the *Anna Elizabeth*, and to sail again for the Pacific, again in solitary. He headed directly for the Marquesas to pick up where he had left off with Rebecca, before she married someone else. He took her to Tahiti. Rebecca gave birth to a daughter, then to a son. Soon afterwards, Rebecca and Ernst set their course, with the children, for Rarotonga in the Cook Islands where they decided to marry officially. They couldn't find any wedding bands in Rarotonga so they used curtain rings. Ernst decided to go to the New Hebrides, just for a two-week vacation. That was in 1954. He has lived in the New Hebrides since. He has had a varied career—director of plantations and captain of boats, navigating throughout the Pacific. Another son. Another daughter. Ernst continued to roam the seas, a free man. A little too free for his wife's tastes. She left him a little before our arrival in the Pacific, to return to Papeete. Ernst told me he had been a bad husband. He liked the cafés too much during his stays on land, and he liked the New Hebridean girls too much.

"When the wife of one of my friends in Santo, Perret, left him, he came to ask me what I did when mine skipped out. So I told him the truth. I got myself three native housegirls."

Ernst wound up marrying a pretty seventeen-year-old New Hebridean. Whether it's a coincidence I don't know, but her name is also Rebecca. As a present on his fifty-fourth birthday, a girl was born to Ernst and Rebecca II, Bertha. Ernst is very proud of her. "I'm not so old as all that. And look how beautiful she is!"

He is happy to be definitively a man of the Pacific. "If I had married young in Holland . . ." he reflected. "Can you see me tied to a fat fifty-year-old Dutch housewife?" When he says such things, Rebecca laughs. She doesn't understand, speaking only her Paama language and pidgin, but she understands the tone.

After leaving Europe, Ernst returned once to see his family. He was already an experienced sailor and a hardened soldier. One evening he met a pretty Dutch girl and slept out, without notifying his parents. During the night his mother called the police to say her son had disappeared and she feared the worst. Damn, said Ernst. If you can't even take advantage of a chance to be with a pretty girl without the cops chasing after your tail, I'd rather stay in the islands. And that's what he did from then on.

Ernie confided other things to me besides. He showed me a wrinkled letter. I first noticed the elegant handwriting and then I read the first words: "Dear Dad." Dear Dad! For the captain it was nothing short of mind-boggling. He didn't know he had a daughter at the other end of the world, in England. During the war he had met a young Englishwoman, and the result, unknown to him for twenty-one years, was a baby. The Englishwoman had made the child believe that her father had been killed in a shipwreck. At twenty, she went to seek her Dutch origins in Holland. She discovered that her father was very much alive and thriving in the New Hebrides. Thus, this letter and a photograph of a pretty girl with long brown hair. Ernst was not at all unhappy to learn this news. He answered right away, offering his daughter a trip to the New Hebrides so they could meet each other. She had not yet decided to venture so far, but her father was confident he'd persuade her to come.

I was dozing in Ernst's cabin. He had offered me one of the berths. He was on deck. He hardly slept at all aboard. He was always on watch to be sure his helmsman kept on course. It's serious business. If you make a mistake, no matter how small, you risk ramming a reef. Since there were no other available berths, Jacques and Kal slept under the dining room table. Here, women have priority for comfort.

The transmitter's clear ring woke me up completely. Despite the open portholes it was so hot in the tiny cabin I could hardly breathe. I went out on deck. The sun and sea dazzled me. In these parts, the weather is often capricious. A little after we left, the barometer started to climb. I heard Ernst's forceful voice. From the railing he commanded his first mate, big Jimmy, a Paama Islander. Jimmy is a bit deaf and he kept stopping to cup his ear, but Ernie's orders got through.

"*Go! You go, you go, you go!*" the captain shouted. "*Quick-time, goddamn. Ship he go long rock!*"

The anchor chain came down, in a metallic din.

"Stop!" howled Ernst.

And the *Konanda* was moored in front of Fona, Ambrym. I was always impressed by the jubilant vegetation tiered up to the sky. The wind barely stirred the coconut palms and *tamanou* leaves.

"Five tons of copra to load," John Woodrow said, with an accounting ledger under his arm.

He was already prepared to go ashore in the first dinghy with his assistant, an Aoba native, who carted the heavy chains and metal bar of the store's balance. They were conscientious. They weighed every bag of copra the islanders brought them.

I settled down on the bridge, protected from the sun by a canvas hung between two awning stanchions. There were two deck chairs, one marked "captain." Island trade excites me and I was all eyes and ears. One team of native sailors worked at the winch. Another went down in two motorized launches which, for hours, would go back and forth between the *Konanda* and the coast. John Woodrow, before leaving, had opened the boat's store where a New Hebridean who knew how to read and write loomed behind the counter amid planks, jars, cans, biscuits, vividly colored dresses hanging from the ceiling, batteries, inexpensive, neatly folded shorts and shirts, boxes of detergent, large cakes of soap, Australian candy, and entire drawers full of *rubber b'long fakfak*, these last in great demand by the natives, probably because of their resemblance to traditional nambas. The *Konanda*'s store is the largest traveling department store in the New Hebrides, the floating Bloomingdale's of the archipelago. You can even buy portable toilets. For the natives of underpopulated islands who have all of nature at their disposal. Beer. Spanish wine in plastic bottles which get dangerously soft under the tropical sun. Ball point pens, sparkling costume jewelry, oil barrels, axes, silks, calico. A forest of shovels and broomsticks hanging from the ceiling, swaying back and forth with the rolls. A welcome whatnot shop. But most of all, there is a freezer full of ice cream. The natives push and shove to buy it. Since they particularly appreciate the strawberry flavor, you're surrounded by dozens of pink black faces. No rum, whiskey, or gin in sight. In this domain, a responsible trader never deviates from the rules. The *Konanda* is loaded with hard liquor, but it is reserved for white gullets. By Condominium law.

The island trading life also means life with the crew. The chief mechanic came out on deck to get some air and talked to me amicably. One of the assistant cooks peeled yams on the stern bridge. An enormous tuna caught with a trailing line was being prepared. The galley's smokestack lived up to its name. We were going to have a good kaï-kaï that evening. The launch's motors crackled away.

"We're going to be here for a few more hours," said Ernst, sitting down next to me.

"All the better!" I replied. I was fascinated by all the movements, all the colors.

Tofor came aboard. He had come down to the coast precisely because he had much to tell us. We were, naturally, forced to buy him a beer. At the same time we offered one to Ernie, but he refused. It's true. On board he drinks nothing stronger than sodas. He is a serious captian.

When we were last on Ambrym, Tofor had placed a taboo on the Marum Volcano. No one could climb it, particularly Europeans. If you broke the taboo you had to pay twenty Australian dollars. For a year or two the volcano had been spouting more ash than usual, seriously damaging the gardens. Tofor thought the presence of outsiders had displeased the volcano gods. Recently, a French Condominium representative went to Ambrym and, despite the taboo, climbed the volcano. Tofor told him, when he came back down, that he had to pay the fine. He refused, saying that the taboos were *"custom b'long you"* but not *"custom b'long me."* Tofor replied that if he were in France he would have to respect its laws. Now the civil servant was on Ambrym in Tofor's territory, and the custom is the law. The Frenchman finally paid up. Tofor told us this story so that we could congratulate him. Then he asked for another beer.

A little later Tofor went down to the store. The ice cream, detergents, and calico didn't interest him. He merely wanted to buy twenty-four cases of beer! Since it hadn't been ordered in advance, the assistant supercargo could give him only eight. Tofor was disappointed. Then he had a brilliant idea. Couldn't we buy him two or three bottles of "medicine"? In other words, rum or whiskey. Since it was illegal and, most of all, knowing he would drink it all in one brief sitting, we said no. He wasn't angry, because he knew the law very well. He had tried his luck *"no more."*

The *Konanda*'s cook is a Fijian. He loves routine. The first meal after leaving Santo and the last meal before returning to port are curries. Roasted chicken Saturday night, ice cream Sunday. He sugars the coffee himself before serving it. He normally puts at least three spoonsful in each cup. If you ask him nicely, he will try to remember not to presugar yours. But I'm sure he thinks that people like us don't know how to drink good coffee.

The chief engineer is also Fijian. Percy. Quite a fellow. He boasted that he has twenty-eight children—three by his legal wife, the others dispersed throughout the Pacific.

Percy had a little problem. He had announced to the captain in port that the auxiliary engine was out of order—not an unusual occurrence. Ernie resigned himself to waiting in Santo for the necessary repairs. He wasn't given any progress reports and began to wonder. "What's the trouble, Percy?" "Oh, we're working on it, captain." After about a month of patience, the average repair time being a week to ten days, Ernie went down to have a look for himself. Nothing was dismantled. Only the water pump was no longer linked to the auxiliary engine. The captain stormed into the chief engineer's cabin. "Okay, Percy, where's the pulley?" Percy confessed. He had given it to the chief engineer of the *Manutai*, Burns-Philps's other ship, who needed one for his main engine. Ernie couldn't get over it. He chided Percy like a child. "It's good to love others and to want to help them out, but before all else you've got to love the ship! Now, the captain of the *Manutai* is a good friend of mine, but I bloody well won't give him my compass!"

Ernie was never quite certain whether Percy had really given the pulley away, or whether he had sold it. But Captain Lamberty's warm heart and sense of humor triumphed over anger, especially since Percy offered to replace the pulley by regular paycheck deductions. B.-P.'s manager, however, hearing the story, was not amused, and was still yelling that the *Konanda*'s chief engineer had to go. Percy could only hope that Ernie's influence in the company was powerful enough.

When we joined Ernie for the local radio broadcasts, which consisted mostly of short announcements in pidgin, we felt like we were deep in the heart of surrealism. Example: a native police force will arrive in Akam village next Monday to inspect the houses *b'long shitshit*. Warning to all who have not yet dug appropriate holes! A friendly word from the Condominium: begin digging your holes at once! Another story in the same category, overheard on the two-way radio: a village elder asked the Delegate to come right away because of an urgent problem. *"Trouble too mass long place here!"* The Delegate replied that he was busy at the moment, and he wanted to know, by radio, what was the matter. The elder did not want to explain. The Delegate, responsible for several islands, could not travel unexpectedly unless the reason was truly serious. He insisted upon having the details. Well. A native nurse sent by the Condominium had demanded that the "rest rooms," which were in the middle of the village, be abolished for sanitary reasons and rebuilt out in the jungle. The order was obeyed. But now the women, accustomed to relieving themselves during the night, refused to go there, since they were too afraid of the forest spirits. So all the village women suffered from abdominal pains, and half of them were constipated. What should be done? The Condominium is perhaps generally not very effective, but sometimes, truly, it's called on to resolve some rather unusual problems.

Ernst had to put himself out for even the simplest manuevers. Just to get a launch lowered into the sea he yelled, *"Boat he go long water row-takem he come!"* But the launch was dropped so quickly and awkwardly that it almost crashed onto the bridge. The captain continued, *"Rock him! Rock him! More . . . more . . . okay, good now! Now down long right, I said! Careful you no spoilem everything! Right!"* The fact that the first mate's hearing was poor complicated matters even more. Ernie certainly earns his pay.

We were surrounded by brightly painted outrigger canoes, many adorned with brightly painted names—*Blue Sea, Pink Crab, Pacific Games*. There was even a small canoe called *Konanda*. Ernst told me there was also an Atchin Island girl who had been named Konanda because the ship, thanks to the captain's attention, had rushed the young pregnant mother, sick, on the brink of death, to the Santo hospital.

It was hard for me to leave the *Konanda* and Ernie. I would gladly have stayed on board for weeks. But we had taken the ship to go to Pentecost and there was no getting around it, we had arrived. I kissed the captain and we all thanked him. An exceptional journey. Now we would see the celebrated Land Dive.

11

The Land Dive

ONCE upon a very ancient time, on the isle of Pentecost, in the Bongwulwul tribe, lived a young woman who found life with her husband, Tamalie, impossible. Several times she ran away, but he always caught her. One day when she was being chased, she climbed a banyan and called to her husband: "I am going to leap to my death. If you dare, follow me. If our lives are saved, then I will believe we were destined to live together, and I will never leave you again." Tamalie, who did not want to be taken for a coward, accepted the challenge. He joined her at the summit of the tree. She jumped. He jumped. He killed himself. She lived happily ever after. What then had happened? While her husband was climbing the tree, the crafty young woman knotted around her ankles two lianas anchored to the trunk. Poor naïve Tamalie hadn't a hope of coming out alive. But the Pentecost men have avenged him since then with the Land Dive.

The Land Dive, in all the local dialects, is called *Gol*, for which the nearest translation would be "jump into the void." The men, braving death, leap from a tower about ninety feet high. Their falls are broken by simple lianas. It is a spectacular and curious rite which is practiced uniquely on Pentecost. In the rest of the archipelago, in fact in the entire world, there is no equivalent to the Land Dive.

The Tamalie legend is not taken too seriously by the islanders. They know that before the first Europeans arrived in the archipelago, Pentecost men did in fact jump from banyan trees. The white men's tools, axes and machetes, permitted the natives to invent and construct their remarkable towers. But the tradition is much older and no one today is certain of its origins.

At some point, the Land Dive became an agrarian rite. On Pentecost the yam is more than the staple food. It is the basis of all ceremonial life. And the Land Dive's purported aim is to assure a good yam harvest for the following year. Normally, the event takes place each year shortly after the first crops come up, around April or May. The sorcerers' secret for determining the exact date lies in the texture of the first yams. When they reach what's considered a good consistency, when they are sufficiently sturdy and moist, the lianas should be strong and supple enough to support a man's weight. The Land Dive can then be scheduled.

The tower is divided into several parts which each bear the name of a part of the human body. The base is called the ankle. The summit is called the head.

There is undoubtedly a relation between the tower and the myth of the origin of yams. The men say that in the time out of mind, an old man named Lingrus cut his fingernails and noticed that they took root in the earth and became yams. He ordered his children to cut up his body after his death and to plant the different pieces in their gardens. The chunks of flesh would also produce yams. Since then, on Pentecost, the different varieties of yams have been named after the different parts of the body. Thus, the name of each yam type corresponds also to the name of a part of the tower. Perhaps in jumping from such and such a level, the men provide for a good harvest of the corresponding yams.

It is interesting to note as well that the three branches that support each platform from which the men leap are called the penis and the two lips of the vagina. The sexual symbolism you are tempted to see in the event is in general confirmed by the explanatory details the islanders can offer if you bother them enough.

It is taboo for women to see the tower's construction. An un-

The Land Dive tower. *Kal Muller*

derstandable taboo, since it was a woman, Tamalie's wife, who was at the origin of everything and who had ridiculed the age-old Melanesian principle of male superiority. Moreover, from the beginning of the construction until the end of the ceremony, a three-week period at least, the men must abstain from all sexual relations with their wives.

The Land Dive tower is a veritable phenomenon of vegetal architecture. Eiffel was talented, but this tower stands without a nail, without a single object coming from the whites. It is made of hundreds of tree trunks and branches which are held together by about ten miles of lianas.

The first problem of the builders is to find a good site. Not too far from the village, since the men return home every evening except the night before the dive; also not too far from the raw materials. The incline of the land is also important. If it is too steep, the construction work will be difficult. If not steep enough, the divers will run higher risks. And then there must be a flat area behind the tower for the dancers. And there must also be a healthy tree at the crucial spot; it serves as the central support.

A dozen trunks are implanted around this tree as vertical supports. Other trunks are attached above these. The body of the tower is rectangular up to about fifty feet, then it slants back. The upper part, not being attached to the central tree, is flexible and sways gently in the wind. All the men work together in the scaffolding. They often sing while working. A festive ambience reigns.

When the tower is almost finished, Tamalie's spirit comes to inhabit it. The men know he's there when they feel certain vibrations in their bodies and when they hear certain cracklings in the tower's framework.

Each man builds his own platform and chooses the lianas which will bind him to the tower. But the choice of lianas, being critical, is supervised by one of the village elders. He estimates, like a doctor examining a patient, their solidity and their elasticity. He cuts them with his machete to the correct length. If the lianas are too short, the diver will remain suspended in air and risk bounding toward the tower's body with enough force to break his bones. If the lianas are too long, he will, quite simply, be smashed into the earth. A difference of five inches out of one hundred feet is cru-

Midway. *Kal Muller*

cial. I wonder how they do it without any measuring rod, given the variable elasticity of lianas. In any case, they don't make mistakes, or only rarely.

During our stay, they swore to us that no one had ever been killed during a Land Dive. There had been a few arms and legs broken, but that's all. However, after our departure from the archipelago, and thus apparently for the first time, a jumper died.

The accident happened during a dive performed especially for the Queen of England during her first trip to the New Hebrides. She must have been expecting an impressive but harmless sports event. And, boom, a man fell and was reduced to mush just in front of Her Majesty because the lianas were too elastic. The lianas were too elastic because the dive was staged earlier then usual in honor of the Queen's visit.

If the men do not normally hurt themselves, it is also because they are trained from earliest youth. Two- or three-year-old boys jump from their fathers' shoulders, papa grasping their ankles firmly. The boys who are a little older plunge from a high rock into the sea, trying to imitate the perfect movements of the real Land Divers. At about five, they start taking part in the construction of a miniature tower, six or seven feet tall. It is an exact model of the large tower in every detail. When a child is eight or nine, the games are over. He is put to the test. It's a first communion, a graduation, a rite of passage in every sense. A boy who jumps from the real tower with his elders becomes a man.

David Attenborough, an English writer and zoologist who saw the event during the fifties, found himself next to a group of women at the beginning. He noticed that one of the women was holding what seemed to be a baby wrapped in calico in her arms. She watched intently as one of the youngest boys climbed the tower, prepared himself, and jumped from the platform. As soon as she saw that the boy was not hurt, she threw the "baby" joyously into the air. It wasn't an infant at all but simply a bundle of calico. The boy who had just jumped was her son, and since he had passed the test, she gave up the symbol of her baby who no longer existed. Her son was now a man. The islanders themselves, however, do not really think of the Land Dive as an initiation rite. For them, its agrarian associations prevail.

During the last days of construction, tension and excitement possess the boys and men. The women are also excited. The virility and courage of their husbands and sons will be measured in public.

When the tower is completely finished, the slope where the divers will land is cleared. The stumps, roots, and rocks are removed and the earth is loosened to a depth of eight or nine inches. The night before the dive, numerous men spend the night next to the tower. They keep guard to prevent sorcerers and spirits from coming to bury objects in the prepared earth. If this were not done or if the taboos concerning women were broken, the divers would hurt themselves. That night, even in the village, no one ever sleeps peacefully, for one reason or another. Late during the night before the first dive we saw, a village man woke me up, calling to me softly from outside our hut. I went out to see him. What's wrong? A problem about the dive? His wife? Someone sick? Not at all. With an embarrassed smile, Alfred explained to me that he couldn't sleep because he was tormented by the white hairs which had begun to appear on his head and he knew the Europeans had products to darken hair. Do me a favor, he implored. Send me a jar of this paint: to Alfred Tavok, Martelli Bay, Pentecost. I will pay you. Alfred had to jump the next day from one of the highest platforms, but he wasn't at all haunted by visions of broken arms and legs. I couldn't help laughing. If I had to jump, I certainly wouldn't be thinking about my hair a few hours before the big moment.

D-Day we climbed the hill at the summit of which was the tower. I walked slowly and painfully, having twisted an ankle stumbling over a coral outcropping in shallow water. When I got there, the dancers were already warming up. The men sang. The women danced next to the men at the base of the tower. Their stamping resounded like tom-toms. The women do not have the right to sing, but they must whistle to encourage the divers. They must do their best to provoke the fall, in the literal and figurative senses, of the men. But now, having learned a lesson from their unfortunate ancestor Tamalie, that poor Melanesian Adam, the men rise triumphantly after the fall.

In a typical dive, between thirty-five and sixty men, according to the importance of the village, jump from the tower. The youngest boys, always nervous and frightened, go first. They aren't theatrical. They get through their numbers as quickly as possible. But even the youngest observe the forms. They clap their hands above their heads and then cross them over their chests and, with rigid bodies, they let themselves be carried away by gravity. In landing they must not uncross their hands. If the lianas were cut to the right length, their heads will just graze the earth.

Each diver is a star. When he steps out onto the platform, the chants, the whistles, and the stamping of the dancers intensify. He braces himself carefully, curving his toes around the edge of the diving board. You wouldn't want to fall before the big jump! Looking at the horizon, standing like a god, he tosses a few croton leaves to the winds. Even before the leaves reach the earth, he lifts his arms, signaling that he wishes to speak. At the bottom of the tower, the music stops at once, the people freeze and lift their eyes respectfully.

The diver profits from the occasion not only by displaying his courage and importance before the women but also by exercising his right to make a little speech before his leap. He talks from the bottom of his heart about his problems, troubles, and secret thoughts, things he would never dare say otherwise. Did he feel insulted by someone? Had he paid one pig too many? This is the time to speak up. Many men complain of their marital difficulties, airing in detail everything they have against their wives. The women may get back at their husbands later, but on this day they keep still and listen stoically.

The speech over, the dancers begin their hypnotic movements again. Back and forth, three steps in one direction, three steps in the other. The chanting and whistling begins again even more strongly, punctuated by unbridled cries, Eh-hey! Eh-hey! The crowd seems completely drunk, not on kava, which is unknown on Pentecost, or alcohol, but rather on emotion. The diver, when he slowly claps his hands three times, seems to be in a state of ecstasy. He leans forward and suddenly throws himself into the void—the Gol—his legs spread and bent like a frog's. When he lands, several men come to help him up and to cut the lianas which still attach him to the tower. The women in his family charge forward to dance around him, whistling frantically, arms thrusting toward the sky. It is the joyous welcome to their hero. If the man is not too stunned by his head having struck the earth rather then skimming it, he bounds to his feet to show everybody that he is not hurt. Otherwise, someone rubs his head and he gets up as best he can. In any case, it's a victory. He has jumped. His family is proud of him.

Often, one or even both of the lianas break. But they have already broken the fall. The diver just gets a rougher shock in land-

The view from the top. *Kal Muller*

ing. Sometimes at the last moment, a man no longer has the courage to jump. No shame. Someone else immediately replaces him. Thus, the most courageous may end up jumping two or three times.

The dive begins around nine o'clock in the morning and ends at about five in the afternoon. Everyone is exhausted, physically and emotionally, after the event. The women and the girls maintain an attitude of utmost respect toward the men. They don't even talk. It's the evening of Father's Day, All Males' Day, and silently they try to please their husbands, sons, brothers, or fathers however they can. The proof has been established: men are superior to women. There is no feast that evening. A simple meal and right to bed, everyone happy as a king—or as a king's servant.

The Bunlap villagers are the last non-Christians on Pentecost. They preserve their traditional life to a large extent, but artificially. According to Robert Lang, a competent and sensitive ethnologist who spent ten months in southern Pentecost in 1953 and 1954, even at that time they were almost as familiar with European civilization as with their Christianized neighbors. They cling to their traditional life, not because the whites' life displeases them—to the contrary, they find and take advantages from it—but because they believe in the ancient principle of a bird in the hand being worth two in the bush. They are very lucid. The missionaries, and the whites in general, do not offer them anything sure. They feel that very often those natives who have converted get trapped between two worlds, having abandoned the one and being unable to cross the threshold of the other. They don't really wish to stay immobile, with an eye toward the past, but they don't see any other reasonable solution. It's interesting to note that those who defend "custom" most are those who know the Europeans best, like the chief, who has even worked in New Caledonia. Unfortunately, once you know another life-style too well, once it has aroused in you certain desires and ambitions, there's no real turning back.

The result in Bunlap is that while the forms of traditional life remain, their substance has been virtually destroyed. Lang wrote, "In my contacts with them, I could not avoid feeling that they are playing at being 'man-bush.'" That was more than twenty years ago. They are still playing the same game, but now it's degenerating fast. A comparison can be made with Tofor and his troop of "false man-bush" on Ambrym. There is a significant difference, however. Tofor has consciously chosen, given the situation, to profit as much as possible from the two worlds, without trying to persuade himself that he belongs totally to either of them. Is he a cynic? A realist? We're no judges. Anyway, he is happy with his life.

Kal was very attracted by Bunlap and the village's chief, Bong. Bong is truly the chief, but even that title is somewhat artificial since the Bunlap people have never traditionally had a chief. It was the Europeans who wanted someone to fill the office so they could deal with a spokesman. Kal and Bong got along marvelously, and Kal was tempted to spend more time in Bunlap than we were. Once he even stayed for several months running.

As everywhere else, Kal and Jacques had asked the villagers in Bunlap for permission to film and photograph. Permission was granted without hesitation. Why? In Bunlap the people know very well that their traditional life won't last much longer and they were aware of one of Kal's fundamental principles: that the films are a means of preserving for the members of the group, for children and grandchildren, as well as for a public who might be interested in them, the customs destined otherwise to be forgotten. Besides, the Bunlap people were thrilled when we showed them on a small viewer the rolls of film already shot in Amok. Ehhey! Incredible! Jacques and Kal had to schedule programs every day. There wasn't the same mystique that existed in Amok. All the men of Bunlap had already been to the movies, on the plantations, in Santo or elsewhere. But they were pleased to see on the screen people who looked like them instead of seeing cowboys, the habitual fare in the New Hebrides.

For Kal, staying alone (or rather, with a French girl he'd brought with him) in Bunlap was a memorable experience. He fit into the village life well, as he had not been able to do on the Big Nambas plateau. He didn't lose any time. He seriously studied the language, the daily and ceremonial lives. He was the first "European" since Lang to live in Bunlap.

Kal is in favor of "custom" and against the entrance of the New Hebrideans into the European system where, nine times out of ten, they are not happy and where, ten times out of ten, they are never completely accepted. But with time, the old traditions give way, too. Even though the Bunlap villagers refused to send their children to the mission or government schools, they asked Kal to teach them how to read. Okay. But not in French, English, or pidgin, said Kal. He codified their language, reducing it to the seventeen most common sounds. He said that after four months, his regular students, five boys and two men, knew how to read and write the simple words, knew a little of the history and geography of their archipelago, and had mastered the basics of arithmetic. One of the boys could even add long columns of numbers without making mistakes. For his own pleasure, the teacher taught a few hardy volunteers how to play chess. They found it an ideal occupation during the rainy season.

Wishing to offer a gift to the village, our friend asked Bong what the people wanted. The response was immediate: a cooperative. Traditional life is turning faster and faster. They would not have asked Lang for a co-op. Kal supplied what was wanted. He had all the necessary merchandise shipped over. Henceforth, at the store in this lonely village you can buy cans of fruit juice or beer, cans of meat or fish; matches, cigarettes, and tobacco sticks; axes, knives, and more. If the villagers didn't have enough money to buy the stock at first, they all have enough to be good customers. The cooperative is a big success.

But since Kal personally wanted to reinforce whatever was left of the "traditional" side, he offered another gift to Bong alone: trips. Not to go enjoy himself in town—Bong can do that without Kal's help—but to see the other "custom" peoples in the archipelago. He took him to the Big Nambas and the Mbotogote. Bong didn't know that these peoples, more firmly anchored in Melanesian life than himself, existed. The meetings between Bong and Virambat and between Bong and Ilabnambenpen were striking. The first thing they noticed, on both sides, was that the other was also dressed in nambas! But not the same nambas! The differences between the penis sheaths, large, shredded pandanus tufts, simple leaves, or pandanus plaited in the form of a rectangle, intrigued the people who were wearing them. The discussions never ended. In your village, do you raise yams the same way we do? How do you carry out the Nimangki? They conversed like cousins who had never met. Kal was very happy. It was the kind of cultural exchange he likes the most.

The presents and attentions were reciprocal. There is now a boy in Bunlap named Kal. It was an honor. Kal, ours, was present when the other was born. The Bunlap people like and fear the whites at the same time. In their language, moreover, the word for "white man" is *isalsal,* "the floating ones." What impressed them most when the first Europeans arrived was not the color of their skins but the fact that the strangers came to Pentecost in large huts that floated over the sea.

An important moment, the most important moment for Kal, came a little later when he received permission to participate in the Bunlap Land Dive. For a year and a half, Kal had tried to get the right to jump in one village or another. It hadn't worked. They all said, one way or another, you foolish white man, you want to break your neck? In Bunlap, he could participate. Kal was going to jump from about forty-five feet up, right near the middle of the tower, not bad for someone who had not been trained from childhood as are the islanders. The Bunlap villagers carry out the dive just like the other Pentecost inhabitants except they wear nambas and not shorts as in the Christianized villages. It is more picturesque. Kal was happy. Jacques didn't have the slightest desire to jump, no more than to be circumcised with a bamboo knife, as Kal had also wanted to do. They still had the same difference in attitude, even though they got along very well in their work. Kal wanted to participate as fully as possible in the native life. Jacques wanted to participate to a certain degree, but he was happy to be a friendly observer sometimes.

The night before the dive, Kal began to get cold feet. The villagers didn't boost his confidence. They kept insisting, *"You think-think you savvy jump? Long tomorrow me think-think you look-look no more."*

Of course that was all it took to affirm Kal's will. He wasn't going to be a coward at the last moment. That much was certain! And when that last moment came, he was up to it. He jumped, and he jumped well, with perfect form. The men charged out to detach him from the lianas. One of them howled as loudly as he could, *"Me look-look! You no fright!"* It was a huge compliment. For Kal, it was one of the accomplishments in his life. One of the lianas broke during the fall, but he wasn't aware of it. The other liana was too tight and he suffered the consequences. For weeks afterwards he was aware of dragging around a leg so numb that even nangolat nettles couldn't bring it back to life.

Kal's Gol high would surely have deflated at once had he suspected how his Bunlap buddies, and relations with them, would turn out. Once the wheel spins steadily, it can really accelerate fast. Only a few months later Bong began organizing the "tradi-

Kal landing triumphantly. *Jacques Gourguechon*

tional activities" of his village for groups of tourists. Even the
Land Dive turned into a commercial enterprise, with admission
tickets, refreshment stands, and a fat fee for taking a photo. Once
they realized that they could cash in on custom, anything was
possible. An Australian girl, an anthropology student but far
more sensitive to the islands than Mike Hallston had been, asked
permission to spend some time in the village. The chief agreed—
for a two-thousand-dollar minimum fee. Then a couple of French
hustlers, seeing a good possibility, convinced Bong that there was
plenty of money to be had out of our team. And so they undertook to sue us, with such contradictory claims as: each Bunlap inhabitant should be paid at professional rates as coproducers of and
actors in our documentary footage; each Bunlap inhabitant should
be paid damages because they represented a "virgin tribe" that we
were raping. We have actually won several trials against Bong and
his virgins. The villagers must have lost all their Land Dive
profits paying their French advisers, a lawyer, and court costs.

12

John Frum,
the American King

O N Tanna Island, the people are waiting for the arrival of their messiah, John Frum, one day. Every evening in strategic locations, men take the watch. They scrutinize the sky and the sea. They survey the volcano's crater. No one knows exactly where he'll come from. At dawn other sentinels will take their places. First and foremost, they watch the comings and goings of the few whites who pass through.

John Frum is the King of America. Maybe. Anyway, he is an American of divine nature. The Tanna Islanders are followers of a very special religion: the Cargo Cult.

Before the Europeans' arrival, the Tannese, like all other Melanesians, had an entire cosmology all their own, with myths and legends that explained the world. There was nothing mysterious about material goods; everything came from nature and was worked by human hands. It was the stone age. The Melanesians also used wood and vegetal fibers, but most of them did not even know pottery.

And then the first Europeans came. On Tanna it was Captain Cook on the *Resolution*. Who were these strange beings who didn't seem to even have toes but who had, among many other unheard-of things, firearms? The resources of local mythology were called upon. The newcomers were undoubtedly spirits. Later, when the first planters and traders settled on the island, the Tannese realized that the Europeans were, after all, no more than human beings. A definite proof: you could even kill and eat them.

But all the mystery remained attached to their fabulous possessions. Over the years, the objects they had became more and more surprising—up to radios and refrigerators. Even the material with which these objects were made doesn't exist in nature. And by what process are they made? How do you shape or weave or build an enameled refrigerator? Or a simple glass? Besides, the whites didn't make these marvelous objects themselves. They arrived miraculously by cargo ships.

Conclusion: these goods are of supernatural origin and were sent to the whites by their gods.

This conclusion facilitated the task of the missionaries, those whites who gladly talk about their God, those generous whites who are willing to unveil the secret of their rites to the natives. Rites which, without a doubt, bring the cargo ships and their fantastic cargoes. Only the missionaries declared that the white men's God does not like pagan rites. To be Christian like us, you must abandon a few practices. Dances, chants, idols, polygamy. Prostitution, because on Tanna, professionals traditionally take care of a youth's sexual initiation. Kava, which the Tannese drank like fish. Their age-old costumes, the penis sheath and the raffia skirt. Above all, hide your flesh! No more mixed swimming in the nude. And, of course, turn your backs on the spirits; there are no good spirits, they're all devils. During those critical years, the Presbyterians ran the show on this island, and they didn't joke around with morality.

To gain access to all these material goods and to the power that goes with them, the islanders would have done almost anything. They renounced all their traditions. They became Christians. And they lived in the hope of seeing cargo ships arrive for them. They were patient. In Melanesia, as in the Orient, people know how to wait. The cargo ships came and went for the whites, but still not for them.

Now, being patient does not mean being duped. The Tannese noticed that the other whites, those who had the most material goods, the planters and traders, didn't follow the missionaries'

laws. They drank, if not kava, at least gin, which was equally forbidden. They were polygamists in their own way, without ever
marrying. And they never set foot in church.

The Tannese, suspecting a trick on the missionaries' part, ap-
pealed to the planters, who affirmed that the matter was simple.
The cargo ships do not come from the sky. To get the things you
want, all you have to do is work. So the natives hired out on the
plantations. They worked, day after day, month after month. But
all they could get for their pains were the simplest objects—
knives, tobacco sticks, plastic combs. And then they noticed that
the planters themselves never seemed to work. They just sat behind their desks. They looked at papers and they gave orders.

So! The planters too were cheats, like the missionaries. They
must all be intervening between their God and us in order to
deprive us of our due. A dirty European plot.

The Tannese reacted vigorously. They became antiwhite and
anti-Christian. They revived certain traditions the missionaries
had forbidden. And they began to talk of a savior, a mythic being,
John Frum. His incarnations multiplied rapidly. Sometimes he
was black, sometimes white, sometimes half-blooded. In any case,
he existed. He spoke Tannese and he communicated with certain
disciples in their dreams. There were even people who saw him,
in the night, by the glimmer of a fire. John Frum! It's he who will
bring the Tannese the material abundance they've been awaiting
for so long. And at the same time he will chase the whites from
Tanna.

It's 1940. The missions and the schools have been deserted. In
1941, the last ties with the planters and traders are shattered when
John Frum let it be known that when the apocalypse came there
would be a Tannese currency, bearing the image of a coconut
stamped by his own hand. To purify themselves and hasten the
arrival of this golden age, all European money must be gotten rid
of and never touched again. The few natives who still worked for
the whites quit, and the Tannese abandoned themselves to a veritable spending orgy. They didn't keep a penny. The chiefs even
spent the gold sovereigns offered by the government as a sign of
friendship near the beginning of the century. The most fanatic did
not want to dirty themselves by giving their money back to the
Europeans. They threw it into the sea.

The English Delegate, representing the Anglo-French Condominium administration in the New Hebrides, James Nicol, was forced to act. He had been on Tanna for twenty-five years, having been sent to replace a too liberal Delegate at the request of the Presbyterian missionaries. These same missionaries now pushed him into action, but he didn't know what to do. He sought out the John Frum prophets. He got hold of someone named Manahevi and attached him to a tree to demonstrate to the population that he didn't have any supernatural powers and that John Frum would not come to his aid. Manahevi emerged with a prestige he had never had before. Nicol went further. He arrested several leaders of the movement and sent them to prison in Port-Vila.

Who knows how the John Frum Cargo Cult would have evolved if the war hadn't broken out in the Pacific? Because it was the war that stirred up the movement and gave it a definite form.

In 1942 hundreds of thousands of American soldiers landed in the New Hebrides, with planes, ships as far as the eye could see, trucks, bulldozers, giant refrigerators, radios of all sizes, in short, with a dazzling wealth of material goods in unimaginable quantities.

The Tannese, who had never seen more than a dozen whites at once, and that was rare, were the least surprised of all the archipelago natives. They naturally attributed this extraordinary event to John Frum.

More than a thousand Tannese volunteered to go work on the American bases. There they found what was really stupefying: black American soldiers! The Tannese thought they had come upon long-lost brothers. But the black Americans were not poor. They had access to all the whites' material goods. Moreover, there were even blacks who gave orders to whites! Decidedly, John Frum's power was infinite.

It should be added that the Tannese were favorably impressed by the American whites as well. They had never been treated similarly by the English or French colonists. On the bases, they were given drinks, food, military uniforms, generous tips for the slightest favors. They climbed into the soldiers' jeeps and they boarded the ships. They went to the army's movie theaters and were dazzled by the films. And the Americans talked to them; not just orders, but real conversations. And some of the Americans

Tannese women in "Friday" dress for the John Frum dances. *Kal Muller*

expressed anticolonist sentiments. Those were without a doubt disciples of John Frum.

For the Tannese, it was a foretaste of the glorious time to come. Since then, they have believed that John Frum is American. Some say he is the King of America. He lives in New California. And he will come back with the American army, dispenser of so much wealth, which this time will be at the Tanna Islanders' disposal.

After the war, they prepared themselves. Rumor spread that the day of the apocalypse was imminent. Here and there they cleared long strips of jungle so that John Frum's plane could land. At all strategic points throughout the island, they planted red crosses, symbol of the cult ever since, coming undoubtedly from the American Red Cross. In front of each cross, the sentinel took his stand.

This was too much for Nicol. He panicked and once again had the leaders of the movement arrested. Moreover, he had an American officer come to explain to the assembled population that there was no one called John Frum in the United States, and that the American army didn't have any intention of landing on Tanna.

He reeled off several bursts from a submachine gun to impress the
natives. He succeeded in scaring them, but not in convincing
them. The Tannese thought this was just another underhanded
trick trumped up by the Europeans.

The John Frum Cargo Cult has had its ups and downs in the
last few years, but contrary to the missionaries' and administra-
tors' hopes, time has not been enough to tone it down. Though it
would be difficult to estimate the precise number of the cult's followers today, one thing is sure: 40 percent of Tanna's population
(which is at least twelve thousand inhabitants) refuse all cooperation with the administration and missions. They adhere to neither
the local councils nor the cooperatives and they do not send their
children to school. These are the practicing John Frumists. And if
you count the nonpracticing believers the Cargo Cult includes almost the entire population.

Arriving on Tanna, we were immediately aware that it was an
island unlike the others. Everywhere else in the New Hebrides,
the people welcomed us with smiles. Here, the smiles were reserved for our little plane, perhaps the same one which will bring
John Frum one of these days. The Tannese, who do not work for
the airline, emerged with rags in hand and respectfully polished
the airplane, an object of veneration.

Kal and I had our American passports. We showed them to the
natives, who don't know how to read but who immediately recognized these little booklets. The smiles broke out, this time for us.
Since the war, the Americans had not come back to Tanna.
Perhaps we were John Frum's ambassadors. We were invited to
the villages.

Among the few things retained from the Christian religion is
the idea of a day of rest, transferred to Friday. To celebrate this
day, the people must play the guitar and dance. John Frum commanded it. On the surface the atmosphere is fairly gay, because of
the island music and the vividly colored costumes. But underneath there is a current of tension, even hostility, which didn't
escape us.

Jacques, though he had only a French passport, was allowed to
be present at these weekly ceremonies. But he could not go
beyond the fence, red like the cross, to see the big annual cere-

John Frum's followers marching in military parade with their bamboo rifles on February 15. *Kal Muller*

mony, sacred above all others. February 15 is Saint John Frum's Day, and Europeans are definitely not welcome.

It was John Frum himself who decreed that his existence must be celebrated and that his return must be prayed for on that day. The rite takes place at Sulphur Bay. It starts with flower offerings before the red cross, exactly as the French and British celebrate November 11 in front of the war memorial in the capital. Then, the prayers. But the principal event of the day, of the entire year, for all the believers is a military parade. Under the orders of a sergeant, about one hundred men participate. They carry bamboo rifles at the end of which are carved bayonets painted red. With their "rifles" they execute military movements. All the participants wear the letters U.S.A. painted in red on their backs and chests. They are the members of the T.A.—Tannese Army—a very special branch of the American army.

These Tannese soldiers had gotten into the habit a few years ago of strutting through all the island villages to announce the imminent arrival of John Frum and to demand pigs and kava in payment for this good news. As their bamboo rifles weren't quite effective enough, they acquired some real ones. Again, the Condominium was obliged to intervene.

Along with the faith—and good faith, too—among most John Frumists there is also some hoaxing among the leaders. They love to mystify the population, for the good cause or for personal reasons. The Europeans suspect that a certain Keoh played the role of John Frum at first. They think he may even have started the whole thing. They know that Keoh did disguise himself as John Frum at least one time, to bewitch a young widow he wanted to marry. His immediate desires were satisfied. But the then demystified widow, disappointed to learn the child she was carrying was not John Frum's, refused to marry Keoh. On Tanna, where single mothers do not figure in the traditions, this incident raised quite a commotion.

Personal ambitions and jealousies still play a role in the Cargo Cult. In this sense, the Tannese have returned to customary rivalries as before the arrival of the outsiders.

Moreover, as in most religious movements, there are schisms. A minority of natives advocate the complete return to Melanesian traditions. They dress in penis sheaths, which have not been worn on Tanna for three generations. The majority think it necessary to drink kava and perform the traditional dances, but to hasten John Frum's arrival, everything material that comes from the whites must be kept. For the custom dances they wear shorts or Mother Hubbards, the muumuu-style mission-imposed dresses, in which fat women and thin women have exactly the same shape. Their faces are painted with colors bought in the trading stores instead of the traditional vegetal colors.

The Ipekel people, at Sulphur Bay, where the February 15 ceremony takes place, have temperaments naturally heated, so to speak, by the Yasua volcano, which is still active just above the village. The Tannese used to believe the volcano housed spirits. Now it is part of the John Frumist mythology. The Tannese believe that John Frum maintains an army of twenty thousand soldiers in the interior of the crater. These soldiers will burst out one of these days, triumphant, to welcome the returning Americans.

In Ipekel we expressed the desire to climb up to Yasua's crater. It's not worth it, said an old man, you won't see anything. What?

Yasua's sentinel. *Kal Muller*

Even from the village we could see the spectacular spurts of fire and lava. But the eruptions didn't interest this good man, who was discouraging us. He explained that we white people didn't have the eyes to see the only thing that was worthwhile, the twenty thousand inhabitants of the crater which he himself had seen a hundred times.

Since we wanted to go up anyway, one of the village chiefs proposed a guide. We protested. No need to put anyone out, we can't get lost. No, no, insisted the chief, you need a guide. We finally understood that this obligatory guide was not to guide us but to survey our actions. Ipekel is the volcano's guardian village, and its inhabitants must keep an eye on all outsiders who climb it so that they do not take any volcanic rocks as souvenirs. These rocks are a source of wisdom, and the Tannese figure the Europeans have already stolen enough.

Long ago, there were many kinds of magic stones, with which a good harvest was assured, the weather controlled, the death of an enemy provoked, and so on. The Tannese accuse the missionaries of having stolen these. But besides refrigerators and cars, John Frum will bring the Tannese other magic stones, even more powerful than the old ones.

The whole time we were on Tanna, we tried to find out the origin of the name John Frum. No one knew, or rather everyone knew, as there were many versions of the story. Some say that Frum is a distortion of broom, because he will sweep the whites off Tanna. Others say Frum is simply "from," John from . . . America. Still others think of John Brown, guessing some American passed through Tanna before the Civil War and spoke to the natives of the abolitionist and what he represented. There may be a fourth version, and it may be the right one.

At last we discussed the Cargo Cult with the island's Europeans. Before it was impossible to do so, because to be accepted by the militant John Frumists, contact with the whites had to be avoided as much as possible. In general, anyway, they are not up on the particulars of the cult, through laziness, prudence, lack of interest, and lack of the natives' confidence. There were two exceptions, more or less, a planter and a missionary, who did have a basic knowledge of the subject.

This missionary, who had followed the cult's evolution for years, drew some parallels, perhaps unconsciously. "They couldn't care less about our logic, or our rational interpretations of their beliefs. After all, in a religion, it's faith that counts above all. Among the youth now there are many who participate in the rites but who are skeptics. Most of the old people are real believers."

He was an honest missionary. "I put myself in their place. If one day someone could demonstrate that Jesus Christ is not the son of God, I would rather die before, without knowing it."

At the volcano's foot is a plain of ashes, a lunar landscape, which the administration uses for an emergency airport. Crossing the plain with a few Tannese, just before leaving the island, we were told the secret of the gods. Even now John Frum lands from time to time during the night on this runway. And he doesn't even need an airplane from the whites to do it. His magic walking stick transforms itself, whenever he wishes, into a black plane.

CONCLUSION

La nuit noire pirate aux cieux d'or debarquant . . .
—Rimbaud

SEPTEMBER. The austral spring—theoretically, at least. Here the seasons follow one another, if you believe the calendar, but they all look strangely similar. Heat. Humidity. The subtlest differences between December and June, and you hardly notice them. The leaden sun. Torrential rains. All the time, all the time. Consequently, this formidable island vegetation. Here it's always flower season, never the season of dead leaves. We talk about a rainy season because it rains even more than usual during December, January, and February; but most of all it's a cyclone season.

The *Tahitien*, announced by Radio Noumea, will be in the Segond Channel, in Santo, in a few days. It's the last voyage of this cargo-passenger ship which for nearly thirty years has rocked across the longest course in the world: Marseilles-Sydney. Jacques came to the New Hebrides on the *Tahitien*. He had such a good memory of this trip and this ship that he wanted to do it again, in the other direction. Forty days at sea. If Jules Verne had known the *Tahitien*, he surely would have made it the setting for one of his books. I'm thrilled by the idea of boarding a ship with such a reputation, and apparently such character.

Three years! For me it's unbelievable. Three years since I landed in the New Hebrides. Time flies even for foreigners in timeless lands. We have shot miles of film, taken thousands of photographs and pounds of notes. Done what we had set out to do, even more. We have loved and hated Santo, our home base. Detested its emptiness, its rotten climate, which transforms you after a while into a tropical vegetable, incapable of even reading a newspaper; which slowly kills you with malarial attacks. At the same time we did find Santo a true terrestrial paradise, far away from all the preconceived ideas, the pressures, the technology that can easily dominate life in our own native lands. On the personal side, we have friends and enemies in Santo. We come and go, between excursions into the jungle or to other islands. We celebrate our arrivals and departures. We know everybody. Albert Goddyn, André Augonnet, and a few other friends even awarded us a giant certificate of honorary citizenship which decorated Albert's bistro for months. But we must leave, of course. On to other projects, places, experiences. We're bringing back masks from Malekula and from Ambrym, a statue from Amok, souvenirs whose lively colors will brighten some dusky European and American winters.

There it is. The enormous *Tahitien*. It's high as an eight-story building, and after all the small boats on which we've traveled around the islands, that's impressive. It stretches almost the whole length of Santo's main wharf. You can hear the hum of the engines all the way down to the Burns-Philp quay. Several hundred passengers lean over the railings on the various bridge levels. I can't take my eyes off this huge ocean taxi that will take us soon to Tahiti and the Marquesas. I don't know why, but I can't really believe we're going on board. However, it is behind one of those portholes and somewhere on those spacious decks that we will cross the Pacific, the Panama Canal, the Sargasso Sea. When we reach Martinique, Europe will be nearer than Melanesia, but there will still be all of the Atlantic before us. At Madeira we'll be in the suburbs. Beyond Gibraltar, we'll be well into November.

The liner, barely docked, looses its passengers from Sydney and Noumea, who swarm over Santo, crowding the cafés and souvenir shops. Conversely, a good part of Santo's population will go aboard to have a drink, either in the first-class bar on the highest deck or the third-class bistro on the lowest. When the *Tahitien* is in port, the classes mix. Tens of thousands of tons of copra must be loaded for Marseilles. There aren't any cranes. Everything is done by loading masts, pulley-blocks, and winches. It will be about three days before the ship is ready to leave.

In Santo, the night before each departure of the *Tahitien*, there's a dance at Mao's. We're going, of course, to this last island blast. The last for us in the New Hebrides, and the last in the New Hebrides for the *Tahitien*, which is to be sold. To the Japanese? To the Americans? For scrap metal? No one knows the boat's fate, but we all know an era is ending in the Pacific. From now on, in the near future anyway, there will be only modern cargo ships, container ships, and tourist liners. Not at all the same as the good old cargo-passengers which have symbolized the charms of the South Seas since the turn of the century. Optimists hope that the Italians will finance a new one, or that the French, who after all are emotionally attached to these Pacific islands, may decide to continue the tradition and thereby perpetuate this aspect of Pacific romanticism.

At the dance nostalgia floats in the air, along with the smoke of English and Hong Kong cigarettes, the latter being much stronger, less expensive, and therefore preferred by New Hebrideans. We dance incessantly. I dance a little with Jacques but more with Ernst Lamberty and members of the *Tahitien*'s crew, mostly Malagasy and Comorians. Jacques dances with Ernst's young wife, Rebecca II, and with Anna Goddyn, who is as beautiful as a storybook black queen. Joseph Santino joins us. He has lived fourteen years in isolation on his plantation far in the Santo jungle, the only European in the region. The spirit of the Pacific's yesteryear. Albert Goddyn had promised to come later, but hasn't. At his age, undoubtedly, he prefers to avoid parties. Anna covers us with shell necklaces for our departure. The big departure. Adieu.

So we turn a page in our lives. The New Hebridean epoch is a closed chapter. Oh, we'll surely come back, but it will never be the same.

What does the future hold for this tiny faraway archipelago? The French have always wanted to keep it. If they lose the New

Hebrides, they risk losing nickel-rich New Caledonia and prestigious Tahiti as well. The British do not want to keep it. For years now they have been trying to get out from under the burden of all their Pacific possessions. But this case is special: they do not want to leave the archipelago to the French. That is basically the policy conflict that has kept the Condominium going up to now. For the British the only way out is independence immediately, or as soon as possible. And they've been doing their best to create the necessary atmosphere.

France has come around to the idea of New Hebridean independence, too. Tahiti doesn't even know the archipelago exists, and there are more French New Caledonians on that island than native ones. Decolonization, oui. But à la français—the slow way—which means creating a French-speaking elite, multiplying French elementary schools, pushing economic development as far as possible, creating little by little the idea of national unity to avoid eventual conflicts between tribes or islands. Achieving these aims would take years and cost a considerable sum, and if France wants to pay the price, it isn't altruism that will guide her decision. The long-range goal is to leave the New Hebrides peaceful, prosperous—and in the French sphere of influence.

The ongoing rivalry is really between French business and British missionaries. The latter are the most ardent campaigners for immediate independence, knowing that they would be able to stay on and, without being hampered by priests or colonists, could bring the archipelago under the Australian sphere.

A journalist from one of the important evening dailies in Paris thinks, like the British, that the time is ripe now. After a short visit to the New Hebrides, spent mostly in the bar of the best hotel in Port-Vila, he was persuaded that practically all the islanders crave independence. As evidence, he signals those who are trying to reclaim lands purchased by Europeans, those who militate for civil rights—a small minority. He doesn't talk about the others. How could he? He never bothered to go meet them. I took the trouble to go see him in Paris, as his articles annoyed me so. But you can't have a real discussion with someone who is determined to see only what conforms to his preformed opinions.

No, monsieur, you can't get away with your facile generalities about colonialism and oppressed peoples. They just have to be modified according to the situation. The fact is, most New Hebrideans do not feel oppressed by the existing government. They don't say it, but their attitude is clear to an outsider. If they were inclined toward adjectives they might call the administration bumbling or paternalistic, but certainly not oppressive. On one island, in exchange for a new road, the Delegate wanted to impose a tax of about twenty-five cents per inhabitant, just as a symbolic contribution. The very idea of the smallest tax so displeased the population that he never brought the matter up again.

The New Hebrideans, moreover, have invented the game of Beat the Condominium, and they are masters at it. Numerous Europeans are adept as well. An example of a good play: say the people of a given region would like a local hospital, know that many others would like one, too, and that all desires can't possibly be fulfilled at once. The chief goes to see his French Delegate; tells him the English Delegate has just offered him a clinic run by a native "dresser," a kind of assistant nurse; says he wonders whether he should accept. Chances are the French official will match the "British offer" immediately and maybe even top it.

I find that the majority of New Hebrideans do not take politics seriously. They're basically too carefree to get upset over anything. They all have their lands, their houses, and no one has ever gone hungry on these fertile islands. The major European companies have already given back some acreage to descendants of the one-time native owners, who often don't even bother to exploit it. Why work for money when it's so hot, when the yams you don't have to pay for are always on the fire, when kava or coconut milk is there for the taking? Some New Hebrideans would rather buy a beer and a can of corned beef, but many are content with what they have. It is a land where the living is good, where a person may worry about an approaching cyclone but won't lose any sleep over how to make ends meet when the first of the month comes around.

A clerk in the Norsup plantation store once confided to me that he always kept an eye on Big Nambas who wandered in, because they steal. Later, coming down with a couple of our Amok friends who were unfamiliar with the coast, I saw what he meant. Without a shilling or a franc, they began picking items off the shelves, opening the packages, and tasting the goods before the clerk stopped them. They couldn't understand that in the Europeans' world you have to *pay* to *eat*. But eating is a natural need, and every man has the right to basic necessities. No? Had the clerk told them they must also pay for their "natural" right to sleep or urinate, they wouldn't have been more astonished.

If the Na-Griamel has lost its punch, Jimmy Stephens having changed principles or loyalties too many times to remain credible, other movements are replacing it. Independence is in the wind, whether most islanders want it or not. And whether or not they desire it, they are going to be pushed and pulled into the twentieth century. More than a few will wind up wondering if the days of local cannibal wars weren't healthier, especially when their future ambassador to the UN has to consider current wars in places of whose existence he is today totally unaware. Vila's slick if small-time operators will undoubtedly persuade some chiefs to stage phony Nimangki ceremonies for tourists, as they already produce phony sculptures. Even most missionaries will agree that it's an excellent source of income for the natives.

The general political picture could change if an important mine was discovered in the archipelago. It's quite possible. They exist all around, not only the fabulous nickel deposits in Noumea, but copper on Bougainville and gold in Fiji.

For the moment, there's mainly just copra, a far cry from a gold mine. Prices dropped but they are rising again, surely because of the scarcity of raw materials in the world. It is not profitable enough for most Europeans, but not too bad for native planters who have no labor costs and a simpler life-style. No one wants to grow coffee or cacao—that's too much work. The Condominium is trying to encourage cattle raising, a possible solution for the European planters, though not a tempting one for many New Hebrideans.

A Honolulu promoter bought an impressive amount of land for a song some years back and sold it dearly, in lots, to thousands of Americans. His hopes were high. He foresaw modern U.S.-style cities in the jungle. It didn't work.

There are more and more tourists, though still relatively few, as the archipelago is not on the major Pacific routes. Vila does have a really first-rate hotel with a charming beach, but how many people are willing to go so far just for a pleasant swim? The powers that be are trying to organize "native shows," Melanesian song and dance sessions, adapted somewhat for the European eye and ear. I shall refrain from comment.

In general New Hebrideans still don't think of themselves as New Hebrideans, except for certain Vila sophisticates you can identify at once by the briefcases (often empty) they carry as a prop. Otherwise, you are a man-Tanna or a man-Santo, and Santo for a Tannese is a faraway foreign land. Some islanders still identify only with their tribe or village.

And what would they think if they knew that many of those powerful "Europeans" now idealize so-called primitive societies? Back to nature, back to mysticism. But they don't know that and are therefore not confused by the resulting conflicts. They do know that Europeans are stronger than they are, because of firearms before, because of money now.

An expansive writer once called the New Hebrides "the jewel of the South Pacific." Perhaps. In any case, I say to you again, in this distant land life is good. I hope it will remain good. I could have been convinced, easily, to stay on, in the jungle, in the villages, on the beaches, and on the boats, for several years more.

BIBLIOGRAPHY

Among the references consulted:

Beaune, Gaston. *La Terre Australe Inconnue: Onze Croisières aux Nouvelles-Hebrides*. Paris-Lyon: Delhomme et Briguet, 1894.

Bougainville, Louis Antoine. *Voyage Autour du Monde par la Fregate du Roi La Boudeuse et la Flute L'Etoile en 1766–1769*. Paris, 1771.

Codrington, R. H. *The Melanesians: Studies in Their Anthropology and Folklore*. London, Oxford: Clarendon Press, 1891.

Cook, James. *A Voyage Towards the South Pole and Round the World, Performed in His Majesties Ships* Resolution and Adventure . . . Tome II. London, 1777.

Craddock Family Papers, 1841–1873. Sydney: Mitchell Library Archives.

Davidson, J. W. "Peter Dillon and the Discovery of Sandalwood in the New Hebrides," *Journal de la Société des Oceanistes*, December 1956.

Deacon, A. B. *Malekula: A Vanishing Race in the New Hebrides*, Camilla H. Wedwood, ed. London: George Routledge & Sons, 1934.

Geslin, Yves. "Les Americains aux Nouvelles-Hebrides . . . ," *Journal de la Société des Oceanistes*, December 1956.

Guiart, Jean. "L'Organisation Sociale et Politique du Nord-Malekula," *Journal de la Société des Oceanistes*, December 1952.

———. "Notes sur la Sociologie Religieuse du groupe dit des 'Big-Nambas,' " *Etudes Melanesiennes*, 1952.

Harrisson, Tom. *Savage Civilization*. London, 1937. (Author's note: for people interested in the subject, Mr. Harrisson's book is fascinating—hard to find but definitely worth the trouble of seeking.)

Johnson, Martin. *Cannibal Island.* New York and London, 1922.

Lane, Robert B. "The Heathen Communities of Southeast Pentecost," *Journal de la Société des Oceanistes,* December 1956.

O'Reilly, Patrick. *Hebridais,* Publications de la Société des Oceanistes, No. 6. Paris: Musée de l'Homme, 1957.

Parkes Correspondence, Vol. 56. Sydney: Mitchell Library Archives.

Paton, John G. *John G. Paton, Missionary to the New Hebrides: An Autobiography . . .* London, 1889–1890.

Politis, Nicolas. *Le Condominium Franco-Anglais des Nouvelles-Hebrides.* Paris: A. Pedone, 1908.

Salomon, R. P. Casimir. Unedited diaries, 1900–1908.

Sautot, Henri. *Grandeur et Decadence du Gaullisme dans le Pacifique.* Melbourne, 1949.

Scarr, Deryck. *Fragments of Empire.* Canberra: Australian National University Press, 1967.

Magazines and newspapers:
Le Neo-Hebridais
New-Hebrides Magazine
Pacific Islands Monthly
Missions des Iles

INDEX